music

THE BUSINESS

THE ESSENTIAL GUIDE
TO THE **LAW** AND THE **DEALS**

ANN HARRISON

Virgin

The law in this book is correct to the best of my knowledge as of 31 March 2000, but the views I expound are mine alone. Although I have tried to give practical examples throughout, everyone's circumstances are different as are the facts of every case. The book is not a substitute for independent legal advice given to you personally. No liability can be accepted by myself or by Virgin Publishing Ltd for anything done in reliance on the matters referred to in this book. – Ann Harrison

First published in 2000 by
Virgin Publishing Ltd
Thames Wharf Studios
Rainville Road
London
W6 9HA

A catalogue record for this book is available from the British Library.

ISBN 0 7535 0433 2

Page design by Roger Kohn Designs
Typeset by Phoenix Photosetting, Chatham, Kent
Printed and bound in Great Britain by Butler & Tanner Ltd.

contents

acknowledgements

THANKS TO:

Debbie Hooker the librarian at Harbottle & Lewis for always coming up with the elusive piece of research I needed with good grace and at very short notice.

Antony Hodgson and Fiona Wharton for their assistance with research into the cases referred to in this book and to Kate Mayne, Richard Gates and Anthony Bebawi in particular for his article on new technology, 'The Digital Jukebox'.

Amanda Gilbert for her Herculean efforts in turning my scribblings and crossings-out into a readable manuscript, and for rescuing my files when I crashed the computer on more than one occasion.

Richard Penfold for his article on trade marks and branding; Emma Reid for her advice on trade marks and domain names; the partners at Harbottle & Lewis for indulging my wish to write this book and the Music Group for putting up with my grumbling about 'that ******* book'.

Last but not least, thanks to David Hitchcock, my husband, for his unfailing patience and support throughout. I couldn't have done it without him.

preface

I qualified as a lawyer in 1983 and began working for a firm of solicitors that did general work but also had a good reputation as entertainment lawyers. At first I just did commercial litigation but I found that I was naturally attracted to the entertainment cases. Somehow they seemed more 'sexy'!

When I moved to another firm to get more experience of the entertainment business I made a big mistake. The firm I joined was good at entertainment work, but in fact wanted someone to clear 180 people off a large holiday camp in the North of England. I spent most of the next two years running 180 separate property cases with no connection to the entertainment business at all. Still, I got to know Scarborough pretty well.

Luckily for me I'd kept in touch with a former flatmate who had become a very successful music lawyer at Harbottle and Lewis. He spent some time trying to persuade me to do the same work that he did. I thought my future lay in sorting out disputes in court and wasn't convinced. Then the law firm I was working for closed and that decided it. Luckily, the job at Harbottle & Lewis was still open and I joined the music department in 1988. But not before I'd gone through about four interviews with different people at the firm, including one where I was asked if I wanted to be the next Madonna. I wish! I don't know what they thought they were getting.

For the next six months I was convinced that this had been the second big mistake I'd made. My litigation training and instincts made it almost impossible for me to appear friendly towards lawyers on the other side, signing letters 'Kindest personal regards' when often I could cheerfully have strangled them. I got over that, though, and became a partner at the firm in 1991.

Since then I've worked mostly for artists and songwriters, managers, small labels and new media companies. Recently I've also been giving legal advice to music business executives and A&R people on their employment contracts. I like working for the creative end of the business. I'm not one for towing the party line. I also like being able to sack a client if the relationship isn't working out for some reason. I couldn't do that if I worked for a company. I've been lucky over the last 15 years to work with some of the leading players in the business. My clients come from every part of the music spectrum from drum and bass, dance and experimental music via classical and opera singers through rock and blues to chart topping 'pop' acts.

If I could go back in time and change anything, would I? Yes, I would have fought harder, earlier to get into this great, exciting often frustrating but incomparable business.

In writing this book I hope I will be able to convey some of that excitement to you.

Ann Harrison
31 March 2000

introduction

When I started work in the music business I had very little idea how it worked. Record and publishing companies were a mystery to me. It felt a little like trying to do a very hard jigsaw puzzle without the benefit of a picture on the lid of the box. I looked for books that might help me but there weren't many around; those that were, were mostly out of date or applied to the USA and not to the UK music business. I had to learn from my colleagues as I went along. I was lucky in that they were very knowledgeable and very generous with their time.

Now there are many more sources of information available on the UK music business and there are full- and part-time media and law courses available to give you a head start. And yet I often find myself wishing there was a good, easy to read guide to how the business works from a legal viewpoint – one that explains what a publisher does and what copyright is. Every trainee lawyer that comes to work with me asks if there's a guide to the music business they can read as a kind of road map through the industry. Managers and artists often ask me the same thing. This book aims to be that guide. Where I've used technical expressions I've tried to give a non-technical explanation alongside. For the legal eagles among you, the detail is there in the footnotes. This book is not, however, intended to be a substitute for legal textbooks on copyright, other Intellectual Property rights or contract. There are many good examples of these sorts of books around, some of which are listed in the Further Reading section at the end of the book.

The music business is constantly changing and evolving, so online distribution, webcasts and other uses of new-media technologies are dealt with throughout the book.

Wherever possible I've tried to illustrate points with practical examples. Because my experience is in acting for the creative end of the business – for the 'talent' rather than the big record or publishing companies – I tend to favour the artist's viewpoint. But I wouldn't have got anywhere in the music business if I hadn't also learned all the arguments that could be used against me by the other side. So I've also tried to give both sides of an argument except where this would have made the text too confusing.

We've all been fascinated by newspaper reports of this or that artist in court over disputes with their ex-managers, record companies or even other members of the band. Are these reports accurate? Do these cases have any long-term effect? Do they matter? In this book I'll highlight the facts of some of the more important cases, what was decided and the effects of the decisions on the music business.

I also have to add a health warning that the examples produced and the guidelines given are mine alone and others may not agree or may have had different experiences.

What I've tried to do is to let you into some of the things I've learned over the last fifteen years in the music business. It's no substitute for legal advice on the particular facts of your case. Chapter 1 deals with choosing your advisers. Please read it. Good advisers will save you from what can be expensive mistakes. Most artists only have one chance of a successful career in this business – make sure you don't lose it through poor advice.

ABBREVIATIONS

In this book the following abbreviations have been used:

FSR	Fleet Street Reports
EMLR	Entertainment & Media Law Reports
CDPA	Copyright Designs and Patents Act 1988
QBD	Queen's Bench Division

I have followed the usual convention of using 'he' throughout. This is not intended as a slur on female artists or on the many excellent women working at all levels in the music business.

1: **GETTING STARTED**

INTRODUCTION

How do you get into the music business as a performing artist or songwriter? How do you get your foot in the door, and how and when do you start gathering your team of advisers around you?

This isn't a book on how to become a star or how to make your band a success, although it does try to help you avoid some of the mistakes you might make along the way. It's about understanding the music business, the deals and how to get yourself started. For books on how to be a star, see the Further Reading section at the end of the book.

CREATING A BUZZ

How do you get your work noticed? The idea is to create a 'buzz' by whatever ways you can. We'll see later that lawyers and accountants can help you to get noticed, but you also need a way to get your work heard.

You can play as many gigs as you can and hope to be recognised by a scout on the lookout for a record or music publishing company, or you can make a demo of your performances or songs and send it to an A&R person and hope.

There's no guarantee of success. As someone said to me the other day, 'Just because you've got a phone doesn't mean anyone will call.'

You could try to improve your chances by using gimmicks. Sometimes bands hire open-top buses and drive past record companies playing as if their life depends on it. Or they dress up as cartoon characters or animals and hang about outside the record company hoping to get noticed. It's still very hit or miss.

You can also shamelessly exploit any and all contacts you have with anyone who has even the remotest connection with the music business, especially lawyers. You can pester these hapless souls to 'get their mate to the next gig' or to listen to your demo. This can improve your chances of at least getting your work listened to but that isn't any guarantee it will lead to a record or publishing deal.

A&R people are bombarded with sackfuls of demos and lots of artists have contacts in the music business promising to do them a favour. You need to be more enterprising than ever to bring your music to the top of the pile. In Internet parlance, to get yourself heard above the 'noise'.

It's true that scouts do find undiscovered talent playing in out-of-the-way pubs. If you happen to be based outside the M25, your chances of being spotted are much slimmer than if you're in London. However, there are other areas of the country that get the attention of scouts – Sheffield, Liverpool, Manchester, Bristol and Glasgow among them. Sometimes you get an ambitious scout who goes and checks out what's happening in a part of the country not on the traditional circuit. When this happens you can get a rash of signings in that area. A recent example of this was the number of Welsh acts that were discovered after one scout crossed the Severn Bridge and found the wealth of talent that existed in South Wales. The number of A&R people heading down the M4 increased 500-fold and suddenly it was the only place to be. Who knows, your area could be next.

A&R people are largely conservative, although there are exceptions and none of them will admit it. They like to have their hunch about an artist confirmed by someone else whose opinion they respect. This could be someone in their own company but, somewhat surprisingly, they will often talk to A&R people from rival companies. You'd think that if they found someone they thought was good they would keep it to themselves until the deal was done. Some do but many seem to need to be convinced that they've got it right, even though this might push up the cost of the deal if the rival company also gets in the running to sign the same artist. For the artist this is a dream come true. He can choose the company that works best for him and his lawyer will play one company off against the other to get a better deal. This is what we call your bargaining power. The more bargaining power you have, the better your overall deal is likely to be.

THE BAND NAME

The name a band chooses is a vital part of its identity, its brand. It's a very difficult thing to get right and it's quite common for bands to go through various name changes before they settle on one they're happy with. It should be chosen for its simplicity and for how easy it is to remember. Why? If you combine a good name with a clever logo then you're already halfway to having the basis of a good advertising campaign. Whether you're selling yourself on the Internet or through the press, TV or radio, a distinctive name makes it that much easier. If it's a name that you can do some wordplay with, so much the better. There has been a tendency in recent years for bands to have short, one-word names – Blur, Pulp, Oasis and Suede, to name but a few. However, a name doesn't have to be short to be memorable. One of my favourite band names is Kitchens Of Distinction (where are they now?).

Finding a good name is easier said than done. I'm sure you've all sat around at some time in the pub after a beer or three and tried to come up with good band names. Despite all my advice on branding I suspect that most bands choose their name for much more down-to-earth reasons, like it sounds cool, or it's the only one they can think of that's not naff and that no one else has already nabbed.

If the Internet spawns the growth we think it will then there'll be even more artists hunting for that elusive, special name. It's already becoming more and more difficult to find a distinctive name that hasn't already been grabbed by someone else. So as soon as you've thought of a name, spend a little money on getting a domain name registered as soon as possible. The costs of registering are coming down all the time. I've recently heard of a company that was offering to register a domain name for £1.99 – but I suspect there may be a catch in the small print.

A potential problem is that you might decide on a name not knowing that someone else has already claimed it. You may then invest a lot of time and maybe some money in starting to develop a reputation in that name. You aren't going to be very happy if you then find out that someone else has the same name. So how do you check if someone is already using a band name?

There are some easy and cheap means of doing this. Firstly, go to the nearest large record store and ask to borrow their catalogue listing all available records. Have a look if the name you want to use appears – the lists are usually alphabetical by artist name, so that's not as horrible a task as it might seem.

If you have access to the Internet you can widen your search. Using a good search engine, check to see if the name you have chosen appears. You could just do a UK search, but if you plan to sell records overseas (and you do, don't you?) then you should do a worldwide search.

THE BAND REGISTER

You can also apply to register your band name with the Band Register (see Useful Addresses). The Band Register is run as a commercial operation and many firms of lawyers subscribe to it as a means of searching for band names on behalf of their clients. Their stated aim is to try to head off disputes over names by acting as a filtering process at the beginning and before a band gets too attached to the name they've chosen. The names that they list are taken from a number of sources. As well as taking the details from people who apply to them they also trawl through the concert listings in the newspapers and add to their database the names of artists who are doing gigs around the country. They do look overseas but not to the same extent as in the UK.

If you apply to register, or simply request a name check, and the search reveals that there is another band with the same name, you may choose to ignore this and go ahead with the name anyway. If you do, remember this: the Band Register has evidence that you knew about it when you decided to go ahead. However, just because a band is listed on the Band Register database doesn't mean that they will automatically succeed in stopping you from using the same name. You have to also look at whether they have a name or reputation, whether they have registered a trade mark or a domain name and whether they have a reputation in the same area of the business as you.

If you choose the same name and the other band objects to you continuing to use it, they may sue you. If they have registered a trade mark they could argue that if you continue to use the name this would be a breach of their trade mark (see Chapter 8).

If they haven't registered a trade mark they would have to argue that they had a reputation in the same area of music, and in the same country as you, and that you were creating confusion in the mind of the public and trading on their reputation. If they *can* establish these things (and that isn't always easy to do), and they can also show that they are – or are likely – to lose out as a result, then they can ask the court to order you to stop using the name and also ask the court to award them damages against you. This is called 'passing off' (see Chapter 8).[1]

1 For a more academic overview of branding see Chapter 21 of *Copinger and Skone-James on Copyright*, Sweet & Maxwell, 1998.

If the other band were registered first and you inquire at the Register, find out that they are already registered and seemingly are active in the business but you go ahead anyway, then that could be evidence that they had the reputation in the name first and that you are passing yourselves off as that band. On the other hand, just because a band has done a gig or two under the same name as you, it doesn't necessarily mean that they have a reputation or that they can satisfy the other tests of 'passing off'. You may have the greater reputation or the greater bargaining power: if you've already got a record deal or are about to release a single or album under that name, you may be able to persuade them that they are in fact trading on *your* reputation and that they should stop using the name.

If you do find another band with the same name then you could do a deal with them to buy the right to use the name. You pay them a small amount (or a big amount if you really want the name) and they stop using it, allowing you to carry on. If you are going to do these sorts of deals you should also make sure that you get from them any domain name that they've registered in the band name and, if they have a trade mark, an agreement to assign the registration to you.

TRADE MARK SEARCH

You can run a trade mark search to see if there is someone else with the same, or a very similar, name in the classes of goods or services that you would be interested in (for example Class 9 for records). In US record deals, the record companies often make it a condition of the deal that they run a trade mark search and charge you for the privilege. They usually add on the cost to the unrecouped balance on your account. If the search reveals another band or artist with the same name, your record company will usually make you change your name.

This happened to the band Suede. They were going to do a tour in the US when it was discovered that there was a female singer who had been using the name Suede for years. So Suede changed their name for the US to The London Suede. Somehow it never quite caught on in the same way.

SHOWCASING YOUR TALENT

Record companies have had their fingers burnt by signing artists (who they haven't seen perform live) for large sums of money and then discovering that they can't play or sing at all. So most record companies insist on seeing you play live. If you're already playing the club circuit, they may just turn up to a gig. If you aren't, they may pay for the hire of a venue. This is called a showcase. The venue will be either a club near the record company offices or a rehearsal studio. Sony Records showcases often take place in their staff canteen. Showcases may be open to the public but usually they'll be invitation only.

You could hire a venue yourself and send invitations out to all the record companies. However, just because you've invited them doesn't mean they'll come. Don't be at all surprised if they say they're coming and then don't show up. It's a very fickle business. They probably got a better offer on the night. The more of a 'buzz' there is about you, the more likely it is that they will turn up – they won't want to miss out on what could be 'the next big thing'.

I once asked the MD of a record company why he was paying for an artist to perform live at a showcase open to the public when he knew that the artist would then be seen by all the A&R people from rival record companies. His answer was quite revealing. He said that he knew how far he was prepared to go on the deal and so wasn't bothered about the 'hyping' of the deal. He felt that if this artist really wanted to be with his record company he wouldn't be influenced by the interest from other companies. If the artist was persuaded to sign to another company then he was not right for his company anyway. Confidence indeed. In fact the artist did sign to him and at the time of writing is still there.

PRESENTING YOURSELF WELL

Here are some tips that may help you showcase your talents successfully. First and foremost, do your homework. Read the music press. Find out the current 'happening' venues, the places that regularly get written up in the music press. Pester that venue to give you a spot, even if it's the opening spot, and get all your mates to come along so that it looks like you've already got a loyal following. You may not get to that stage immediately. You may need to start out in the clubs outside the main circuit and work your way in.

You should also find out what nights the venue features your kind of music. If yours is radio-friendly, commercial pop you don't want to get a gig on heavy metal night.

Make sure the songs you play (your set) represent a good cross-section of what you do. What goes down well with your mates in the local may not work for a more sophisticated (or uptight) urban audience.

Be professional. Rehearse, rehearse, rehearse. Think about your image. Is it shoe-gazing indie rock or in-your-face punk? Dress accordingly. Don't send mixed messages. Practise your attitude to the audience. If yours is the 'say nothing, the music will speak for itself' style, that's fine – but make sure you're sending that message clearly to your audience. We all like a 'personality'. If your band has got one, make sure you use him or her.

Always tell your audience who you are at the beginning and end of your set. You'd think this was obvious but you'd be surprised how many gigs I've been to where it's been impossible to tell who the artist is unless you've seen them before. The line-up of the bands on the night can change and no gig ever starts at the time it's supposed to so you can't even make an intelligent guess. Make life easier for us – tell us who you are.

Try and get your local press behind you. I know of one Nottingham band that did this very successfully. They made a fan of the arts reporter on the local newspaper and kept him up to date on what they were up to and when they were playing. This made sure they got good reviews. A scout read one of these and went to the next gig. This led to a gig on the outer London circuit. The band took 'rent-a-crowd' with them and were spotted by an A&R man, who had been tipped off by the scout. A record deal followed. The local reporter was the first one they told – after their mums, of course.

SHORT CUTS

It's a long haul and it needs determination and dedication to plug away on the gig circuit like this. Are there any short cuts? Yes, there are some. There are 'battle of the bands'-type competitions and if you get through to the final three, or even win, then that will give you valuable exposure and should ensure a number of follow-up gigs in the local area and some useful publicity. They don't often lead directly to deals although, if you win, you may get free studio time to make a demo (see below).

There are also 'open mike' evenings at clubs, when anyone can turn up and ask to play one or two numbers. In London these are held at places like Cairo Jacks, West 14, the 12-Bar Club and the Kashmir Club. Scouts regularly visit these venues because there are reasonable chances of them seeing a good act.

Music industry organisations – such as the Performing Right Society Limited (PRS) or its US equivalents The American Society of Composers and Publishers (ASCAP) or Broadcast Music, Inc. (BMI) – occasionally arrange nights at a Central London venue to showcase two or three acts who are either unsigned or have signed a record deal but not a publishing deal (or vice versa). Again these are popular with A&R people because someone has already filtered out a lot of the rubbish for them.

There is also an annual UK music industry convention called In The City. Attached to it is a series of showcases for unsigned acts at venues in the city where the conference is being held. Its base is Manchester but it does visit other places. In 1999 it was in Liverpool and, in previous years, Glasgow and Dublin have hosted it with varying degrees of success.

It's quite expensive to register for the conference but it's often possible to get into the bar of the main conference hotel where the executives meet to relax. You could get lucky and meet one or two A&R people and get your demo to them. Remember, however, that their bullshit level tends to increase proportionately to the lateness of the hour and the number of pints of beer drunk. They'll probably need to be reminded who you are with a follow-up call a few days later.

If you're chosen for one of the unsigned showcases, it will guarantee that at least one A&R person will be at your gig – even if he's there to see someone else. In past years Suede, Kula Shaker and Oasis have all played 'In The City Unsigned'.

THE DEMO RECORDING

One thing most short cuts have in common is that the organisers have to hear a recording of your work first. The demo recording is your calling card, your way of introducing a stranger to your work. It should be recorded to the best standard you can afford.

STUDIO DEALS

What if you haven't any money – how do you afford to make a recording? One way is to beg down time off your local recording studio. This is time when the studio isn't being hired out commercially. It's usually at really unsociable hours such as 2 a.m. to 8 a.m. But who needs sleep – you've got a record deal to get.

The studio may give you the time cheaply or even free. In reality they're more likely to let you have the time in return for promises of what they'll get when you get your first deal. The studio owner may want some of the income (the royalty) you earn from the sale of your records. This is sometimes called an override royalty. This is fair if you get a deal using recordings made at the studio, but take care that the studio isn't being too greedy and asking for too much. A 1% override royalty is enough. By that I mean that if you are offered a 12% royalty then you have to give 1% to the studio owner, leaving you with 11%. Some studios try and get royalties on your second and third album too. They argue that you wouldn't have got your chance to record at all without their generosity. This is true but there comes a time when your success has nothing to do with that original generosity. One album is plenty.

The studio may also want a guarantee that you use their facilities when you make your album. Or the studio owner may want to produce your album. You should be careful about agreeing to these sorts of conditions. Record companies don't like package deals on studio and producer. They like to have some say on these things themselves.

The demo should feature a good cross-section of your work. Most people think that it should contain no more than three or four different pieces, with your best one first, your second best one last and contrasting style pieces in the middle. The opening number should have immediate impact in case the listener fast-forwards it before you've got into your stride. Many A&R people listen to demo tapes in their car. If you don't grab their attention they'll hit the eject button and move on to the next in the pile. The case and the tape/CD/DAT should both contain details of who you are, the names of the pieces, who wrote them and, most importantly, a contact number. I get loads of demos where the name and number is only on the case so that when, inevitably, the case gets separated from the CD or tape itself, there's no way of telling who it is and how you get hold of them.

If the A&R person likes your tape he'll undoubtedly want to hear more. He may want to pay for some studio time for you to record some more material or to try out different versions of what you've already recorded on your demo. He may offer you a demo deal.

DEMO DEAL

The deal will usually guarantee you a certain amount of time in a professional or in-house recording studio. Many record and publishing companies have their own studio facilities, which they may offer to make available. Perhaps you shouldn't look a gift-horse in the mouth but if the studio doesn't have the equipment you need to show yourself off to best advantage then you should say so and either ask for that equipment to be hired in or ask to go into a commercial studio. Cheeky, yes, but you can do it politely and it's your big chance, so don't blow it.

The record or publishing company will expect to own the copyright in what you record (see Chapters 3 and 4). The company will want to own the right to control what happens to the recording. A record company won't usually expect to own rights in the song, but a music publisher might. Try and take advice before you agree to give away rights in the song. At the very least, they shouldn't own the song unless they offer you a proper publishing deal (see Chapter 4).

The company offering you the deal will also own the physical recording or 'master'. This is fine as long as they don't stop you recording the same song for someone else if they don't offer you a deal. They should also agree that they won't do anything with the masters without first getting your permission. This is important. When you finally sign your record deal you'll be asked to confirm that no one else has the right to release recordings of your performances. The record company will not find it funny if a rival company releases the very track that they had planned as your first single. The company who paid for the demo will usually agree that you can play it to other companies if they decide not to offer you a deal.

The record or publishing company will normally want some exclusivity in return for the studio time they're giving you. They may want you to agree not to make demos for anyone else or to agree not to negotiate with another company for a period of time.

They may be slightly more flexible and want the right of first negotiation or refusal. This means that they will want either to have the first chance to try to negotiate a deal with you or to have the right to say yes or no first, before you sign to another company. This is a difficult call. You'll no doubt be excited, and perhaps desperate not to risk losing the deal, but before agreeing to exclusivity or these negotiating options you need to be sure that the exclusive time period isn't too long. If they tie you up for months, you may miss your moment. If they have first negotiating or rejection rights then they should tell you as soon as possible where you stand. If they're not interested then you need to move on as quickly as possible.

Bear in mind, though, that the record company has to go through a number of stages before they can make a decision. They have to listen to the recording, probably then discuss it at a weekly A&R meeting and then maybe also with their immediate bosses or even overseas colleagues. All this takes time and they may not want to risk losing you to a rival company. So you need to get a balance between the needs of the two sides.

Don't be surprised if, after you make the demo, the company decides not to offer you a deal. Don't get too depressed. I know several artists who got demo time from two or three record companies and ended up with an excellent set of demos that they took to another company who then signed them up. What you don't want to happen is that people feel that you've been around for a while and are sounding a bit stale. This is a difficult balance to strike.

On a more positive note, the first company may love what you've recorded. The demos may confirm the A&R man's faith in your abilities and he may be ready to do a deal with you. You've passed go and, after you've read the rest of this chapter on getting yourself some good advisers, you should go straight to Chapter 3 (What Is A Good Record Deal?).

GETTING HELP AND PUTTING TOGETHER YOUR TEAM

All of this may seem a bit daunting. Don't be worried about negotiating or signing a studio or demo deal. There are people that you can turn to for help. You should be looking to put your team of advisers and helpers in place as soon as you start to get a bit of a 'buzz' about you, so that you're ready to move quickly.

THE LAWYER

A good lawyer with experience of the business can be of enormous help to you. So where do you find one and what can they do for you?

Finding a lawyer

You can ask the Law Society for their suggestions (see the Useful Addresses section for details). They have entertainment firms on their referral lists but make no judgement on the quality of the advice.

Many law firms have their own websites. You can search for them on the Internet. Most websites will tell you a bit about the firm and its areas of expertise. The websites usually contain an email address, so you could try sending them a message or ask for further information.

Some websites contain details of the last big deals the firm did and, where their clients allow them to, list the names of some of their clients. It isn't necessarily a bad thing if there aren't many clients mentioned. Professional rules mean we have to keep client information confidential and not even say that someone *is* a client without that person's permission or unless it's public knowledge. If a client is kind enough to give me a credit on the album sleeve then I take it that he's happy for people to know I'm his lawyer.

Directories

There are two main books listing UK legal firms – *Chambers*[2] and *Legal 500*.[3] The guides can be found in most of the larger public libraries. Both have a similar approach, breaking down the lists into areas of the country and particular specialisations. Most UK music lawyers are based in London but there are one or two elsewhere, such as Manchester and Glasgow. *Chambers* features short pieces on those it thinks are the leading players in a particular field. *Legal 500* operates on a league principle. When it interviews lawyers it sees which names are mentioned most frequently by others in the business and grades the firms accordingly.

The *Music Week Directory* also lists UK law firms, but an entry in the directory isn't any guarantee that they are any good.[4]

Managers and accountants

If you already have a manager or an accountant, they may be able to recommend a lawyer to you. You should check if your manager has the same lawyer. Most managers realise that for some things (for example, negotiating the management contract) you have to have a separate lawyer from the manager. There is a conflict in the interests of the two parties, which means you must be separately advised. Where there is no conflict of interest there is nothing wrong in having the same lawyer as your manager.

Other bands

Other bands or contacts in the business may well be able to recommend someone to you. They may recommend their own lawyer or someone they've heard others say is good. We lawyers love personal recommendations as a source of new work. It means we must be doing

2 *Chambers*, published by Chambers & Partners Publishing, Tel: (020) 7606 1300. Fax: (020) 7600 3191.

3 *Legal 500*, published by Legalese. Tel: (020) 7396 9302.

4 *Music Week Directory*, published annually by Miller Freeman Entertainment. If you subscribe to *Music Week*, you are entitled to a free copy of the directory and a free entry in it.

something right. Recommendations based on a job well done are about as good as it gets really.

Other sources of information

Other sources could be the Musicians' Union, the International Association of Entertainment Lawyers and the Music Managers Forum. See the section on Useful Addresses at the back of the book.

How do you go about choosing and employing a lawyer?

Like everyone else, lawyers can have their moments when they're in the public eye because of a particular high-profile piece of work they've done and then everyone wants to have them as their lawyer. You must, however, try to find out whether the lawyer is experienced and not a one-hit wonder. How do you do that? Ideally you should have two or three names on your list possibly gathered from a variety of sources. You should call them, tell them you're looking for a lawyer and ask to meet with them. Be wary of lawyers who promise the earth. We don't have all the answers. Before you meet up with the lawyers have some questions ready for them. Ask how long they've been doing this and who their main clients are. As we saw, they may be a bit coy about this because of their duty to keep clients and their business confidential.

You should also ask the lawyers the all-important question of what they charge, when they expect to send you a bill and when they expect it to be paid. Will they accept payment in instalments and, if so, do they charge interest on the balance? Can you pay by credit card? Beware a lawyer who is reluctant to discuss his costs. If he tells you what he charges by the hour, you may need a stiff drink afterwards. But quoting hourly rates doesn't really help you to compare two firms, as one lawyer may work faster than the other. A better way to do it is to ask them to give you a ballpark figure for what it usually costs for them to do a record or publishing deal. If you ask each lawyer the same question you'll have a better basis for a comparison. Don't necessarily go for the lowest price. It may be that the deal gets done faster but it's a short-term view. Where the lawyer really comes into his own is when something goes wrong in six months' or a year's time. Then the thoroughness with which he's done his job in protecting your interests really gets put to the test.

Your lawyer is a fundamental part of your team. Take your time in choosing one and don't be afraid to say if you're not happy with a piece of work, including voting with your feet and changing lawyers if it doesn't work out. The same goes for your accountant and any other advisers you have. We're only as good as the last job we did for you.

Potential problems

There are firms of lawyers that work mostly for record and publishing companies and others that work for what we call the talent (the creative end of the business). It's important to know this. If the record label interested in you uses the same firm for their own legal advice there will be a conflict of interest which will make it difficult for that firm to work for you if you're in a dispute with the record company. Some say it's possible to build Chinese Walls (artificial barriers where, in theory, one lawyer within a firm knows nothing about what another is doing so can't be influenced in any negotiation). When things are going well this can work, provided everyone knows it's happening. When things aren't going so well will you feel confident that your lawyer is looking after your interests?

Another potential problem area concerns fees. The Law Society now recommends that your lawyer send you a letter setting out the basis on which he is going to work for you, including details of what he expects to charge. The letter should also tell you whom you should complain to within the firm if you can't get the problem sorted out by speaking to your own lawyer. If the worst comes to the worst you can ask for a Remuneration Certificate (provided you ask for it within a month of getting the bill). You can also ask the court to tax (i.e. check) the bill. As a last resort you can appoint another firm of lawyers to sue the first. The Law Society can recommend firms to you that do that sort of work. But this is all very negative. In the majority of cases there isn't a problem that can't be sorted out with one phone call.

Beauty Parades

When you go to meet lawyers, it's only fair to you tell them that you're seeing other firms. Lawyers call these meetings 'Beauty Parades', as we set out to impress you. There's nothing worse than spending an hour giving advice to someone you think has already chosen you as their lawyer only to be told as they walk out of the door, 'Thanks for that, I'll get back to you when I've seen the other firms on my list.'

If you're asked what other firms you've seen, you don't have to say. However, if you do, it helps that lawyer, who then knows who he's in competition with and can adjust his 'sales pitch' accordingly.

When you've decided on the lawyer you want to work with, you should tell the others, who have given up an hour or more of their valuable time, that they are out of luck. You never know, you may want to change lawyers at some point and there's no harm in keeping things civil.

What does your lawyer do for you?

A trite answer may be to say whatever you instruct him to do (provided it's legal). We do work 'on instructions' from you but that's really not a true picture of all that we can do for you. We are there to advise you, to help you decide what's the best deal for you. We give you the benefit of our experience of similar situations. In larger firms, where there's more than one music lawyer, you are also getting the benefit of all their experience, as we share information on who is doing what deals and for how much.

If you want, we can help you to target companies that our experience tells us should be interested in your type of music. This can help you to be more focused. This doesn't mean to say that we act as A&R people, although I have come across one or two lawyers who do think they are, including one large law firm that employs at least one lawyer in an A&R role to 'spot' new talent that's likely to be successful and bring in lots of work and fees.

The type of music you are into shouldn't influence your lawyer. Your lawyer should be able to represent you whatever style of music you make, provided it's not so out of his area of expertise that he doesn't have the necessary experience or knowledge. For example, if you were a second Nigel Kennedy or Charlotte Church and your lawyer has only done rap or techno deals before, he could do the legal work for you but he wouldn't be much use to you as a source of commercial advice, on whether the deal is good, bad or indifferent.

Our role can be as wide or as narrow as you want it to be. If you're already clued up on the type of deal you want, or have a manager who is, then you won't need the benefit of that sort of advice. If you're quite happy about negotiating a deal direct with the record or publishing company then you bring your lawyer in later, when the commercial terms are agreed and you need to get the legal contract in place. On the other hand, if you're new to the business and aren't confident enough to negotiate commercial terms then you'll want to involve your lawyer at a much earlier stage.

I work differently with different types of clients. If it's a new artist that either doesn't have a manager or has a manager who isn't very experienced, I run with things right from the beginning, when the record company says it wants to do a deal. I contact the record company, get their deal proposal and, after talking to the client, I go back to the record company with any counter-proposals, continuing this process until the deal is in its final form. I then get the draft contract, check it, make any necessary changes and negotiate those with the company until the contract is in a final form ready for me to recommend to the client for signature.

With other clients there may be an experienced manager on board who knows exactly what his bargaining power is and what sort of deal he'd ideally like to end up with. My role at the beginning is just that of an adviser. The manager will usually make sure I get a copy of the proposal and any counter-proposals but won't want to involve me directly in the negotiations. He may call from time to time to ask if I think Company X can do better than what they are offering. I'll tell him what I think based on other deals I, or my colleagues, have done with that company. We keep the details and the names of the clients confidential but we can say whether we know they can do better on a particular point or not. Once this type of client is happy with the commercial terms I'm then brought in to do the negotiation of the contract itself.

You should establish with your lawyer what kind of relationship you want to have. This may well change from deal to deal as you grow in experience.

I like to take an interest in my clients' work. I'm delighted to be sent a copy of the new album or single before it's released. It helps to cement the relationship between us. I also like to go and see my clients play live. I have to admit, though, that when I'm in the middle of a very long week at work and a client rings up and says, 'Hi, I'm on stage tonight at the Laughing Cow at 10.30 p.m.' (which means 11 p.m. at the earliest) then my wish to support the client is tested to the full.

What you don't want to happen is for your advisers to embarrass you. And yes, it does happen. I can still remember a gig a few years ago at the Forum in London. Four members of a top entertainment accountancy firm were standing proudly in the front row wearing the band's T-shirt over their work suits. The band was The Fat Lady Sings. Their name comes from the American saying, meaning that an event isn't over until the singing of the national anthem by the obligatory large opera singer. On this occasion, the sight of these accountants in the audience must have been enough to make the band feel like rushing straight to the last few verses of 'God Save The Queen' before dashing off stage.

When should you get a lawyer?

There are a number of different views on this. Some say that there's no need to get a lawyer until you have a contract in front of you. Funnily enough, I think you should get a lawyer as early as possible. I think that the whole process of getting a deal is so much of a lottery that anything you can do to reduce the odds must be worth doing. Most of us are happy to give initial advice and guidance for free or only charge you when your first deal is in place. Just be careful and check this before going ahead.

The lawyer can also help you to find a good accountant.

ACCOUNTANTS

This leads me neatly on to discuss how you find a good accountant, and what they can do for you.

The Institutes

The accountancy profession doesn't have one society, unlike the legal profession and its Law Society. The Institutes of Chartered Accountants in England & Wales, Scotland or Northern Ireland and the Association of Chartered and Certified Accountants can recommend firms to you (see Useful Addresses). What is important is that the accountant is a qualified Chartered or Certified accountant.

Directories

There isn't any general guide like *Legal 500* or *Chambers*. The accountancy profession is broken down into the big five international firms, such as Ernst & Young and Deloitte & Touche, medium-sized national firms with international networks, such as BDO Stoy Hayward, and smaller local firms.

You can also check in the *Music Week Directory*, which has a section on accountants. The directory is not a recommendation that they're any good, but it is a good starting point. See the Useful Addresses section for contact details.

AMIA

You could always go to the Association of Music Industry Accountants (see Useful Addresses). They will be happy to recommend accountants from within their own membership and, as their name suggests, they are all associated with the music business.

Music Managers Forum

The MMF can give you recommendations for accountants as well as for lawyers but they'll probably point you in the direction of the accountants who sponsor them or are corporate members (see Useful Addresses).

Lawyers

Your lawyer should have had dealings with a number of accountants and should be able to recommend two or three to you. Lawyers are a very valuable source of clients for accountants. This probably explains the many invites I get to accountants' parties. The idea of a boat ride on the Thames may seem attractive but once you've been trapped on the boat with a hundred other lawyers and accountants for hours the novelty tends to wear off.

Bank managers

Your bank manager may have one or two names of accountants he can suggest – but it must be someone who is familiar with the music business. Certain banks, such as Coutts and some branches of Barclays, NatWest and HSBC, concentrate on the entertainment industry and they would certainly be able to suggest some names to you. It is also important that you find a sympathetic bank manager who will understand that your income doesn't come in neat monthly wage cheques. Your accountant can put you in touch with those he has found to be helpful.

Other sources of information

Your A&R contact or your friends in the music business may be able to suggest some names and it's always good to get a recommendation from someone who rates a particular accountant highly.

How to choose an accountant

You should see more than one accountant. You should ask them the type of work they can do for you. Some have their strength in tour accounting or in auditing (inspecting) the books and records of companies. They may also do general bookkeeping and give tax advice – but, then again, they may not, so ask.

If you expect to do a lot of touring, it's worth having an accountant who is experienced in putting together tour accounts and is familiar with tour budgets and all the necessary arrangements to deal with VAT on overseas tours and taxes on overseas income (see Chapter 10).

It's less important that your accountant's offices are in the same place as the record and publishing companies. They don't have to be in London. The main thing is that they are familiar with the music business and how it works. They must know the sources of income and how and when it's paid. They need to know how to read and understand a royalty statement. These things are often, literally, written in code. You need to know what country A is and what the code for CD sales is. Your local family accountant can, of course, do the basic accounting work as well as the next man but this isn't enough. Just as you need a lawyer with specialised music business knowledge, so you need the same expertise from your accountant if he's to be able to properly look after your interests. The basic accountancy and tax rules do, of course, apply to artists and songwriters but there are a number of specialised rules and regulations aimed at them. Your accountant must be up to date on these rules.

Some accountants don't claim to be experts in tax planning or advice and, if that's an area that you need to have covered, you would be best advised to go to an accountant that can provide that and then get a specialist accountant in to do the tour accounting or auditing.

Business managers

There is another breed of accountant that could provide the sort of services you are looking for and that is a business manager. This is a term that has come across from the US where they're quite common. In the US they generally act as the business and financial adviser alongside a personal manager who looks after the day-to-day and creative aspects of the artists career (see Chapter 2).

In the UK, the term means something slightly different. They provide day-to-day business advice and bookkeeping services. They will do your VAT and tax returns for you. They can provide business plans and advice and some also do tour accounts. Most don't provide international tax planning or audits. Their argument is that this makes them more cost-effective as you aren't paying for a full tax planning and audit service. This means they can charge less than the bigger firms of accountants do. When specialist tax or international advice is required they make use of their contacts with more than one of the bigger accountancy firms and other financial advisers and can refer you to the right company for you – to get the advice you need when you need it.

How do they charge?

Accountants should charge fees rather than commission. They may quote you a rate per annum for advising you. Some of the bigger accountancy firms run special schemes where the first year's work for you is done at a special, discounted rate. You don't have to stay with them after the first year. If you are tempted by these schemes you should ask what exactly is covered by the discount rate. It's likely that you won't get the same service as the full-price one. You should also ask what the non-discounted rate would be after the first year so that you can decide whether you think you would be able to stay with them afterwards or will have to start the search for a new accountant, which could be disruptive.

You should ask them what their experience is and who will be doing the work. Often you find that the person who sees you and does the hard sell is the partner or even the marketing person. Someone quite different, and possibly much less experienced, may be doing the work. This sort of thing is more likely to happen in the bigger firms, particularly those that are offering a discount rate. You can be reasonably sure that it won't be a partner that'll be doing the cut-price work.

What does an accountant do?

Accountants can do a number of things for you. They do the books for you, advise and help you to complete your tax return. They register you for VAT if necessary and can do your quarterly VAT returns. Depending on their level of expertise, they may also do the tour accounts for you and help prepare a tour budget.

Your accountant will advise you on whether you should be a sole trader, in partnership or a limited company (see Chapter 11). He can prepare partnership or company accounts. Some accountants can also act as the auditor of your company books and many can also act as the company secretary. They can arrange for the company's registered office to be at their offices. Incidentally, this is also a service that your lawyer can often provide, so you might want to compare costs and see which offers the best value before automatically plumping for one or the other.

Your accountant can act as your financial adviser, telling you where is the best place to invest your money. Because this area is very closely regulated, not all accountants are authorised to provide financial services advice. You should ask if your accountant is. If he isn't, you will need a separate financial adviser.

Your accountant can be your tax adviser and help plan with you such things as whether you could consider putting your income in an offshore tax haven or, indeed, if you could, or should, become a tax exile.

Can your accountant help you get a record deal? Yes, he can. You can use accountants in the same way as lawyers. Use their contacts and pick their brains for information on companies and A&R people. Accountants also send out demo tapes on behalf of artists and songwriters.

If your accountant does find you a deal then he shouldn't charge you a commission for doing so. He should just charge for any accountancy advice that he gives you on that deal. If your accountant offers to get you a deal, ask him on what basis he's doing it before you give him the go ahead.

The accountant should be able to work as part of the team with you, your manager and your lawyer. It's important that you keep your accountant in the loop about how the deal could be structured as tax-effectively as possible. You should let him know before you sign anything and get his input on how best to structure the deal.

All accountants should give you a letter of engagement setting out the basis on which they will work for you and how they will charge. They should give you the name of someone in the firm that you can complain to if you have a problem with your accountant. If the complaint is about fees then you can ask for a breakdown of the bill. The professional body that your accountant belongs to is the next port of call for complaints about your accountant. If they don't deal with the complaint to your satisfaction, you can take it to court. This is again very negative and most relationships proceed smoothly.

Your accountant can have conflicts of interest just as your lawyer can. If your accountant acts for one of the major record or publishing companies and you then want to do a deal with that company, the conflict may or may not arise at that stage. However, if later on you aren't sure whether the company is accounting to you properly and you want to send someone in to look at (audit) the books then your accountant will have a conflict of interest and you'll probably have to take that work elsewhere. There are in fact specialist firms of accountants who only do audits. Sometimes it's best to use their specialised knowledge, even if there isn't a conflict of interest with your own accountant.

So now you've got your lawyer and your accountant lined up. You have two members of your team – getting a manager could be the critical third stage. I'll deal with this in the next chapter.

CONCLUSIONS

- If you hope to get noticed through doing live work, do your homework first. Investigate your venues and rehearse thoroughly. Tailor your material to your audience and tell us who you are.
- Consider short cuts like industry-organised showcases, open-mike evenings or music conventions.
- Make sure your demo is the best quality that you can afford and that it contains a good cross-section of your work. Put your name and contact number on the tape or CD as well as the packaging.
- If you do a deal with a studio for studio time, make sure it's for no more than 1% and do everything possible not to agree they can be the producer on the first album.
- If you do a demo deal, keep the exclusive period as short as possible and make sure that they can't do anything with the recordings without your agreement.
- When picking a lawyer or accountant, arrange to see two or three and ask them for estimates of their charges for a particular piece of work. Find out their expertise and who their clients are.
- When you appoint a lawyer or accountant, get written confirmation from them of their charges.
- Your accountant and lawyer are vital members of your team – take your time to choose the right one.

2: MANAGEMENT DEALS

INTRODUCTION

In this chapter I'm going to look at how you find a good manager, what to expect from a manager and what you have to think about when doing a management contract. I'm going to look at it from the artist's point of view, but when we get to the contract part I'm also going to put the manager's side of the argument. The section on what to expect from a manager should also be useful to managers. It'll give them an idea of what is reasonable to expect from them.

It gives me a real thrill to team up the right manager with the right artist. It really is like watching a well-oiled machine going into action. It's also great to work with a good artist/manager team. Everyone's pulling in the same direction.

HOW TO FIND A MANAGER

How do you go about getting the right manager? Once again I'm going to look at it from the artist's point of view, but the ideas apply just as well to managers. As a manager you might also want to know how you go about finding artists to manage. This section should help you as well.

Directories

The main music business directory in the UK is the *Music Week Directory*. It lists managers and the acts they manage. *Gavin* is a directory for listings of US managers.[1] The *Musician's Atlas* lists managers in the independent sector of the US music business. For details of how to get hold of these directories, see the section on Useful Addresses.

Although they can be a good starting point, the drawback with all directories is that they don't give you any clues as to whether the managers listed are any good. The information you get from them needs to be backed up from other sources.

Music Managers Forum

One such source is the Music Managers Forum (MMF).[2] The MMF doesn't act as a dating agency for setting managers up with artists. It does, however, publish a directory of its members and is helpful in putting you in contact with individual managers.

Membership of the MMF isn't any kind of recommendation that a manager is any good but, if a manager is a member, it at least shows that he's interested in talking to other

1 *Gavin* is published annually by Miller Freeman. It is one of the leading directories of information on who's who in the US music industry and can be a useful source of information if you are looking for managers with American connections or offices in the US.

2 The MMF was formed in the mid-90s by a group of like-minded managers who felt that they could achieve more, both for their artists and for themselves, if they grouped together. It has only recently changed its name from the International Managers Forum (IMF). They act as a lobbying group on behalf of their members in relation to national and international issues facing the music industry. The MMF is now branching out to establish links with managers in Europe.

managers and in keeping up to date with what's going on in the outside world that can affect the music business and their or your livelihood. The MMF also runs very good training courses for wannabe managers (see Appendix 4).

It can be lonely out there so, if you're a manager yourself looking for like-minded individuals, the MMF runs a group for new managers, called MMF 2000, which meets each month at a central London location. The aims of MMF 2000 are to educate and inform less experienced managers but not in any kind of 'preachy' way. Most meetings are held in the pub.

Endorsements

You may by now have quite a lot of information about various managers, but you still might not know if they're any good or even if they're looking for new artists to manage. What you need are personal endorsements (references if you like) from people who've worked with a particular manager or know him by reputation. Where do you get these? You can ask around among other bands to see if they've any good or bad experiences of particular managers. Bad reports can be as useful to you as good ones. At the end of the day you'll have to make up your own mind whether to trust a particular manager, but if people who know him keep saying bad things about him, you can't say you weren't warned.

Lawyers and accountants

If you've already found yourself a lawyer or accountant then they should be able to tell you what sort of reputation a particular manager has. They are also good sources of information and can put you in contact with managers that you may not have discovered on your own.

As with all major decisions, you shouldn't rush into anything. In particular, if a lawyer or accountant has recommended someone, you should try to find out what the relationship is between them and that manager. If, for example, they get most of their work from that manager, just how independent are they and is there any conflict of interest? They can't advise you independently if the rest of the time they're advising the manager. But just because a lawyer recommends a manager that they regularly work with doesn't mean that there is necessarily a conflict of interest. You just have to be clear who is looking after your interests.

Surgeries

The Performing Right Society Limited (PRS) holds regular 'surgeries' (see Chapter 15). These are meetings where professionals, such as lawyers, managers and A&R people, discuss particular topics and answer your questions. These are very sociable events, held in a pub or club (surprise, surprise) and are good places to meet other songwriters and music business people. Details of their meetings are given in the PRS Newsletter or direct from the PRS.

A&R contacts

Record or publishing company scouts or A&R people can be an excellent source of information on managers and whether a particular manager is looking for new artists to manage. They can put you in contact with managers. In fact they may insist on you getting a manager before they're prepared to discuss a possible deal with you.

Managers

There is always the possibility that a manager will approach you direct. They may have heard about you from an A&R contact, a lawyer or accountant or they may have seen you play live. It's not unheard of for a manager to come up to you after a gig to say that he wants to manage you. A word of warning: just because a manager approaches you doesn't mean they're any good, nor does it mean that you have to leap at the chance of being managed by someone, regardless of who they are. You still have to do your homework and make as sure as you can that this is the right manager for you.

You should always ask for a trial period to make sure that the relationship is working. It's a new relationship and it does take time to build up the necessary trust between you. The manager should agree to that, but he will be looking for commitment from you before he spends any significant amounts of his own money on you. He will certainly be looking for you to confirm that you want him to manage you before he approaches record and publishing companies on your behalf. If he's prepared to commit time and money on you then it's reasonable to expect some commitment from you in return.

Having discussed how to find managers, we should now look at one or two of the principles behind the artist/manager relationship. These are what make it tick. Many of the principles have been developed and applied to management contracts through a series of cases involving some of the leading players of their time.

THE PRINCIPLES

The first thing you have to understand is that it's a relationship based on trust. If the trust is lost then there's little hope for the relationship. The contract won't hold you together if the trust isn't there. All that a management contract will then do is to tell you what your rights are and what happens if you part company.

This loss of trust has led to many disputes between managers and artists over the years. Some end up in court but many more settle before they get that far – even at the doors of the court. Most people don't want to air their dirty linen in public. It's not a pretty sight when you're sitting in court and the reporters are all lined up on the benches behind you ready to take down every sordid detail. One time I was in court I found myself sitting next to a journalist from one of the tabloid newspapers. He was obviously bored with the lack of juicy scandal and kept popping in and out of court. In one of the gaps in the proceedings I asked him if he'd been going out for a cigarette. 'Nah, love,' came the reply, 'I'm checking with my bookie who won the last two races at Sandown Park.' He then asked me if I fancied a bet on the outcome of the trial and could I tell him what he'd missed when he was outside on the phone. Ah, British journalism at its finest.

Anyway, the cases described below *did* get to court. Two of them were written up in the Law Reports, which means they can be quoted and relied on in later cases. The third one was unreported but within days every decent music lawyer had a copy of the judgement because its effects were so far-reaching. The judgements in these cases helped to establish what lies behind the relationship in legal terms, what duties the manager has towards an artist and what's acceptable in a management contract.

- One of the leading cases on management fall outs and the breakdown of trust is *O'Sullivan* v. *Management Agency and Music Limited.*[3]

Gilbert O'Sullivan (yes, he of the flat cap and mournful expression) signed a management contract with Management Agency and Music Limited (MAM) in 1970. He was young and unknown at the time and had no business experience. This theme comes up time and time again in music disputes. MAM and the man behind it, Gordon Mills, already had an international reputation. Mills managed the superstars Tom Jones and Engelbert Humperdinck. Through MAM, Mills also had interests in a number of other music companies.

O'Sullivan trusted his manager completely and at Mills's suggestion he also signed recording and publishing contracts with those related music companies.

O'Sullivan didn't have any independent legal advice on these contracts. He wasn't told that it would be a good idea for him to get such advice. It seems that he trusted Gordon Mills to such an extent that it didn't cross his mind to get a second opinion. If his manager told him to do something then he did it. I wonder if he'd have gone as far as putting his hand in the fire if Mills had told him to?

The agreements tied O'Sullivan to Mills and to his companies completely and the terms were far worse than if O'Sullivan had done the deals with independent companies and if he'd had independent advice.

O'Sullivan's debut single on MAM was the very successful 'Nothing Rhymed'. Early UK successes were followed by a Top 10 hit in the US with 'Alone Again (Naturally)'. In 1972 he had two No. 1 singles in the UK with 'Clair' and 'Get Down'. His second album reached No. 1 in the UK and he had a number of further hits but by the mid-70s his career seems to have been on a downward path.

By 1976 O'Sullivan's relationship with Mills had broken down; he'd lost his trust in him. This might have been because, for all these hits, he didn't seem to be making much money. He sued Mills, arguing that the various contracts should be treated as if they'd never happened (that they were void) because Mills had used his position of trust with O'Sullivan to wrongly influence him to sign them. He also argued that the terms of the contracts were so unreasonable that they unfairly restricted his ability to earn a living. These concepts of undue influence and unreasonable restraint of trade come up often in music contract disputes.

The court decided that Mills did owe a duty to O'Sullivan. This is called a fiduciary duty – a duty to act in good faith. Mills had a duty to put O'Sullivan's interests first. The court also decided that the contracts were void and couldn't be enforced. If O'Sullivan chose to ignore them, Mills couldn't do anything about it. The court tried to put O'Sullivan back in the position he would have been in had the contracts not been signed. It ordered all copyrights that

3 [1985] QBD 428.

had been transferred (assigned) by O'Sullivan to be returned to him as well as all recordings of his performances (masters).

This was a dramatic decision and it caused uproar throughout the music business. Record and publishing companies were afraid that if this decision were allowed to stand there would be a rush of other artists making the same claims and trying to get their rights back. They knew that many of the contracts around at the time were no better than those that O'Sullivan had signed. They were really worried that all the deals they had done for the records or songs would be void and unenforceable. It's no exaggeration to say that the whole basis of the music business, and the financial security of many, was at risk.

Unsurprisingly, Mills and his associated companies wanted to have this dangerous precedent overturned. They appealed against the decision that the companies owed any duty to O'Sullivan. They argued that the record and publishing companies hadn't used any influence over O'Sullivan. They also argued that the contracts should be declared voidable and not void from the outset. If the Court of Appeal agreed with them, the contracts would be valid but could be set aside later if they were found to have been signed through undue influence or to be in unreasonable restraint of trade. Because the companies had already acted as if the contracts were valid, they argued it would be impossible to return everyone to the position they would have been in had the contracts not existed. They said that the copyrights and master recordings shouldn't be returned to O'Sullivan but that he should be compensated by payment of damages.

In a very important decision for the music business, the Court of Appeal decided that the associated companies *did* owe a fiduciary duty to O'Sullivan because Mills was effectively in control of those companies and was acting in the course of his employment by these companies when he used his undue influence over O'Sullivan. The court also confirmed that it *was* possible to set these contracts aside, even if the parties couldn't be put in exactly the same position that they would have been in had the contracts not been signed. The court thought that this could be done if it was possible to reach a 'practically just' result for O'Sullivan.

So far so good for O'Sullivan you might think. I'm sure his lawyers were rubbing their hands with glee at this stage of the judgement. They must have thought they were home and dry. But there was a sting in the tail. The Court of Appeal decided that a 'practically just' solution would be for the copyright in the songs and master recordings already in existence to remain with the publishing and record companies subject to suitable compensation for O'Sullivan. They also said that the contracts were voidable rather than void, that they were an unreasonable restraint of his trade and that O'Sullivan was freed from them but only for the future. What he'd written and recorded before stayed with the record and publishing companies.

The music business breathed a collective sigh of relief. The refusal of the Court of Appeal to order the return of the copyrights has made it very difficult, if not impossible, to successfully argue for a return of copyrights in cases of undue influence or unreasonable restraint of trade.

● At about the same time, another important case was reaching the courts: *Armatrading* v. *Stone and Another.*[4] It involved Joan Armatrading, a guitar-playing singer-songwriter who some

4 1985, unreported.

people have compared with Tracey Chapman. She is still recording today. The case was about an agreement that Armatrading signed when she was young and relatively inexperienced and before she became famous. There's that theme again.

Stone was a partner in the Copeland Sherry Agency, which had signed a management agreement with Armatrading in March 1973. This was shortly after she released her debut album, *Whatever's For Us*, which was produced by Gus Dudgeon, who also worked with Elton John. Copeland is Miles Copeland, who managed The Police and still manages Sting. Stone advised Armatrading on business matters. She took charge of most creative issues herself. It seems she was confident enough to select studios and producers without needing advice from her managers, but she didn't have a clue when it came to the business end of things.

In 1975 Armatrading released her second album, *Back To The Night*. It didn't reach the charts. She then began work on an album that turned out to be the first to bring her properly to the public's attention.

In February 1976, as the term of the original management contract was about to run out, she signed a new contract under which Stone was to manage her on his own. I'm sure he must have been worried that she would go off to another manager when the original contract ran out and just as her career was starting to take off. Although he denied that in his evidence, the album that she released in 1976, *Joan Armatrading*, went into the Top 20 in the UK and one of the singles released off it became her most famous and successful song. It was called 'Love And Affection' and it reached the Top 10.

Things continued to go well for her at first and in 1980 she released her most successful album to date, *Me Myself, I*, which also contained the hit single 'All The Way From America'. Shortly after that she seems to have become disillusioned with Stone and commenced proceedings for the management contract to be declared void because Stone had used undue influence to get her to sign the contract and on the basis that the terms were unreasonable and a restraint of her trade.

It became clear from the evidence given in the case that the lawyer who drew up the contract had been introduced to Armatrading by Stone and had done some work for her. Coincidentally, I worked with that same firm of lawyers for a couple of years. The contract was done before my time there but the court case was going on when I was there and I know it caused a lot of strain on the lawyer concerned. When preparing the management contract it seems the lawyer acted on the instructions of Stone and not Armatrading. In particular, Stone asked for two specific things to be added to the draft contract. The lawyer billed Stone for the work and it's clear from the description on the bill that he thought he was only acting as Stone's lawyer.

At a meeting on 4 February at the lawyers' offices, Armatrading received a copy of the draft contract to take away with her. She returned the next day to sign it. She didn't ask for any changes to be made to it.

Stone claimed that the lawyer acted as lawyer for both of them. When he gave evidence, the lawyer said that he thought he was just acting as lawyer to Stone. A very confusing state of affairs. Stone and Armatrading were both present at the meeting with the lawyer on 4 February when the contract was discussed. That must have been very awkward. If a manager turns up at a meeting I'm due to have with an artist to discuss a management contract, I insist on him staying outside while I take the meeting. I can't be open with the artist about what I think about the contract, or the manager, if the manager is in the same room. The same would apply the other way around.

The contract was also strongly biased in Stone's favour. It was for five years and, during that time, Armatrading was exclusively tied to Stone as her manager. The contract didn't say that Stone had to do very much at all for her. He could manage other artists. Stone was to be paid a management commission of 20% (which, as we will see, is quite common) but 25% on any new recording or publishing deals she signed (which is not). He got 20% commission on touring whether or not the tour made a profit. The court thought this was particularly harsh, as was the fact that Stone's right to commission was open-ended. For example, if Armatrading signed a new record deal in year three of the five-year management term, Stone would be entitled to 25% commission. He might stop being her manager two years later but he'd still go on earning at 25%. If Armatrading got herself a new manager and he negotiated some improvements to the recording contract in return for, say, a two-year extension on the record deal, Stone, not the new manager, would get commission at 25% on the extended term. Not much of an incentive for the new manager. And expensive for Armatrading if she had to pay out two lots of commission to the original and the new manager.

When he gave evidence, Stone agreed that he knew that he had a duty to act in Armatrading's best interests and that she had trust and confidence in him. This fiduciary duty already existed when the 1976 management contract was being discussed. Stone knew that his interests under this contract weren't the same as Armatrading's and yet he still seemed to think that the same lawyer could act for both of them.

Stone admitted that it was very likely that Armatrading didn't realise she should have separate legal advice. Even though he accepted his fiduciary duties existed, he didn't seem to accept the idea of a conflict of interest and couldn't seem to see that if something in the management contract was in his interests it wouldn't necessarily be in Armatrading's best interests. This doesn't mean that a manager can't look out for his own interests, just that it's up to him to make sure that the artist has separate advice and is able to come to an informed decision.

The court found Stone's evidence was very contradictory, and I have to agree. It decided that Armatrading relied heavily on Stone in business matters. She trusted him and he had told her that he would look after her. The court thought it was clear that he had influence over her. She didn't look at the detail of the contract. She relied on Stone, who told her that it was a standard and fair contract, even though he'd asked for two specific changes to be made to the draft.

The court decided that the contract should be set aside by reason of undue influence by Stone. The terms of the contract were said to be unreasonable ('unduly onerous and unconscionable' in the words of the judgement). The contract was voidable and not void from the outset. On this point, they came to the same conclusion as in the O'Sullivan case.

The fact that Armatrading didn't have separate legal advice was seen as very important. On its own, this wouldn't have been enough to set aside the contract. For example, if the contract had been a perfectly reasonable one, so that any lawyer who advised on it would say it was all right to sign it, then the absence of that advice wouldn't have been fatal. The absence of separate advice coupled with the particularly harsh terms of the contract was enough to convince the court to set it aside. The court found that although she had some experience of the music business, because she concentrated on the creative side it was important that she be given a proper understanding of the business side of the contract. She hadn't understood the implications of the open-ended commission clause and hadn't been able to form an independent view after full, free and informed thought. She had signed the contract relying on her manager's claim that it was fine. He'd failed in his fiduciary duty to her. She was freed from the contract and went on to record several more successful albums.

Although this case wasn't reported in the Law Reports, it had a very significant and practical effect on management contracts. We lawyers still use it as a yardstick to measure the reasonableness of management contract terms. It's also quoted as an authority for saying that artist and manager should have separate lawyers when discussing the management contract and whenever their interests are not the same.

After this case it became usual to add a clause to management contracts saying that the artist has been advised to take independent legal advice. I don't think this goes far enough. Just advising someone they should get advice and then not making sure that they do is not enough. I think that the manager should insist on the artist having separate legal advice from a lawyer who understands the music business and should make sure he understands what he's being asked to sign.

The Armatrading case also cast doubt on whether a five-year contract term was reasonable. After the case, some managers decided to go for a shorter term or otherwise tried to make their contracts more reasonable. No manager wants to risk having an artist walk away from a management contract at the height of his or her success.

The judge was also quite critical of the 25% commission rate on new record and publishing deals. As we'll see below, 25% rates are now rare. He was even more concerned about the fact that Stone took commission on touring money even if the tour made a loss. Music business lawyers reacted to these criticisms by introducing new protections for artists in this area.

• Another case on management contracts that was reported in the tabloids, as well as the Law Reports, involved Elton John: *John* v. *James*.[5]

Elton John signed a series of publishing, management and recording contracts starting in 1967, when he was still under age and unknown. Although these themes come up quite often in these cases, each one played its own part in developing how the business operates and how contracts have to be adapted to deal with criticisms made by the judges.

Elton John and his lyricist Bernie Taupin were originally taken on as sort of in-house writers for James's new publishing company, DJM. It's said they were on wages of £10 per week. It took quite a while for them to be commercially successful. The first successful album was produced by Gus Dudgeon and was called *Elton John*. The 1972 album

5 1991, F.S.R. 397.

contained the now-classic work 'Your Song'. Seven consecutive No. 1 albums followed in the next seven years.

Although Elton was making a lot of very successful records, he didn't seem to be seeing much of the proceeds. For example, the publishing set-up consisted of a number of interrelated companies, each taking its own slice of the income, so that a very small amount was left for Elton. What he did get, he had to pay management commission on.

He sued to try and recover his copyrights and damages for back royalties. He relied on the tried and true arguments that he had signed the contracts under undue influence and that they were an unreasonable restraint of his trade.

He hadn't taken separate legal advice before signing any of the contracts. He'd placed trust and confidence in James. The contracts weren't anywhere near as good as they could have been had they been with independent companies. The publishers could take rights in the songs and not have to do anything with them. They could be shut away in a drawer and never seen again and Elton couldn't do anything about it. He was signed up exclusively. He couldn't take his songs to another music publisher.

The court decided that in these circumstances it was to be assumed that there was undue influence at work and that it was up to the manager to show that he didn't use his influence in the wrong way. The court found that James had failed in his fiduciary duties to Elton. It felt that James couldn't be acting in the best interest of Elton if James's publishing and recording companies were also entering into contracts with him. How could James be advising Elton as his manager while he also had an interest in making as much money as possible for his record and publishing companies out of those contracts?

Once again the decision in this case had a knock-on effect on the music business. It was fully reported in the Law Reports, so had authority, and it confirmed the existence of the fiduciary duty owed by not only the manager but also any companies under his control. It also brought home the importance of separate legal advice.

The other important thing it changed concerns what happens when your manager also has a record or publishing contract he wants you to sign up to. If your manager also has an interest in a record or publishing company the management contract will now usually ask the artist to confirm that he won't consider it a failure of the manager's fiduciary duty to him if he signs up to the record or publishing company on the manager's advice. I don't think this would be enough to get the manager off the hook if he did in fact break his duty to the artist – especially if the artist hadn't had separate legal advice. There's also usually a clause that says the manager can't take a double hit on the income from the record or publishing deals. For example, if the artist releases a record on the manager's record label, the manager should get his money from the label's profits on the record sales. He shouldn't also take a management commission on the artist's record royalties.

● Not all disputes involving managers are claims by the artist against the manager or vice versa. Sometimes the manager has to look after the artist's interests in other ways. One such case involved Elton John's manager at the time, John Reid (*John Reid Enterprises Limited* v. *Pell*).[6]

6 1999 EMLR 675.

Mr Pell is a colourful character who, it is alleged, comes by confidential or interesting information on people in the public eye by, among other things, rummaging in their dustbins.

Mr Pell supplied material to the *Daily Mirror* about Elton John's spending habits, including information that was from sources expected to be confidential, such as a letter from a firm of accountants. John Reid Enterprises Limited (JRE) was Elton John's management company at the time and it seemed that the 'leak' of the information could be traced back to someone within JRE. JRE wanted to know who it was, so that they could be dealt with and the clients' belief in their ability to keep things confidential could be restored.

JRE brought an application to the court for an order that Mr Pell deliver up all information and papers he had so that they could find the source. Mr Pell applied for no such order to be made on the basis that he was an investigative journalist with many sources of information that it was important for him not to disclose.

The court decided that it was of the essence of the trust relationship on which JRE's business was based that it could assure its clients of confidentiality. The court takes it as being of less general importance that a source is protected where information has been obtained unlawfully. The court refused Mr Pell's application.

WHAT TO LOOK FOR IN A MANAGER

This all depends on what you expect your manager to do for you. You may only need a manager to advise you on business matters. You may want that but are also looking for creative advice, comment and guidance. Some artists already have a clear idea of what they are doing creatively and have a good business sense and grasp of contracts. They don't want an all-round manager and may only be looking for a good organiser. We saw in the Armatrading case (above) that Stone only looked after Armatrading's business interests. She looked after the creative side herself.

You may be looking for a Svengali, someone who will come up with the cast-iron plan for world domination in three years. Such managers do exist. People like Tom Watkins, who has successfully managed acts like The Pet Shop Boys and Bros to considerable success. Then there are managers like Simon Fuller, whose marketing background meant that he could see the worldwide possibilities of an act like The Spice Girls and who seems set to do it again with S Club 7. When you expect a manager to devise an all-encompassing gameplan, and then to implement it, you can't expect to get away with no effort on your part. You and your manager will have to put enormous amounts of time and energy into making the plan work and both of you must completely buy-in to the whole idea behind it.

IS IT ESSENTIAL TO HAVE AN EXPERIENCED MANAGER?

No, it isn't. Someone who hasn't managed anyone before can make a good manager if they have the flair for it. They may have been a musician themselves, a tour manager, a producer or may have worked in-house at a record or publishing company. They will have seen how the music business works and can bring valuable experience to the job of manager. However, the skills that make a good producer are not necessarily those that make a good manager, so be careful. In 1960s Cliff Richard movies, the 'fifth member' of the band, who can't play or sing but who wants to do something, may turn out to be a successful manager, but it rarely happens in the real world.

QUALITIES TO LOOK FOR IN A MANAGER

The manager has to be a diplomat, motivator, salesman and strategic planner – and has to have the patience of a saint.

Record and publishing companies like to have managers around to act as middlemen so they don't have to have unpleasant conversations with you. They'd like you to choose someone that has already successfully steered an artist through getting a deal, getting a record made and someone who has already done the whole touring and promotion side of things. This doesn't mean to say that they won't work with an inexperienced manager, just that they'd prefer one who wasn't. They'd also like you to be managed by someone they already know, someone they know they can work with. This doesn't necessarily mean that that manager will be in their pocket. It could mean that they have a healthy respect for him for being tough but fair, someone that gets the job done. But, if you are being pushed by your record company towards a particular manager, take the time to stop and ask why and to do some research of your own before meekly accepting their choice.

WHAT DOES A MANAGER DO FOR YOU?

PERSONAL MANAGERS

A personal manager looks after your day-to-day needs. This usually includes some advice on the creative side of things. The personal manager also acts as go-between with the record and publishing companies and the outside world. A personal manager is usually someone who organises your life and tries to make everything run smoothly but doesn't necessarily get involved in day-to day business decisions or strategic plans. They put into action plans others have come up with.

BUSINESS MANAGERS

A business manager doesn't usually involve himself in the day-to-day business of running your life. He leaves it to the personal manager to make sure that you have your personal needs attended to, that your fridge is full when you get back off tour and that you get to where you're meant to be at about the right time. It's the job of the business manager to work out where you should be in terms of business planning and to help you put the plan into action. He will liaise with the record and publishing company but usually more at the level of negotiating deals, changes to the contracts, setting video and recording budgets and getting tour support when it's needed (see Chapters 3 and 10).

It's much more common in the US to have a separate business and personal manager. There the business manager is often an accountant or financial adviser. The idea of these roles being filled by different people hasn't yet become popular in the UK. What tends to happen here is that one person will do both jobs.

PERSONAL ASSISTANTS

As you become more successful, so the manager may employ someone to act as your personal assistant (PA). If the PA is working full-time for you, the manager will expect you to pay their wages. If they work some of the time for you and the rest on general work for the manager or for other acts that he manages then the cost is likely to be shared between you. If the PA works most of the time for the manager and only occasionally runs errands for you then you'd expect the manager to bear all the cost.

If you do have separate business and personal managers, you need to be sure that you aren't paying too much by having two people on board instead of one.

Don't assume that because you have a business manager you can do away with the need for an accountant. You'll need one to oversee your tax and possibly VAT returns and someone to prepare company or partnership accounts (see Chapter 11). Bear this in mind when you agree what to pay your business manager. If you're paying your business manager 20% of your income, your personal manager another 10% and then paying an accountant, you haven't got a great bargain.

The manager is there to advise you, to guide you through your career in the music business. A successful career as a performer or composer can lead into other areas such as films, television, writing or modelling. One of the many things you have to consider in choosing your manager is whether the manager can also look after these other areas of your life.

The manager should spend a reasonable amount of time on your affairs and your career. He should help you to get a record and/or publishing deal, live appearances, sponsorship and merchandising deals.

The manager should advise you whether or not you should take up a particular offer. It may not fit in with the gameplan that you and the manager have worked out. Putting together that gameplan is a very important job for your manager and you and he need to be on the same wavelength.

FIDUCIARY DUTIES AND PROBLEMS WITH BANDS

As we saw in the section on the cases (above), the manager has to always act in your best interests. He has a fiduciary duty to you, which means that he has to always act with the utmost good faith towards you.

This duty can cause problems when dealing with a band. Something that may be good for the band as a whole may not be good for one of the band members. There's a very narrow line that the manager has to tread. Sometimes you may feel that the manager has stepped the wrong side of that line.

- This issue was one of several behind the recent dispute between Nigel Martin-Smith and Robbie Williams (*Martin-Smith* v. *Williams*).[7]

I have to declare an interest here as this was a case I inherited when I became Robbie's lawyer a few years ago. Martin-Smith was the manager of Take That from the early days to the

7 1997, unreported.

height of their success. Take That was made up of five members, including Robbie. He became fed up at the direction his life was taking and was thinking about leaving the band. His version of events is that he was prepared to see his commitments to a major tour through to the end before leaving the band. He says that, on advice from Martin-Smith, the band sacked him. The other members and Martin-Smith say he walked out.

When Martin-Smith later sued Robbie for unpaid commission (Robbie had refused to pay him) one of the arguments that Robbie used was that Martin-Smith had failed in his fiduciary duty to Robbie and wasn't acting in his best interests in advising the band to sack him.

Martin-Smith acknowledged that it was very difficult in such circumstances to advise a band when he also had a duty to each of them as individuals. He admitted that he'd had discussions with the other band members about Robbie and how disillusioned he was but he said he also tried to advise Robbie on what was best for him. He said that he'd acted in the best interests of the band as a whole while trying to balance this against the interests of the individual members. He denied that he'd advised the band to sack Robbie.

The judge accepted his evidence that he had acted in good faith and was not in breach of his fiduciary duty to Robbie. The judge acknowledged the difficulties that a manager faces in such circumstances but decided that in this case Martin-Smith had stayed the right side of the line.

WHAT IS IN A MANAGEMENT CONTRACT?

Once you've found yourself a manager you think you can trust and who'll do a good job for you, you need to think about what goes into the contract between you.

This will be different depending on whether you're an artist or a manager. As before, I'm going to take the artist's viewpoint, but in my time as a music lawyer I have acted for both artists and managers and so I'll try and present both sides of the argument.

INDEPENDENT LEGAL ADVICE

As we've already seen, when negotiating a management contract the artist must have separate legal advice. The manager may decide not to take advice on it. He may be experienced enough to feel comfortable with the deal he's prepared to do and doesn't need advice. If he's experienced with management contracts then this isn't really a problem. If you decide that you don't want legal advice then this is a problem for the manager (see the Armatrading case, above). The manager should insist on you getting separate advice from someone who is familiar with the music business and with management contracts.

What if you haven't got the money to pay for a lawyer? The Musicians Union (MU) has a limited cheap legal advice service for its members but you can't expect it to be as detailed as if you were paying proper rates for it.

Some managers will loan you the money to take independent legal advice because it's in the manager's interests to make sure you're properly advised. If the manager does loan you money to get a lawyer, he will usually put a limit on how much he'll contribute. You'll either have to get the lawyer to agree to do the work for that much or you will have to put some in as well. The manager will get his contribution back out of your first earnings.

TERRITORY

The first thing you have to decide is what countries the contract will cover. We call this the territory of the deal.

The manager will probably want to manage you for the world. This isn't just so that he can get as much commission as possible. He may want to keep overall control of the gameplan, which he won't be able to do very easily if he only manages what you do in one part of the world.

You may be fine about this because you're confident that he can look after your interests around the world. But you must bear in mind that the way the music business operates in the US in particular is very different from the UK. Does the manager have an office in the States? Does he have an associate there? Or will he be spending half his time on planes crossing the Atlantic? If he is, who's going to end up paying for that? Sometimes it'll be the record company, sometimes it'll be part of a tour budget, but sometimes it'll be you.

If you don't think that the manager can successfully look after your interests worldwide, you could insist that he only manages you for part of the world: for example, the world outside North America.

Even if you aren't sure if he's up to being a worldwide manager you could still give him the benefit of the doubt. You could make it a worldwide deal to start with and if he's not up to it you could insist that he appoints a co-manager, probably for the US but possibly for other parts of the world like Japan, to look after your interests there. Because this is a very personal thing, both you and the manager should agree on who this person should be.

The co-manager is usually paid out of the commission you pay to the manager. Apart from the co-manager's expenses you shouldn't end up paying out more in total commission just because there's a co-manager on board.

There are several ways that the manager and co-manager can split the commission between them. They could just take the total worldwide commission and split it down the middle. They could each just take commission on the income earned by you in their particular areas of the world. For example, the co-manager could take commission on the income you earn in North America and your original manager on the rest of the world income. Or the manager could decide not to share his commission but to put the co-manager on a retainer or pay him a fee. It's a complex subject and the manager should take legal advice on it.

ACTIVITIES COVERED

The next thing to think about is whether the contract will cover everything you do in the entertainment business or just your activities in the music business. You might start out as a songwriter or performer and later move into acting or writing books. The manager may be perfectly capable of managing you for all those activities or he may be an expert at the music business and know nothing about the business of writing books or acting. If you aren't convinced he can look after your interests across the whole of the entertainment industry you should limit it to the music business only. The manager may be unhappy about this. He may think that it'll be his management skills that will help turn you into a success in the music business which will in turn open doors to acting or writing books. He may feel that he should share in your income from those other activities. On the other hand, you may be concerned that he isn't up to representing your interest and may want a specialised acting or literary agent involved.

Many managers will agree to compromise and say they have no objection to you bringing in specialised acting or literary agents if you are acting in roles or writing books that have nothing to do with you being a successful musician or songwriter first. If the acting role or book is directly connected to the fact that you are an artist then they will want to share that income and manage those projects. For example, if you're asked to write a behind-the-scenes look at your time out on the road with the band, the manager will expect to take commission on your income from that book. If, however, you're asked to write a book on Lowland Gorillas that clearly has nothing to do with your fame as a successful musician or songwriter, the manager may agree not to take commission on that income.

By the time you get a manager you may already have established yourself in another part of the entertainment business. For example, you may already be a successful TV actor or model. The manager may agree not to manage those areas of activity. He may also agree not to manage or take commission on work that comes from a particular contact, such as a recording studio, that was in place before he came along. But if you ask him to manage projects that come from that source – for example, by chasing them for payment for you – then it's only reasonable that the manager should be allowed to take commission on that work.

EXCLUSIVITY

Once you've decided what activities he's going to manage and in what parts of the world, the manager will expect to be your only manager for those activities and those areas. He will want to be your exclusive manager. You won't be able to manage yourself or to ask someone else to manage a particular project unless he agrees. This is not only reasonable – it's practical. You can't go around accepting work without referring it to your manager – it might clash with something he's putting together for you.

KEY-MAN PROVISIONS OR, HOW DO YOU MAKE SURE THAT YOUR MANAGER IS THERE FOR YOU WHEN YOU NEED HIM?

What happens if your manager manages other acts or is part of a management company that manages a number of people? How can you make sure he'll be there for you when you need advice? How do you make sure you aren't fobbed off on to someone else because your manager is busy with the others he manages? Well, first of all you make sure that your management contract says that he has to spend a reasonable amount of time, on a regular basis, on managing you.

You could possibly go further and insist on what we call a 'key-man' clause being put into the contract. I think this term comes from insurance policies that are taken out on the life of key individuals in an organisation, which pay out if the key-man dies or is unable to work. You name the manager as a key-man and say that if he's not available to you as and when you need him, you can bring the contract to an end.

Your manager may be very flattered at being named as a key-man but he may also feel that it's a bit harsh to allow you to end the contract so abruptly. He may want to say that you can only terminate the contract if he's regularly not been available to you or has been unavailable to you for over, say, six weeks at a time. But you have to be sensible about this. If you're buried in a residential studio in the depths of Wales writing or rehearsing material for your next album then it may not be reasonable to expect your manager to be there all the time. If you were in the middle of a major renegotiation of your record contract, you can reasonably expect him to be around.

These key-man clauses are also sometimes put into record or publishing contracts but the companies hate them because they give the artist and the key-man a huge amount of power. If they sack the key-man then you can end the contract. Rumour has it that Oasis had a key-man clause in their record contract with Creation Records. When Sony came to look at buying the remaining shares in Creation they are said to have backed off because Oasis could have walked out of their contracts at the height of their success if the key-man at Creation Records, Alan McGee, was no longer in control at the label. I can't confirm if this is true but, if it is, it's a lovely example of the little man beating up the big corporation.

TERM – HOW LONG SHOULD THE CONTRACT RUN?

The contract could be open-ended, just carrying on until one side or the other decides it's over.

It could be for a fixed period of, say, one or two years and then if everything is going well it could continue until someone says stop.

More usually it's for a fixed period of three to five years and at the end of that time the contract is renegotiated or it just ends.

Until the early 1980s, terms of five years or longer were common, but the Armatrading case cast some doubt on that. More recent UK cases, including one last year involving Shaun Ryder of the Happy Mondays, have made it clear that a term of five years or longer is not acceptable here.[8] Personally, I'm not happy advising an artist to accept a five-year term. I feel three years is long enough. If it's working then they can renegotiate at the end of the three years.

I can be persuaded to agree to a three-year term with the manager having an option to extend it for one or two years. But the right to exercise that option should be linked to the manager achieving something for the artist – what I call hurdles.

Hurdles

A hurdle could be that the artist has to have a record or publishing deal or have earned a

8 Again this is not the case in the US where terms of five years or longer are still common.

minimum amount of money in the first three years, although it's difficult to say what the right minimum level of income is.

It's also possible to put hurdles in at an earlier stage of the contract. You could have a get-out if the manager hasn't got you a decent record or publishing deal in the first twelve months. Or if he got you a deal in that time and it's come to an end and he hasn't got you another one within, say, six or nine months.

Album cycles

This is a US concept. There the term of a management contract is often linked to an album cycle. An album cycle starts with the writing of the songs to be recorded on an album, runs through the recording of the album and all the promotion that then goes on after its release. The cycle ends with the last piece of promotional work.

There are one or two lawyers in the UK who now favour this way of measuring the management term. My problem with it is that it's very difficult to say how long it will last. You don't know at the beginning how long it will take to write, record and promote an album. I'm uncomfortable with agreeing to two- or three-album cycle deals, which could easily run for five years or longer. If you are offered this type of deal, I advise you to put a time backstop on it, for example, a two-album cycle or three years, whichever comes first.

THE MANAGER'S ROLE

I've already explained a little of what you can expect the manager to do for you. What you can't do, though, is to list every single thing that you expect a manager to do. Sod's Law says that it will be the very thing that's not listed that causes the problem. There are some contracts that try and list things they expect the manager to do: for example, that the manager will advise you on clothes, image, voice training, etc. I think these have an old-fashioned feel about them. I end up imagining what the reaction would be if Oasis' manager tried to advise Liam Gallagher on his stage image or told him to get singing lessons. My management contracts just say that the manager will do all he reasonably can to further the artist's career and to do all the things expected of a manager in the entertainment or music business.

WHAT IS THE MANAGER PAID?

Some would say too much, but if you ever saw a manager working round the clock, seven days a week to make an artist successful with not even a thank you from him then you'd say it wasn't enough.

The average rate of commission for a manager is 20%. If you're very successful the 20% could be negotiated down to 10–15%. Some record producer managers only charge 15–20% because there is less management of projects or a career than there is with performing artists. Although a 25% rate was criticised in the Armatrading case, there are some circumstances in which it could be justified. The manager may have invested a lot of his own money in making you successful and may want to get that back in commission as soon as possible. He may agree to reduce his commission to 20% when you're successful and he's got his investment back. That is in fact what happened with Nigel Martin-Smith and Take That.

Percentage of what?

A percentage of your gross income is the simple answer. For example, if you were paid £100,000 on signing a record deal, the manager on a commission of 20% would take £20,000.

What if you have to use some of that money to record your album or pay a producer? What happens if you are advanced money by your record company (which they get back or recoup from your royalties) to make a video or to underwrite losses on a tour? Is it fair that the manager takes 20% off the top? The answer is no, it's not. There are a number of exceptions. It's *not* usual for the manager to take commission on monies advanced to you as recording costs, video costs, payments to record producers or mixers, sums used to underwrite tour losses and sometimes monies advanced to you to buy equipment.

Example: The record company sets a budget of £200,000 for you to make an album, plus £50,000 to make a video and £100,000 for you to live on for the next year. The manager often won't take commission on the £200,000 or the £50,000 but will take commission on the £100,000, i.e. £20,000.

Depending on the manager and the contract, he may say that if you decide to use £20,000 of your £100,000 to buy some equipment then that's your choice and he's still going to take commission on the full £100,000. Or he might treat the £20,000 spent on equipment as an exception and take his commission on the balance of £80,000.

Commission on earnings from live work can be a problem. The manager usually has to work very hard putting together and running a successful tour. He may feel that he should take his 20% off the top from the income that comes in from that tour. What if the expenses of putting on the tour are so high that the tour makes little or no profit? For example, you take £50,000 in ticket sales and the expenses are £40,000. If the manager took his 20% off the £50,000 (i.e. £10,000) there'd be £40,000 left, which would be wiped out by the expenses. As an artist performing every night of the tour, you may start to resent the manager making £10,000 when you are getting nothing. As we saw in the Armatrading case, the judge was very critical that Stone took 20% of gross income on touring, regardless of whether the tour made a profit.

What tends to happen is that the manager takes his commission on net income after some or all of the expenses are taken off. There are various formulas that different managers favour for how to arrive at a fair compromise. Your lawyer will advise.

Post-term commission

This means how long after the end of the management contract the manager continues to get paid commission. It has two sides to it. Firstly, should the manager take commission on albums made or songs written after the end of the management term? Secondly, how long should he earn commission on albums made or songs written while he was the manager.

Dealing with the first, until the early 1980s it was quite usual to see management contracts that allowed a manager to go on earning on things the artist did long after he'd stopped being the manager. If he negotiated a five-album record deal while he was the manager and he stopped being the manager after two albums, he'd still take commission on the remaining three albums because that contract was done while he was the manager. Some contracts also allowed him to continue to take commission after he stopped being manager if someone else negotiated an extension of or substitution for that original contract. Again, because he'd done the original work. This led to some very unfair situations. The new manager had no incentive to improve upon deals because it was the earlier manager who got the commission. Artists found it difficult to get new managers and were forced to stay with the original manager. Or the artist ended up paying out two lots of commission. This situation was strongly criticised in the Armatrading case and led directly to a change in the way UK managers operated. They began to accept that they would only get commission on work done, recordings made and songs written while they were the manager.[9]

How long should the manager continue to receive commission?

After it was established that managers should only take commission on what was recorded or written while they were the manager, the question then came up of how long they should go on earning commission on those recordings and songs.

Many managers take the view that they should go on earning commission as long as the artist goes on earning income from a particular song or recording. I can see the logic in this but again it can lead to some unfairness. A manager might have only been around for one album's worth of recordings. It may be a second manager that made the artist successful. Fans of successful artists want to own all the artists' back catalogue of records and so buy the first album. Or a track from the first album may go on a Greatest Hits album. The first manager has done nothing to help on-going sales of that first album. Should he get full commission on it? Some managers insist that they should but these days most accept that after a period of time their influence can't be affecting continuing sales of early records so they agree to a reduction in their commission rate. Most also agree that it should stop altogether after a given time. For example, the first manager could agree that his commission on the first album drops to 10% after five years after the end of the management term and stops altogether after ten years. This means the artist can give the second manager an incentive by giving him 10% of the income on the first album after five years and 20% after ten years. Or the artist makes the saving himself and gives nothing to the second manager.

These periods of five or ten years are negotiable. There are all sorts of variations but I don't agree with some music lawyers who insist that the commission stops after two or three years. This is too short.

WHAT HAPPENS IF THERE'S NO WRITTEN CONTRACT?

Some managers prefer to work without any written contract. They say they'd rather work on a good-faith basis, trusting you to do the right thing by them.

9 In the US it is still common for managers to expect commission on the first if not the second album made after they've stopped being the manager.

It's also possible for a manager to work for you for a trial period and then not carry on. No written deal is done but you still have to deal with what he gets paid for the work he did.

You and the manager may have discussed the basis on which you'll work together but never get around to writing it down.

It is of course perfectly possible for there to be a verbal contract in place. The difficulty with verbal contracts is that it's very difficult to prove what exactly was agreed.

If it's not possible to show that there was a verbal agreement the manager has to rely on what would be a fair price for the work he has done (a *quantum meruit* claim). If you and the manager can't agree this and there is a court case, the judge would take expert evidence of what's the norm in the music business and will make an order of what he thinks the manager should be paid. It's rare for the court to order payments going forward. The court will order payment for the work already done. For example, if the manager got a record deal for you then the court might order that he's paid a percentage of the money payable on signing that deal. However, what the court rarely does is to order that the manager is paid a share of on-going royalties. So the manager would not usually get a share of post-term commission. Therefore, it's usually more important for the manager to have a written contract to protect his commission on future royalty income than it is for the artist.

ACCOUNTING – WHO COLLECTS THE MONEY?

It's very important to know who's looking after the money. The manager may be unhappy at the thought of you looking after the money because you're an artist. Artists are notoriously bad at hanging on to money (they say). 'They can't even keep the money back to pay the VAT or the taxman; how can I trust them to keep enough back to pay me?'

On the other hand, you may feel you've got a fantastic head for figures and are very responsible with your money. So why aren't you an accountant then? You may not want your manager controlling your money, but do you really want to have the bother of looking after it yourself?

A compromise would be for you to appoint an accountant (see Chapter 1). The money is paid into a bank account in your name, which the accountant looks after. The manager sends in an invoice for his commission and expenses. The accountant checks the sums are right and writes out a cheque for you to sign. If you've asked him to, he'll deal with your VAT and he'll almost certainly tell you to keep some money back for tax. What he does with the rest of the money depends on what you've told him to do. He could pay it into another account for you or leave some there to meet expenses.

EXPENSES

On top of his commission, the manager is entitled to be repaid his expenses for working for you. That doesn't mean everything he spends. The costs of running his business, his office, staff, computers and so on are all paid for by him. These are called office overheads. But if he pays for a taxi to pick you up from the recording studio or for a courier to deliver your demo to an interested A&R man then you can expect him to reclaim that money from you.

He should keep receipts and bills and have them available for your accountant to check.

He should also agree that he won't run up expensive items without checking with you first. I wouldn't expect him to buy a plane ticket to New York without checking you're all right with him spending your money in that way. On the other hand, it's not practical for him to have to come running to you for every small item of expenses. If he's going to spend £250 or more he should check with you first. Alternatively you might agree a float account. This is a special account with a fixed sum of money; say £500 in it. The manager is authorised to draw money out of that account for expenses and the account is then topped back up to £500 on a regular basis; a bit like a float in a till of the pub or a shop.

TAX

You are responsible for you own tax and National Insurance and for paying the VAT man. Don't expect the manager to do it for you. As we saw in Chapter 1, your accountant is a very important part of your team. Your accountant will keep your books, do your VAT returns and prepare your tax return for you. This doesn't mean you can sit back and do nothing. You have to tell your accountant what's come in and give him receipts for anything he might be able to reclaim or recharge. He'll tell you the sort of things he's looking for. Your accountant will also advise you of what you can expect to have to pay in tax and ways in which you can, legitimately, pay as little tax as possible. But remember, there are, they say, only two certainties in this world – death and taxes.

SIGNING AGREEMENTS

It's practical to allow the manager to sign one-off short-term contracts in your name. For example, when you do an appearance on *Top Of The Pops*, the BBC needs you to sign a short-release or consent form before you can appear and get paid. You are busy rehearsing. It's all right for the manager to sign that form for you.

What isn't acceptable is for the manager to sign a long-term contract or indeed anything more that a one-off. It's dangerous for you – you won't know what's in it, what's been agreed. It's also dangerous for the manager. You may not object at the time but when you find something in the contract that's not to your liking you can be sure you'll blame the manager for not telling you.

You should take responsibility for your career and for what is being done in your name.

CONCLUSIONS

- Different lawyers must advise the artist and the manager.
- Treat with caution any term capable of running for longer than five years.
- 20% is the average management commission for artist managers.
- Commission is on gross income. If exceptions are to be made, these must be spelt out in the contract.

- Commission on 'live' work should be after deduction of some or all of the expenses.
- The management deal does not need to be for the whole world.
- Who is collecting the money?

3: WHAT IS A GOOD RECORD DEAL?

INTRODUCTION

Everybody's idea of what is a good deal is different. For some it's a question of how much money is on the table. For others it's how much commitment there is from the record company. Some artists are more interested in how much control they have over what sort of record they make. We call this creative control.

I'm going to look at these different ideas of what's a good deal. I'm going to do it from the artist's point of view because that's what I know best. But because I've negotiated so many record deals over the years and I've heard all the arguments from the record companies, I'll try and put their side too.

There is more than one type of record deal. I'm going to look at three basic types of deal – the licence, the development deal and the exclusive recording contract.

To understand record deals properly you also need to know some law, so I'm going to look at the basic performer's rights, at copyright and at what rights a record company needs in order to exploit your recordings.

Incidentally, in the music business we use the word exploit quite a lot. Some people react badly to the use of this word. They associate it with exploitation in the bad sense – oppression of the weak and that sort of thing. When we use it we generally mean 'to use', 'to sell' or 'to make money from' your recordings or songs. It's a positive use of the word, not a negative one.

You won't be surprised to learn that there have been a few celebrated cases over the years to do with recording contracts. I'm going to look at three in this chapter to see what the problems were, what the courts decided and what the music business learned from them.

THE HYPE

We've all read in the press about new, unknown acts supposedly being signed to million-pound deals. Can you believe what you read? Well, I guess in one or two rare cases it could be true but it's pretty unlikely if it's a completely unknown artist.[1]

What is much more likely is that the deal has been 'hyped' up in the press to make it seem bigger than it is. If you add up all the money that the record company could spend on making an album then you could arrive at the figure of a million pounds. That would include the recording costs, the cost of making one or two videos, marketing and touring costs. The artist might only see a fraction of that money himself in personal advances against his royalties.

When the record company is making up its mind about what to offer you it will look at a number of things. First, and most importantly, how much they want to sign you to their

1 The Americans are more likely to go for telephone number-size deals. But then the rewards are much greater for the record company. In the US, a successful album will sell many millions of copies. Here, a platinum-selling record is only 300,000 copies.

company. If they desperately want you, they'll pay over the odds to get the deal done. If you've got more than one company fighting over you then you have much greater bargaining power. Your manager and lawyer can play one company off against the other and get you a better deal. Or you can say to one of the companies that they won't do that if they offer the deal you want.

If the record company is doing it scientifically, they'll use various formulae to work out what's a reasonable deal to offer you. There are computer models that they can use. They look at the type of act you are, at how much they think it's going to cost to record the album and to make videos. They also look at other commitments, possibly to touring. They put these estimates into the model and it tells them how many records you'd have to sell before they break even. If they think that's an unrealistic number they may scale down the offer to you. Well this is the theory anyway. I suspect that they do this number crunching and then go with their hunches anyway as to how well they think you're going to do.

We saw in Chapter 1 some of the ways in which you can get a 'buzz' going for you. The 'hotter' you are, the more the record company is likely to pay or the better overall deal you will be offered. The better your lawyer is, the less likely it is that the record company will get away with paying below the odds – a very good reason to get a good lawyer on your side.

Your manager should sit down with you and discuss what's important to you. Are you only interested in big money advances or would you prefer to go for a smaller advance in return for creative control or more commitment from the record company? Once he knows what you want, your manager can make his 'pitch' to the record company along those lines.

It should be a balanced contract where the record company can reasonably protect its investment but also one where you get some commitment from them and the chance to earn a decent living from the deal.

THE PRINCIPLES

Before I look in more detail at these questions of money, commitment and creative control, I need to run through one of the guiding principles in deciding what is a good record deal.

RESTRAINT OF TRADE

We've already seen in the cases of *O'Sullivan* v. *MAM*, *Armatrading* v. *Stone* and *John* v. *James* that the courts can be highly critical of clauses in contracts that are unfair on the artist.

In deciding whether a contract is fair, the court looks at a number of things. It'll look at the bargaining power of the artist and the company. It will also look at whether the artist had independent specialist advice before he signed it and it will look at how experienced the artist was in the music business at the time the contract was signed. It does this against the background of what was the norm for these contracts at the time.

The other main guiding principle behind the court decisions is that of the doctrine of restraint of trade.[2]

2 For a more detailed description of the general principles of restraint of trade, see *Chitty on Contracts*, Sweet and Maxwell.

For years it has been well known that the doctrine applied to ordinary contracts of employment or contracts for someone to provide their exclusive services. The leading case on the subject was one to do with garages.[3] What we didn't know until a 1974 case was whether the doctrine could apply to recording and publishing contracts.

The basic principle behind the doctrine is that where someone has to provide services or be exclusively employed and the contract contains restrictions on what they can and cannot do, that contract is automatically a restriction on their ability to earn a living or trade. Because it's an exclusive arrangement, the person concerned can't earn money in any other way than through that contract.

In the UK it was decided long ago that these contracts were contrary to public policy. A man should be free to earn his living wherever he can. The courts recognised that there would be circumstances where it was commercially necessary to have restrictions in a contract. They decided that such restrictions would be allowed if they were reasonably necessary to protect the legitimate business interests of the person imposing the restrictions. If the restrictions were unreasonable they couldn't be enforced – the contract would be unenforceable.

● Because it was so important to the music business, the case of *Macaulay* v. *Schroeder*[4] went all the way to the House of Lords before it was finally clear that the doctrine did apply to recording and publishing agreements.

Macaulay was a young and unknown songwriter who entered into a publishing agreement with Schroeder Music Publishing Ltd. It was an exclusive agreement for his services for five years. The contract was in a standard form used by the publisher. Macaulay's copyrights in the songs he wrote were assigned for the life of copyright throughout the world. The contract specifically prevented him from working as a songwriter for any other music publishers during this five-year period. There is nothing wrong in signing someone up to an exclusive deal. However, because that exclusivity restricts that person's ability to go and work for anyone else, we have to look at whether, as a whole, such a contract is fair. Do the restrictions that an exclusive contract places on someone still allow that person to earn a reasonable living? The House of Lords looked at the specific terms of that agreement to see if, taken as a whole, they were reasonable. It found they were unduly restrictive and an unreasonable restraint of trade. They did not enable Macaulay to have a reasonable chance of earning a decent living from his trade of songwriting. The George Michael case (see page 46) is an example of an exclusive contract that was found to contain reasonable restrictions.[5]

When negotiating a contract, you can often use the argument that a particularly harsh term could make the whole contract unenforceable if it stays in. This often helps to get the offending term removed or toned down.

3 *Esso Petroleum Ltd* v. *Harper's Garage (Stourport) Limited* [1968] AC 269.
4 *Macaulay* v. *Schroeder Music Publishing Co. Ltd* [1974] 1 W.L.R. 1308, HL.
5 The particular provisions that were found to be unreasonable are discussed in more detail in Chapter 4.

Now that we've got this general principle out of the way we can look more closely at what's a good deal.

CREATIVE CONTROL VERSUS LARGE ADVANCES

DO YOU GO FOR THE MONEY OR TRY TO PROTECT THE INTEGRITY OF YOUR ART?

Of course it's important for you to be able to eat, to have somewhere to live and transport to get you to and from gigs, rehearsals and the recording studio. But it may not just be a question of money. For many artists creative control of their work is at least as important. The right to make a record with minimal interference from the record company is crucial to some artists.

If creative control is the most important thing for you then getting that control would mean you had a 'good' deal, even if it meant there was less money on the table. Some record companies are more flexible than others on questions of creative control. If this is an important issue for you, you need to look at this at the point when various record companies are still courting you. You should ask them what their attitude is to this issue. What is their track record? You should talk to other artists signed to the record company, if you can, to find out their experiences. You should also ask if the record company is prepared to guarantee creative control in the record contract.

Your wish to have creative control must be balanced against putting so many restrictions on what the record company can do with the recordings that they can't sell your records properly. If that's the case, they may choose to use another artist's recordings – one who isn't so particular about creative control. For example, a proposal comes in from an ad company to put one of two tracks into a major new jeans campaign. Band A has full creative control in its contract and is known to be completely against the idea of its work being used in ads. Band B, on the other hand, has an eye to the integrity of their work but realises that a campaign like this, if done properly, can really break it into the big-time. Band B reacts positively and the record company puts their track forward, not Band A's.

You may be very interested in getting as much commitment as possible from the record company. If so, you'll concentrate on getting their commitment to release a minimum number of singles off each album, to make one or more videos, to commit to a specific figure in marketing 'spend' or to underwrite tour losses up to a fixed amount. The record company may be reluctant to do this. They would be in trouble if there weren't enough tracks on the album suitable for release as singles. It's expensive to make videos and they may not want to commit to making one that only gets played once on *Live and Kicking*. They don't like putting figures on marketing spend. They say they'll spend what it takes. They might commit to the principle of underwriting tour losses but may not want to put a figure on it. They would prefer it if it were discussed at the time. If these things are an important part of your gameplan, you will want to push for some or all of them to be included in the contract.

Whatever your particular needs (and it may be a mixture of all three), if you get a reasonable number of them in your record contract then you will have what is a good deal for you.

This whole issue of creative control versus money has caused a lot of problems over the years. It's one of the reasons why Prince became Symbol became The Artist Formerly Known As Prince and now just The Artist. He believed that by changing his name he could use a loophole to get out of his record contract. He was probably also hoping that it would show his record company, Warner Bros., the strength of his feeling over the type of records he wanted to make.

- The same issue led to a very acrimonious case between George Michael and his record company, Sony Records: *Panayioutou* v. *Sony Music Entertainment (UK) Limited.*[6]

As we all know, George Michael was part of the very successful pop duo Wham! along with Andrew Ridgeley. The first exclusive record deal that George and Andrew signed was with the record company Innervision, owned by Mark Dean, in 1982. Yes, you guessed it; they were young, unknown and inexperienced. The record deal was for up to ten albums, which was a lot even in those days. They were exclusively tied to the company until they had delivered all the albums that Innervision wanted from them. Applying the doctrine of restraint of trade, you can see that the restrictions in the contract were immediately contrary to public policy and unenforceable unless they were reasonable.

Innervision was a small record company. It had a deal with Sony whereby Sony provided funding and facilities for the manufacture, sale and marketing of Innervision's records. So the Innervision contract with George and Andrew also included Sony's standard business terms. If the Innervision contract was criticised as being unenforceable and an unreasonable restraint of trade then this was also an indirect criticism of Sony's terms of business.

At first, things went well and their second release, 'Young Guns', was a UK Top 10 hit in 1992. This was followed by 'Bad Boys', 'Club Tropicana' and the chart-topping album *Fantastic*. By 1983, however, the relationship between Wham! and Innervision had broken down. They sued the company to get out of the contract, arguing that it was an unreasonable restraint of trade. The case settled before it got to court. It was part of the settlement that George and Andrew signed an exclusive recording contract direct with Sony label, Epic Records. Again that contract contained Sony's business terms but an experienced music business lawyer negotiated it on George and Andrew's behalf.

Once again things went well at first. Their first single on Epic – 'Wake Me Up Before You Go Go' – went to No. 1 in the UK and was followed by four further No.1s in quick succession.

In 1986, George and Andrew parted company. Andrew eventually left the music business and for a time was racing motorcars. George embarked on a solo career with Sony.

And it was a very successful one, although not until 1988, with 'I Want Your Sex' a deliberate move to break with the playboy Wham! image. His first solo album, *Faith*, was a huge success, selling over 10 million copies. On the back of that success, George renegotiated his contract with Sony – again with the help of that experienced music business lawyer.

In return for a substantial sum of money, George agreed to record three solo albums in the first contract period and gave Sony options for up to five more albums. *Faith* counted as the

6 [1994] EMLR 220.

first of the three albums and he went on to record and release a second hugely successful album, *Listen Without Prejudice (Vol. 2)*, which also sold millions. His star was also rising in the US, where he had a No. 1 with 'Praying For Time' off that album.

Not surprisingly, Sony wanted George to continue in the same style with his third solo album. By this time George wanted to move away from the out-and-out commercial pop style of records. He wanted to be regarded as a serious artist.

Because the contract ran until he'd delivered up to six more albums, or for a maximum period of fifteen years, George couldn't record for anyone else. Sony also had the final say on whether an album by him met the necessary artistic and commercial criteria. They could go on rejecting more serious material from him. Deadlock.

George sued. He argued that the record contract was an unreasonable restriction on his ability to earn a living, that it was an unenforceable contract.

He refused to record for Sony and instead did a number of projects with other artists that were within the terms of his contract – just. For example, he did guest spots on other people's albums. He also concentrated on live work.

The case finally came to trial in 1994. The decision to throw out George's case was made on somewhat surprising grounds. The judge ruled that in order to decide if the 1988 renegotiation of the contract was an unreasonable restraint of trade he would also have to consider the earlier 1984 contract. He decided that he couldn't re-open a review of that contract because it had been entered into in order to settle a dispute. It's contrary to public policy to re-open something that was agreed by the parties as being a final settlement of a dispute.

An appeal by George Michael seemed pretty likely. Perhaps the judge realised this because, even though he had decided that he couldn't look at the 1988 contract, he went on to say what his conclusions would have been if he had done.

The contract was an exclusive worldwide deal. It was for potentially a very long time and Sony had the absolute right to reject recordings and a limited duty to do much with any recordings that it did accept.

On the face of it, you'd think this was enough to make the judge decide the contract was unfair and unenforceable, as being an unreasonable restraint of trade. Not so.

The judge looked at the relative bargaining power of the two sides. By 1988 George was a very successful and powerful artist and well able to stand up to Sony. The judge also saw that George had had the benefit of advice from his long-standing lawyer, who was very experienced in music business contracts. Finally, he looked at what George would get out of the contract. Financially he got a great deal.

Balancing out all these factors, he decided that the benefits George got out of the contract meant that the restrictions in it were reasonable to protect Sony's investment and its legitimate business interests.

Sony, of course, was delighted, but it was seen by most of the 'talent' in the business as a blow for creative freedom.

Interestingly, while the case was going on it was much easier for me to get improvements in Sony contracts, particularly those parts that George was specifically attacking. For example, on CD sales, Sony only pays 75–80% of the royalty. While the case was on they were much more inclined to agree a full 100% royalty rate. As soon as Sony won the case it was business as usual.

George, as expected, appealed. The thought of prolonged, expensive litigation with an artist who clearly wasn't going to record for them led to a settlement before the appeal was heard. George was released from the contract and signed to Virgin/Dreamworks in return for a payment back to Sony. As part of the settlement, he later recorded some new tracks or new versions of old tracks for a Greatest Hits album that was released on Sony.

Once you've decided what is important to you in a contract, you need to know what types of deal may be on offer. You'll also need to know what basic rights a performing artist has, what copyright is and what rights the record company needs in order to release records.

TYPES OF DEAL

Although there are many variations, there are three basic types of record deal – the licence, the development deal and the exclusive long-term recording contract.

Let's look first at the difference between a licence and the other two. To do this, I need to explain some legal principles before we go any further.

LEGAL PRINCIPLES

Licensor is the technical term for a person or company who owns rights, which it is licensing to someone else. I'm going to use the word 'owner' instead, as it fits more easily into the text.

Licensee is the term for the person or company to whom the rights are licensed.

A **licence** is an agreement to allow someone to do certain things with the rights that an owner has to a particular product – a recording, a song and so on. A licence can be for as long as the life of copyright (see below) but is usually for a much shorter period. The owner continues to own the rights but gives someone else permission to use some or all of those rights.

An **assignment** is an outright transfer of ownership of rights by an owner to someone else. It is usually for the life of copyright although sometimes the rights are returned (reassigned) to the owner sooner than that. The assignment can be of some or all rights or have conditions attached.

An **assignor** is the owner of the rights being assigned. The assignor no longer owns the rights once they've been assigned. Again I'm going to use 'owner' instead.

An **assignee** is the person or company to whom the rights are assigned.

Life of copyright is now the same throughout the EU. For literary and musical works (i.e. songs) it's 70 years from the end of the year in which the author dies. For sound recordings and performer's rights it's 50 years from the end of the year in which the recording was released or the performance was made.[7]

7 Sections 12 and 13A CDPA.

The rights I'm talking about are intellectual property rights of copyright and also performer's rights.

The **author** is the first owner of the copyright.[8] The 1988 Copyright Act says that in the case of sound recordings it's the producer. This could be confusing and for a time record producers were going around claiming they were the copyright owners. It was soon clarified that the position was the same as before the 1988 Act. The copyright owner of a sound recording is the person 'who made the arrangements for the recording to be made'. This is generally taken to mean the person who paid for the recording to be made.

What is **copyright**? It's the rights that an author has to prevent anyone else doing certain things with his work without his permission. The basic rights of copyright are the right to copy the work; the right to issue copies of the work to the public; the right to rent or lend out copies of the work to the public; the right to perform, show or play the work in public; the right to broadcast the work or include it in a cable programme; the right to make an adaptation of the work. The right to do any of the above acts in relation to that adaptation.[9] Before anyone can do any of these things with a copyright work they have to get the permission of the copyright owner.

Performing rights are the rights performers have to prevent someone else from doing certain things with their performances or with recordings of their performances without their permission. The basic performing rights are in some respects similar to the rights of copyright. They are the right to prevent someone making a recording of a live performance; the right to prevent the making of a broadcast or its inclusion live in a cable service programme. It's also a performer's right to prevent someone from making a recording of his performance directly from the broadcast or cable programme.[10] The performer's permission has to be obtained to do any of the above.[11] Recordings of performances for personal use are allowed. The performer also has the right to refuse to let someone make a copy of a recording; to issue a copy of a recording to the public; to rent or lend copies of the recording to the public; to play a recorded performance in public or to include it in a broadcast or cable programme service.

LICENCE VERSUS ASSIGNMENT

With a licence the owner keeps the underlying copyright. He only gives the licensee permission to do certain things with the copyright for a period of time (the licence term).

It's clear from the Gilbert O'Sullivan case that even where the court finds that a contract is unenforceable, it won't usually say that it is void but *voidable* and it won't usually order the return of copyrights or other rights that have been assigned.

If it's a licence then the underlying rights haven't been assigned; there is nothing that needs to be returned to the original owner because it never left him.

If O'Sullivan had licensed his rights rather than assigned them, he wouldn't have had such

8 Section 16(2) CDPA.
9 Sections 17–27 CDPA.
10 Sections 181–184 CDPA.
11 Section 185 CDPA.

a problem. The licence would have come to an end because MAM were in breach of its terms and he would still have had his copyright in his songs and masters.

So, from the point of view of an artist, a licence should always be preferable to an assignment.

There are two problems with this. The first is that the record company will probably be the one who made the arrangements for the recording to be made (i.e. paid for it) and so will be the first owner of copyright. The artist may have his performing rights but will probably not own the copyright in the sound recording. The second is that record companies don't want to do licence deals if they can do an assignment of rights instead. They have investments to protect. It can take half a million pounds to launch a new act. They will want to own the copyright outright. They can't risk losing their rights if a licence ends.

The more successful an artist is, the more chance he has of being the owner of the copyright in the sound recording and in a position to license it to the record company.

The other time when you may find a licence rather than an assignment is when one record company (perhaps a small label or an individual) has paid for a recording to be made and then licenses the copyright to another (perhaps bigger) record company either non-exclusively or exclusively.

I think that in time, and particularly as a result of changes in how records are made and new methods of distribution such as the Internet, this situation will change. Artists and smaller record companies won't need as much, if any, direct financial investment from a bigger record company (see Chapter 7). They will be able to fund it themselves more cheaply and efficiently. This could see a shift in the balance of power in favour of artists doing more licence deals.

EXCLUSIVE AND NON-EXCLUSIVE DEALS

When a record company is putting out a compilation ('The Best Dance Records In The World Ever Vol. 3' or similar) then you might license rights in a recording that you own to that company for that compilation only. You would probably want to license the rights on a non-exclusive basis. You might want to put the recording out yourself or license it to another company for a different compilation. You couldn't do that if you'd given the first record company an exclusive licence.

On the other hand, you may be an artist or a small label that has recorded a track or an album yourself, so you own the copyright in it. You may not have the financial resources to do anything with that recording. Perhaps you can't afford to press up copies of it to sell or you can't promote it properly. You might go to another record company for those resources. If they agree then the licence is likely to be an exclusive one to protect their investment.

THE LICENCE TERM

How long should the licence last? If it's non-exclusive it probably doesn't matter too much. An exclusive licence could be as long as the life of copyright (see above) or as short as a year.

Three-year licence terms are common. The licensee wants to have long enough to get a reasonable return on his investment, but if it's a short licence term the owner will get the rights back sooner and may be able to re-license them to someone else (perhaps with a new mix) or release them himself.

TERRITORY

It could be a worldwide licence or it could be limited to particular countries. If, for example, you've already licensed the rights exclusively to a company in the US, you can only then grant other licences in the same recordings for the rest of the world outside the US.

Although exclusive recording contracts can be for limited countries, this is more common in licence deals.

There are people that go around trying to get you licence deals for particular countries. They usually take a commission from you of 2–5% of what you get in advances or royalties and sometimes they also take a fee off the licensee for bringing the recording to them. These are called 'finders' fees'.

The main problem with individual country deals is that you have to keep on top of a number of different licensees. There's not just one company to chase for payment of royalties. The main advantage is that you can license the recording to the company that most wants it in each country.

OPTIONS

When you're doing a non-exclusive licence of a single track for a compilation, you don't usually give the licensee any options to any further recordings you may make. It's usually a one-off.

If it's an exclusive licence, the licensee may be keen to get follow-up products. The licensee may be encouraged to invest more in promoting the first track if they know they are going to get the follow-up.

When doing your exclusive licence deal you can agree upfront the basis on which you're going to give them any follow-up product. Or you can leave it to be agreed at the time they exercise the option. This can be to the owner's advantage if the first track has been successful. His bargaining power will be higher. It isn't a very certain state of affairs, though, and often leads to problems, so I don't generally recommend it.

Another possibility would be to give the licensee an option, which gives the licensee the chance to be the first to try and do a deal with you for the follow-up. For example, you might deliver a demo of the follow-up and give the licensee the exclusive rights, for two weeks, to try to negotiate a deal with you. If they don't succeed in that time, you can take it into the market place. This is called a first negotiating right.

Or you could give the licensee a matching right. This is the right to match any offer for the follow-up that you get from someone else. You have to tell the licensee the details of the offer and if the licensee matches or betters it you have to do the deal with them. Again you would usually give them a week or two to come up with a matching offer.

DEVELOPMENT DEALS

These take two forms.

THE TRADITIONAL FORM

In its traditional form this is precisely what it says. You may still have to develop your skills and musical direction. The record company may not want to put too much pressure on you in the early stages while this is happening. The deal is usually a low-key one. In the early stages the personal advances offered to you will be low to reflect the fact that you're not yet ready to make and promote an album. Recording costs will probably be paid on a track-by-track basis until, say, five recordings have been finished and the direction in which you are developing is becoming clear. At this point the record company usually has to decide whether or not to commit to a longer-term record deal with you.

Rights

Traditional development deals are usually exclusive worldwide deals. The record company will usually expect you to assign any copyright you may have in the recordings made under the deal. It's very likely that you won't have any because the record company will have paid the studio and will be the first owner of the copyright.

You will probably have performed on the recording and so will have performer's rights. If the deal develops into a full-blown exclusive recording contract, you may be happy to give your consent as a performer to your rights being exploited by the record company. If it doesn't, and the record company doesn't go ahead with the deal, then you won't want them to be able to release the recordings. You could stop them from doing this in a number of ways. You could, for example, withhold your performer's consents for the recordings to be used commercially. You could also require the record company to reassign the copyright in the sound recording to you if they don't do a full deal with you.[12] The record company may be happy to do this with no strings attached. Or they might say you can have the copyright if you repay to them the recording costs.

ALTERNATIVE MEANING OF A DEVELOPMENT DEAL

It could be a cheap exclusive recording contract dressed up as something else.

The record company may not be quite convinced that you've got star quality but they believe that there's enough there to make it worth them doing an exclusive deal with you. They'll want to be able to get out of it at an early stage and their investment in recording costs and payments to you will be low. They won't usually commit to a big spend on recording or video costs or in supporting you on tour.

They'll usually want an assignment of all your sound recording copyright and unconditional permission to use your performances. If the deal doesn't progress, they're unlikely to automatically reassign copyright to you. They'll probably want their recording costs

12 Reassignment doesn't have to be in writing but it is wise to have it recorded. The original assignment must be in writing – Section 90(3) CDPA.

back or a share of any royalty that you make from exploiting the recordings (an **override royalty**).

WHY SHOULD YOU DO ONE OF THESE DEALS?

Well, you may not have much choice. This may be the only offer on the table. You may decide to take it and see if you can manage to make it a success. If it is, you can hope to renegotiate the terms.

If you aren't desperate for a deal, you might decide to hold out for a proper exclusive recording contract – perhaps by doing a publishing deal first to keep you going (see Chapter 4). Or you might decide to find the money to make some recordings yourself and license them to another company or release them yourself (see Chapter 6). This is becoming easier and cheaper to do with advances in technology. The increasing availability of digital recordings over the Internet may present the greatest challenge for some time to the traditional record company means of distribution (see Chapter 7).

EXCLUSIVE RECORDING CONTRACT

This is the third type of record deal and the one that most new artists want to get. This type of deal gives you the greatest potential investment and commitment from a record company. In return, of course, the record company will expect to be able to protect its investment. You won't be able to walk away from it when you choose.

It will be up to your advisers to make sure that the contract is a fair one. It should also be in the record company's interest. If the contract is so unfair that it's an unreasonable restraint of trade then it will be unenforceable and you can walk away from it.

Although it's likely that the record company will own the sound recording copyright, the contract will usually make sure by making you assign any copyright you may have to the record company. The record contract will also make sure that the record company will be able to exploit your performances by getting all necessary performers' consents from you. Your lawyer ought to make sure that you have plenty of creative control over what the record company can do with the recordings and with your performances.

One thing you might not want them to do is to put your recording with an advert for a product that you don't approve of. I was once involved in a case where Sting was furious that a recording of his track 'Don't Stand So Close To Me' was used in an advert for deodorant.

TERM OF THE CONTRACT

It will usually be for an initial period of one year (possibly six months if it's a singles deal rather than an album deal). The record company will usually have a number of options to extend the contract term. In each contract period they will expect you to record a minimum number of tracks. It could be single tracks or enough tracks to make up an album. If you really want to make money then you'll want your record company to commit to recording albums as early as possible in the contract. In the first contract period the record company may want a couple of singles first, but they should also then commit to the number of tracks required to make up an album (usually at least ten tracks in total).

Each contract period is usually extended for three to four months after you deliver the last of the recordings the record company wants. The slower you record and deliver recordings, or the longer it takes to release them, the longer each contract period will be.

WHY IS IT ONLY THE RECORD COMPANY THAT HAS OPTIONS?

The record company will have invested a lot of money in making your records. It will probably also have made videos and may have supported you while you've been out touring. These costs are recoupable (i.e. the record company gets some or all of them back from your earnings or royalties from sales of your records). If you don't sell enough records or you walk out of the contract before you have given the record company the chance to recoup their investment then these costs would be down to the record company.

Over and above this are the promotional and marketing costs which, for a major release, can run into hundreds of thousands of pounds. Most of these costs are non-recoupable.

Then there are the manufacturing and distribution costs, which again are usually non-recoupable.

If you could just up and walk away from the contract whenever you felt like it, the record company would not be able to protect its investment, its business interests. If you could walk away at any time, they wouldn't invest anything like these amounts of money in you. So the options are in their favour, not yours.

That said, various labels, including one set up by George Michael, are trying to do deals that do give you the option to walk away after you've completed all the promotional work needed on a particular record. The problem is that there is a great deal of suspicion about these types of deals and investors are unwilling to invest large sums of money.

WHY CAN'T YOU GET YOUR COPYRIGHT BACK?

I can understand why a record company justifies its ownership of copyright in the recording by the fact that it's invested a lot of money. What is less easy to understand is why the company won't transfer that copyright to you once they've recouped that investment. George Michael argued this point in his case with Sony but the way the case went meant that there isn't a definitive decision on the point. Given the reluctance of the courts in cases like O'Sullivan to upset the economic order, it seems that the courts would be very unlikely to order a return of copyrights.

Record companies say that the vast majority of artists don't recoup their investment (depressing thought but let's press on). They also say that they have to spend a lot of money in researching and developing new talent. If they had to return the copyrights of successful artists, they say they won't be able to invest as much in new artists in the future and that the culture of the nation will suffer as a result. Well, I can think of a few bands that made barely a dent in the cultural richness of my life, can't you?

Some record companies, mostly those owned by former artists or managers, do offer to return copyright to an artist that has recouped his costs after a period of time, usually at least fifteen years, but there are often lots of conditions attached.

If you are a very successful artist, you may get some or all of your copyrights back when you renegotiate your record deal.

HOW MANY OPTIONS SHOULD THE RECORD COMPANY HAVE FOR FUTURE ALBUMS?

Most major record companies in the UK want options on four or five further albums.[13] Independent record companies may accept less.

The number of options, and therefore the overall length of the contract, is a key issue when considering if a contract is an unreasonable restraint of trade.

- This issue was at the heart of a major court case between Holly Johnson of Frankie Goes To Hollywood and his record company ZTT (*Zang TumbTum Records Limited and Perfect Songs Limited* v. *Holly Johnson.*[14]. He also had a similar dispute with the sister publishing company, Perfect Songs, which I'll deal with in the chapter on publishing deals below.)

Holly Johnson and the other members of Frankie Goes To Hollywood were unknown when they attracted the interest of the directors of ZTT, Jill Sinclair and her husband (the highly successful record producer Trevor Horn). They were broke and were very keen to work with Mr Horn. They were told that ZTT would only do the record deal if they also signed an exclusive publishing deal with Perfect Songs. Now you might detect a whiff of undue influence here but in fact this point wasn't seriously argued in the case. The band signed up to both deals. Although they were inexperienced and had very little bargaining power, they were represented by a lawyer who was experienced in music business contracts.

Frankie Goes To Hollywood had two very successful singles with 'Relax' and 'Two Tribes', both of which attracted a great deal of controversy because of the subject matter in the case of the first and the video for the second. At one stage the two tracks were Nos. 1 and 2 in the UK singles charts. The band's first album, *Welcome To The Pleasure Dome*, sold well and produced two more hit singles. They failed to make a success of it in the States and by 1986 the pressure was on them for the second album to be a success.

The band had a lot of trouble with the recording of this album, to be called *Liverpool.* Trevor Horn controlled the recording costs; he was the record producer and the recordings were being made in his studios. The costs were escalating alarmingly and the band were horrified by how much they'd have to recoup. After a lot of problems the band split up but ZTT (and Perfect Songs) wanted to hang on to Holly Johnson.

Johnson didn't want to continue with them and sued on grounds that both the recording and publishing contracts were an unreasonable restraint of trade.

The term of the record contract was for an initial period of six months and was extendable by two option periods and up to five contract periods all in favour of the record company. Each contract period was to be for a minimum of one year and extendable until 120 days after they fulfilled their minimum obligations to the record company (known as the Minimum

13 In the United States, options for six or seven further albums are commonplace.
14 [1993] EMLR 61.

> Commitment). There was also no maximum extension of the contract period. It was open-ended and depended entirely on when the band fulfilled its Minimum Commitment.
>
> The Minimum Commitment was one single in each of the initial and two option periods and one album in each of the third through to seventh option contract periods. This is a very odd way of structuring a contract but, basically, it meant that if the record company exercised every option, the band had to record three singles and five albums.
>
> The record company was free to bring the contract to an end at any time. The record company also had the right to reject recordings delivered to them by the band. As the term continued until after delivery of recordings that were satisfactory to the record company, this meant the record company controlled how long the contract lasted. There are echoes of this in the George Michael case.
>
> The court decided that the contract was so one-sided and unfair that it was an unreasonable restraint of trade and unenforceable. It thought that the potential term of the contract was far too long; it could easily last eight or nine years. In that time the court felt that the band wouldn't have had the opportunity to earn a decent living from their work. The record company was not obliged to do very much with the recordings. There was no commitment to release them. They freed him from the contracts and awarded him substantial compensation.

As a result of this case, record contracts now usually contain a clause committing the record company to releasing records in at least the home country. For example, if you did a UK record deal, you'd expect to be able to insist on your records being released in the UK. If they aren't released then the contracts usually give you the right to end the contract and sometimes to get your recordings back, possibly in return for an override royalty. The term of UK record contracts also became shorter and maximum backstops are now usually placed on the time each contract period can run.

TWO-ALBUM FIRM DEALS

This is the other side of the coin. It's possible to get a record company to commit in advance to a second album. These types of deals are called two-album firm deals. Record companies are more likely to agree to these types of deals when they are in competition with another record company. Most record companies don't want to give this commitment. They want to see how the first album does before committing to a second. These types of deals go in and out of favour. Some artists and managers favour them because they provide commitment and certainty, which allows them to do some forward planning. Others feel they only work if things are going well. If things aren't going well, the record company will probably try to get out of it after the first album. If your only alternative is to sue the company for failing to honour their side of the bargain then you'll probably agree to accept the offer they make to end the contract, so the commitment may not mean much in the end.

TERRITORY AND SPLIT-TERRITORY DEALS

Long-term exclusive record deals will usually be offered on a worldwide basis. This may be perfectly acceptable to you, particularly if the record company has a strong presence in most major markets of the world. However, because the US is a very different market place from that of the UK, an artist sometimes asks for what is known as a split-territory deal.

This means that you do one deal with a record company for the world excluding the US and another deal with another record company for the US. To make these types of deals work, the artist and his manager have to juggle the demands of two record companies. If you get it right it means that you have two companies protecting your interests in the two main English-speaking music markets in the world. Record companies don't like doing these types of deals because they say they need a worldwide market in which to recover their investment. They will also say that their own companies are strong worldwide and should be given the chance.

Split-territory deals are usually offered to artists with considerable bargaining power, to those with an already established track record and occasionally to new artists managed by a manager with a track record for finding and developing new artists.

If you're thinking of doing a deal with a smaller record company, you may find that they don't have branch offices or companies in other parts of the world. They may have a network of licensees in different countries. Those licensees might take all the records they produce. These are called catalogue licence deals. Or the UK company may look for different licensees for each artist. For example, the UK record company could do a deal with Atlantic Records in the US for all their acts or it could do a deal with Atlantic for their mainstream acts and with a smaller label for its 'indie' acts. Whatever the situation, you need to know who the licensees are going to be. They need to be well-established, trustworthy companies that will do a reasonable job of selling your records in the country concerned. If the licence deal isn't in place in a particular country when you do your record deal, you should have the right to approve that part of the licence deal that affects you at the time the licence deal is done.

Smaller companies use overseas licence deals to help to fund their operation in the UK. For example, a company in Germany could pay an advance against the royalty it expects to pay on sales of records in Germany. It may also pay a contribution to the cost of making a video in return for the right to use the video in Germany. If the artist does a promotional or concert tour in Germany, the German licensee will usually provide some financial back-up. If you have a small low-key deal in the UK with a label that can't afford to pay you very much upfront, you could ask that some of the advances paid by overseas licensees of your recordings should be paid through to you. For example, if the German licensee paid an advance against royalties of 100,000DM you might get 25% (i.e. 25,000DM). This will help to make up for the low advances in the UK. This is something that should be negotiated at the time the original UK record deal with you is done.

Now that I've looked at the three main types of deal and some of the things that distinguish them, I want to look at some aspects of contracts that are common to all three types.

DELIVERY REQUIREMENTS – MINIMUM COMMITMENT

Each type of record contract has a minimum that it requires from you. Licence deals can be for single tracks or albums. Development deals may start out as being for four or five tracks and then develop into a commitment to record albums. Exclusive album deals can either be for a single track or an album initially with options to acquire further product. One of your obligations will be to deliver the required minimum number of recordings.

Your obligation may be simply to deliver the master tapes of these recordings to the record company. More often, however, your commitment is not fulfilled until the record company has agreed that the recordings meet the required standards. As we saw in the George Michael case, if these standards aren't met then the company can reject the recordings and make you re-record them until they meet the necessary standard. It's important that these standards are realistic and that they are set out in the contract. They could either be technical requirements or commercial ones or a combination of both. What you should try to avoid is a subjective standard. This is someone else's view of whether you meet the required standard or whether the recording is commercially satisfactory. What a record company executive thinks is commercially acceptable may not be anything like your own views on the subject. It's best if you can try to set an objective standard, a standard against which the quality of your recording can be measured. For example, measuring it against a recording that the record company has previously accepted as being satisfactory.

It is also usual to try to put a time limit on when the record company has to give you an answer as to whether a recording is satisfactory. That must be a realistic time period, as the company may have to go through various stages and processes before it can give you an answer. Your A&R man will have to listen to it and probably play it to his colleagues at the weekly A&R meeting. He may talk to the producer of the record to get his view of how he thinks the recording sounds. He will probably talk to your manager and get his views. He may have a hunch that the record could be improved if one or more tracks are remixed by someone other than the record producer or original mixer. Depending on the contract, he may have to get your permission before he does that. The contract with the record producer may mean that he has to give him the first chance to remix the track in question. This process takes time.

If it makes artistic sense then you're going to agree to one or two remixes, but this can cost more than £10,000 a time for a good remixer. Some or all of this may be recoupable from your royalties, so you don't want to do too many remixes or it will get very expensive for you. Until these have been done and accepted you may not have fulfilled your Minimum Commitment.

Once the record company is happy with the standard of your recordings it may say that the recordings have been accepted and that you have fulfilled your Minimum Commitment. But most companies want more information from you before they do that.

Acceptance of fulfilment of Minimum Commitment usually means that the record company has to start planning the release and maybe has to pay you a further instalment of your advance. The record contract may set a last date by which the record must be released. The record company won't want that time to start running until they are in a position to start the processes for a release. This means that they usually require you to hand over a number of other things before delivery is said to have taken place and before they accept the recordings. These could be artwork for the packaging of the records, details of who performed on the masters and confirmation that those performers have given their performer's consents. If there are samples of anyone else's recordings or songs in your masters then the record company will want to know that you've obtained permission from the copyright owners of those recordings or songs to use the samples (see Chapter 13). If permission to use the samples hasn't been agreed then the record company can't put your recordings out without being in breach of copyright.

Because it's vital to know when a recording has been accepted, I often ask for the record company to agree that the recordings are said (deemed) to be accepted if the record company has not said that they aren't within four to six weeks of you delivering the masters, artwork and so on to them. Depending on how long they think it will take for them to go through the acceptance process, they may agree to this or they may not.

ADVANCES

For many artists this is the most important issue. Remember that these monies will have to be recouped out of the royalties you earn from exploitation of your recordings. Unlike a loan, however, advances are not usually repayable if the record company doesn't sell enough of your records. That's the record company's risk. But, if you take their money and then don't deliver a single recording, they may try and come after you to get the advance back. If you've spent it and haven't got any money then they may not bother to sue you because it would cost them more in legal fees than they would get back. I wouldn't like to rely on them not suing though.

If you take their money, it's only reasonable that you deliver some recordings to them. Obviously this is sometimes out of your control – if the band splits up or the singer gets ill, for instance. But I have seen artists who cynically wait to split the band up until after they receive the first instalment of their record advance. One band I know waited until they'd delivered the finished album to the record company and had taken the advance they were due on delivery. They then split up before the record was released. The US record company that they were signed to was furious. Here they were, having spent all the recording costs and paid all the personal advances due to the band only to have an album with no artist to promote it. They were so angry that they sued the band for return of the advances and breach of contract. We had to settle it by agreeing to give them an override royalty on the next album they released.

What is a good advance?

A good advance is one that meets your needs. You may only care about getting as much money as possible and aren't concerned if you never sell enough records to recoup. There are a lot of cynical managers with that view in the business – take the money and run. In that case, you'll just be looking for the most money you can get upfront. It's a short-term view because the greater the record company's investment in advances, the more pressure there is going to be on you to perform and the more likely it is that the record company will want to dictate to you. If you go for a more reasonable advance, payable in reasonable instalments, the record company is going to put you under less pressure to deliver. You should also recoup the advances sooner out of your royalties. Because so few artists recoup advances and costs, this will put you in a strong bargaining position with the record company.

A good advance is going to be one that allows you to live and have a roof over your head for at least a year, and preferably eighteen months, while the recordings are being made and then promoted. It's a good idea for you or your manager to do an outline budget of what you may need.

If your manager is only interested in getting as much of the advance as possible, as early as possible, you should be suspicious. Is he only concerned about his commission? Is he only in it for the short-term? Doesn't he expect to be around when the record is finished or when

Outline budget for a record deal:

Personal Advances: Wages to cover your basic living requirements, such as food, rent/mortgage and personal expenses, multiplied by the number of members of the band and on a monthly basis over, say, 18 months. The record company may bargain you down to 12 months, but 18 is more realistic.

Example: A 4-piece band needing £1,000 a month each would need a total of £4,000 × 18 = £72,000

Equipment: You may need to invest in certain equipment, for example, microphone stands, a better PA or guitars, an upgraded drum kit and so on. This throws up arguments about who owns this equipment. The record company usually retains notional ownership and in theory could require the band to return it once the deal ends, but this is rarely enforced.

Example: Say £5,000

Transport: You may need to buy or upgrade a transit van to get to gigs or to and from the studio.

Example: Say £5,000

Rehearsal Time: You may suggest a sum of money to cover the cost of hiring a hall or rooms to rehearse. You might argue that a long-term rental is cheaper than hiring commercial rehearsal rooms. One band I know took a lease on a room over the local chip shop to rehearse in.

Example: Say £500 a month for 12 months = £6,000

Debts: It would be unusual if you had reached this stage without running up an overdraft or other debts. If you were looking for justification for a particular level of advance then an amount to repay debts would be a valid item to include in the budget.

Example: Say £2,500 per artist × 4 = £10,000

Professional management fees: Don't forget you're going to have to pay a lawyer and an accountant.

Example: Say £7,500

Management Fees: If you have got a manager you will also have to allow for him taking a 20% commission of the gross amount, so you should uplift your total figure to allow for this.

The Hype Factor: This is unquantifiable. My suggestion would be for you to look at your basic budget first.

Budget

Personal Advances	£72,000
Equipment	£5,000
Transport	£5,000
Rehearsal time	£6,000
Debts	£10,000
Professional Fees	£7,500
	£105,500
Management Commission	£16,900
	£122,400

Say: £125,000

Add the 'hype' factor, which is whatever your instincts or your advisers say the deal can be pushed to.

Say: **£160,000**

Be prepared to be flexible.

it is time for the option to be exercised? Whose interests is he looking after – yours or his? It may be a perfectly legitimate approach but don't accept it without question.

You may accept a lower advance in return for other things, such as greater creative control. It is possible to get both, but usually only when you have a lot of bargaining power. If you go for a lower advance, you should also be able to argue for a higher royalty.

Min-max formula

The level of advances payable could be calculated according to a formula (called a min-max formula). Under this formula a minimum advance is payable to you and a limit is also set on the maximum the company will pay. The actual amount is calculated as a percentage of the royalties you earned from sales of the last recordings released of your performances. For this reason the formula usually applies from the second contract period onwards.

At the beginning of the second contract period the record company looks at how much you have earned from sales of the recordings you made in the first contract period. The company then takes a percentage of that and if the amount then arrived at is more than the minimum and less than the maximum then that is the advance payable for that period. For example, in the twelve months following the release of your first album you may have earned £100,000 in royalties. The formula for calculating your advance for the second contract period is linked to 66% of those earnings. 66% of £100,000 is £66,000. The minimum advance payable in the next contract period is, say, £50,000. You are above that. The maximum advance payable is, say, £100,000. You haven't got to that point. So the advance you get is £66,000.

These formulae can work and many record companies favour them because they give them a degree of certainty for budgeting purposes and a payment linked to success. If you are offered a deal with this type of formula for calculating advances then you need to make sure that the minimums are enough to meet your minimum living requirements. In the example I gave, could you live on £50,000 for a year or longer in the second contract period?

The maximums are usually double the minimum but may be more in later contract periods. Is the maximum a reasonable advance if you're doing very well? To be honest I don't worry about the maximums as much as the minimums. If you're hitting maximum advance figures it's because you're doing well and the record company is more likely to want to keep you happy by renegotiating these figures upwards.

There are a number of variations on how you calculate what has been earned in the previous contract period. The actual percentage can change. It can also make a big difference whether income earned but not yet credited to your account is taken into account (so-called pipeline income), as can the period over which it is calculated. It's wise to take your lawyer's advice on these kinds of deals.

Payment terms

Advances are normally paid in instalments – one on signing the deal, another when you start recording the Minimum Commitment for that contract period and the final instalment either on delivery of the completed recordings to the record company or commercial release of the recordings. As the release could be some months after delivery, you will want the final instalment to be paid on delivery. The record company may want to protect itself by only paying the last instalment when the record is released, when there is a reasonable prospect of record sales reducing its financial exposure.

A lot can happen between delivery of the finished masters and their release. Only recently a client of mine delivered finished masters to the record company and they were accepted. A few months later, and before the last date on which the record company had to release the recordings, the company closed down and the copyright in the client's recordings was transferred to another record company. That record company then hesitated for a few months more about whether or not they were going to release the album. In the end the artist's manager asked me to send the record company a formal notice under the terms of the record contract requiring the record company to release the album and pay the final instalment due under the deal. When the record company got the notice they rang me up and said that they had decided that they didn't want to release the album. They offered to give my client the copyright in the album back in return for an override royalty until such time as they had recovered the recording costs that had been spent on the album. At the time of writing the client and his manager are still trying to decide what to do. More than seven months has passed since the recordings were delivered and there seems to be very little prospect of the artist getting the advance due on release of the album.

Costs-inclusive advances

The advances I have been describing so far are called personal advances. They go towards the artist's personal needs. The costs of making the recording are separate recoupable amounts. The record company may offer you an advance that includes the costs of making the recordings. These costs-inclusive deals are called recording-fund deals. Both you and the record company have to be quite careful that the amounts advanced under a recording-fund deal are at the right level. You have to be sure that you can make the album you want to make with the available fund and still have something over to live on. The record company has to know it's not being too generous but also that you won't run out of money before the recording is finished. If you do, the record company inevitably ends up paying out more money if it wants to get the recording finished. Recording-fund deals can work for established artists, for those with their own recording facilities or more mature artists who can be relied on to make the recording without spending all the money on themselves.

RECORD BUDGETS

If a record company isn't offering a recording-fund deal and you have a development or exclusive recording deal, you will need to have some idea of how much it's going to cost you to make the recordings. You need to know that the record company is committed to spending that amount of money. If you are doing a licence deal then you will usually have already finished making recordings and so the issue is less relevant.

The budget must take into account how much it will cost to rehearse the material, do any necessary pre-production (preparation for recording, perhaps programming a drum machine or a computer to produce certain sounds), record the material in the studio, have it produced, mixed and edited. Some record companies include the cost of cutting or digitally mastering the recording in the budget. This can add £1,000-plus to the deal so, if the budget is tight, try to get them to pay for that separately. You also have to bear in mind the cost of hiring in specialist equipment and engaging the services of additional musicians and vocalists. The budget also usually includes what are called *per diems*, a Latin expression meaning a daily expenses payment to cover food and drink and sometimes also transport to and from the studio (see Chapter 5).

The record company may commit to a guaranteed minimum spend on recording costs in the contract, but most are reluctant to do that. This is either because they are afraid they may get it wrong or because setting a minimum figure means you tend to spend that amount of money whether it's necessary or not. On the other hand, you will want to know the record company is committed to a particular level of spend so that you know that you can make the kind of record you want. Both sides have to be realistic. It's no good a record company thinking you can make an album for £5 but neither is it any good you thinking the record company will let you have a blank cheque. This is where a decent recording budget is invaluable.

Recording costs are usually fully recoupable. There are, however, some elements of the recording costs budget that may be wholly or partially non-recoupable. A classic example is the costs of remixing. Mixing costs are very expensive. As I said, it's common to pay £10,000 or more to a well-known remixer. If you are on a tight budget then these costs can take a lot out of the total. The record company may want to commission a remix that you don't think is necessary. Who's to pay for this and are the costs to be recoupable? Some record companies will agree that the first mix comes out of the recording budget, as does any remix that you want to do, but if the record company wants to do a remix then they pay that on top of the recording budget. So, you know what to do – make sure it's the record company that asks for the remix, not you. Steer them into suggesting it.

ROYALTIES

This could be the subject of a whole book in itself. No two companies calculate royalties in exactly the same way. This is an area where there really isn't any escaping the need for experience and legal advice.

Record company executives usually have guidelines as to what is or isn't allowed. Certain top artists may have been given 'favoured nations' terms. This means that they have the best deal that the record company can offer on that particular point. If any other artist is offered better terms by that record company then the artist with the favoured nations provision must also be given these better terms. As this has potentially huge financial implications for the record company, an executive crosses these boundaries at his peril. It may be impossible to do so and will definitely require agreement from someone high up the corporate ladder.

Retail versus dealer price

You need to know what price basis the record company is using to account to you. An 18% royalty on the retail price of a CD would be good, but 18% on the dealer price of the CD would be just average.

Until about five years ago, the majority of UK record companies calculated their royalties as a percentage of the retail price of the record in question. However, the retail price isn't within the record company's control and varies considerably. Most UK companies have, therefore, moved over to using the dealer price of the record as the basis of calculation.

The record company will usually tell you what dealer price they charge for each type of record – vinyl, tape, CD and so on. If there isn't a dealer price available or the record company still calculates its royalties on a retail price basis and you want to make a comparison then, as a very general rule of thumb, in the UK you can work on the basis that the retail price is about 130% of the dealer price of an album.

Outside the UK and in particular in countries like Japan and the United States, they have very different methods of arriving at a dealer or 'wholesale' price basis. In order to make a proper comparison you should ask the record company to give you the actual figures they are talking about so you can do what is sometimes known as a 'pennies' calculation. This means that you can calculate roughly what you will get from each record sold. This calculation is essential when you are trying to compare offers from more than one record company. It's also important for a record company executive trying to make a deal to know how much he will have to pay in record royalties per record sold. He or his finance officer will need to calculate how many records will need to be sold before the advance they offer will be recouped. It has to make some kind of commercial sense even if the A&R man is so determined to do the deal that he wants to pay over the odds. At least he will know what he has to aim at in terms of record sales.

Here is an example of a pennies calculation:

Pennies calculation:

	Company A	Company B
Price basis	Dealer	Retail
Price	£8.49	£12.49
VAT	17.5%	17.5%
Percentage of Sales	100%	90%
Packaging Deduction	25%	25%
CD Deduction	20%	0%
Royalty Rate	18%	15%

Then insert figures into these calculations:

Company A:
1 £8.49 – 17.5% (VAT) (£1.49) = £7.00
2 £7.00 × 100% = £7.00
3 £7.00 – 25% (packaging) = £5.25
4 £5.25 × 18% (royalty) = £0.945
5 £0.945 × 80% (CD deduction) = £0.76 royalty per CD

Company B:
1 £12.49 – 17.5% (VAT) (£2.18) = £10.31
2 £10.31 – 25% (£2.58) = £7.73
3 £7.73 × 90% (% of sales) = £6.96
4 £6.96 × 0% (CD deduction) = £6.96
5 £6.96 × 15% (royalty) = £1.04 per CD

What percentage of sales?

Is the royalty calculated on all records sold or a lesser percentage? Virgin Records still calculates on 90% of sales and yet it is part of the EMI Group of companies, which calculates royalties on 100% of sales. This is a hangover from the early years of the record business when records were made of acetate that broke easily. A 10% breakage allowance was built into the calculation. In these days of CDs and even online distribution these allowances are clearly irrelevant. They are, however, still built into the way some companies calculate royalties. In working out if it's a good royalty, this difference must be taken into account. Again, a pennies calculation may help.

PACKAGING AND OTHER DEDUCTIONS

The most common deductions are packaging deductions, sometimes also referred to as container charges. This is a charge supposedly to cover the cost of making the cases or other packaging in which the record is sold. In reality, the actual cost is usually far less than the average packaging deduction and is a way by which the record company artificially reduces the royalty paid to you. These deductions must be taken into account in order to compare offers from different companies. An average packaging deduction for CDs is 20%, although many companies charge 25%. Other companies, such as V2, make a virtue out of having no packaging deductions. Their royalty rate may seem uncompetitive until you take this into account.

Other traps for the unwary are the reductions that some record companies apply to certain types of records. For example, some companies, most notably Sony, calculate their royalty at 80% of the royalty rate on CDs, and in some earlier contracts at 75%. If you were on a 20% royalty, that royalty would go down to 16% on sales of CD copies of your record at 80% of the rate. As this is now the main format for most types of records sold, this is significant – especially when you also take into account the packaging deductions.

There is also usually page after page of types of recording or methods of distribution that involve a reduction in the basic royalty rate. For example, sales by mail order, through record clubs or at budget prices will be at a lower royalty rate. The principle behind all these deductions is that where the record company gets less than the full price for a sale it will reduce the amount payable to you on that sale. For example, a record sold as a budget record will usually attract a 50% reduction in the royalty rate. 50% reductions also often apply to records advertised on television, sold by mail order, or through record clubs. The reduction in the royalty for mail-order sales is important when you think that many companies will now offer mail-order sales over the Internet. If this becomes the established method of selling records then we ought to look again at whether or not a 50% reduction is appropriate (see Chapter 7).

A detailed exploration of all the royalty reductions is beyond the scope of this book. Your lawyer and accountant will be familiar with these. Most UK record companies usually apply the principles behind the reductions in a similar way but the details will differ a great deal. For example, some record companies will pay you a full royalty on sales of compilation records they put out featuring one or more of your tracks. Others will only pay you 66% of the royalty.

WHAT IS A GOOD ROYALTY?

As a very general guideline, a basic royalty of more than 18% of the dealer price, calculated on 100% of records sold, with no reduction for CDs and a packaging deduction of no more than 20% would be good. It's unusual to see royalty rates of more than 23% of the dealer price for new signings to exclusive record deals. However, royalties on licence deals could well exceed 20–22% on the above basis because the record company is getting a finished recording. It can assess the commercial potential upfront. The record company also hasn't taken any risk on the recording costs. On non-exclusive licence deals between record companies, the royalty may well be more than 18% of the dealer price with no packaging deductions because they recognise the deduction for what it is.

NET PROFITS DEALS

Smaller record companies often offer these deals. You share the responsibility for costs such as manufacturing or promotion costs, which the record company wouldn't normally be able to recover from you.

Everything that's earned from all uses of the recordings is brought into account. This might include advances paid by overseas licensees. It will depend on the deal you do. All costs involved in the making of the recording are then taken out of that total income. As well as the obvious ones of recording costs and the costs of making a video, manufacturing, press and promotion costs are deducted as are, often, payments to music publishers (see Chapter 4) and even legal and accountancy charges. There are many subtleties as to what may or may not be deducted that are negotiated on a deal-by-deal basis. Any net profits made after those deductions are then split between you and the record company. The usual division is 50:50, but it may go up to 55–65% in your favour and even to a 75% share to you of overseas profits.

At the outset, net profit deals can work quite well for the record company, as that is when costs are high. The record company still bears the risk on the costs initially but it doesn't pay out anything to you until the deal goes into profit. Also the record company gets to recoup costs it wouldn't normally be entitled to offset against you, such as manufacturing costs. You can still receive an advance to live on. This would be an advance against your future share of profits.

Where these deals start to become less attractive to a record company and much more attractive to you is when the initial costs have been recouped and ongoing costs are going down. If the record continues to sell well and you are on 50% or more of profits, you are doing considerably better than you would be if you were on a straight royalty basis.

RELEASE COMMITMENTS

Obviously, once you've got your album delivered and accepted you need to have some kind of assurance that it's going to see the light of day and not just sit on the shelf. You need a commitment from the record company to release your record in at least the home market and preferably also the main overseas markets. The release should usually take place within three to four months of delivery of the masters. If it doesn't, the usual remedy is to serve a notice on the record company telling them that if they don't release your record within another two to three months then you have the right to end your contract with them and not have to deliver any more masters. Even better would be if you could get a commitment from them to return your unreleased masters to you, perhaps for an override royalty until the recording costs have been recouped.

Some record companies don't want to do this because they don't want to have to anticipate in advance what sort of deal they'd want to do with you. They may also want, perversely, to hold on to the masters in case another company has better luck in making you successful. They then have back catalogue material they try to release to cash in on the success. This is pretty daft because, although the tried and true fans will buy all records, there's no artist to promote the record, so it's unlikely to go very far. Perhaps they will want to hold on to it in order to try and sell it to your record company later.

Overseas, if your record isn't released within three to four months of the UK release then you can serve another notice of 30 to 60 days, and if there then hasn't been a release you may have the chance to find a licensee and make them license it to that company to release. They're unlikely to automatically give you your masters back as they know it's difficult to make their overseas companies or licensees release recordings.

ACCOUNTING

You should get paid at least twice a year, possibly four times with smaller companies doing their own distribution. The accounts statements will be sent to you 60 to 90 days after the accountant date. If you have recouped all your advances the statement will have a cheque with it – yippee! If you aren't certain what the statement says, check it with your accountant. If he doesn't think it's right, you should challenge it – but don't leave it too long as you probably can't object after a period of time, say one to three years. You have the right to audit (inspect) the books at least once a year. Send your accountants in to audit if you've had a successful period or at the end of a deal that has gone well.

This has been a general overview of the main points of a record deal. In Chapter 11 I deal with the parts of the record contract that cover what happens when a band splits up. The sections on payment of mechanical royalties are dealt with in Chapter 4.

CONCLUSIONS

- There are three main types of record deal – licences, development deals and exclusive recording agreements.

- With each type of contract you need to work out how much exclusivity you are going to give and what territory the contract is to cover.

- Advances against royalties could include recording costs or these could be separate. Recording and personal advance budgets are useful in setting the level of the deal.

- Royalties could be calculated on the retail or the dealer price of the record. It is important to establish which as it makes a lot of difference to the deal.

- Every record contract contains reductions in royalties on certain types of sale or method of distribution.

- Net profits deals work for the record company at the beginning but the scales tip in favour of the artist after the initial costs have been recouped.

4: WHAT IS A GOOD PUBLISHING DEAL?

INTRODUCTION

In this chapter I'm going to look at what rights a songwriter has and what he can expect from the various types of publishing deals. As usual I'm going to look at it from the point of view of the talent, the songwriter, but I will try to give the publisher's point of view. I'm also going to look at whether you need to do a publishing deal at all. If so, whether, ideally, it should be before or after you've done your record deal.

Before I go into any detail about the contract we need to look at how you find a music publisher, what rights a songwriter has and what a music publisher actually does. You'll not be surprised by now to learn that the doctrine of restraint of trade comes up here too. I'll look at three cases in this area and one that was a straight dispute between band members about who had written what.

HOW TO FIND A MUSIC PUBLISHER

Music publishers employ A&R people and scouts in the same way as record companies do. These people are on the lookout for talented songwriters who either also perform in a band or as a solo artist or who mostly write songs for other people. They go to live gigs just like record company A&R people.

Hopeful songwriters send demos to publishing companies in the same way as record companies.

You can find lists of UK music publishers in the *Music Week Directory*. You can also assume that all the major record companies will have well-established music publishing companies as part of the group. For example, there is an EMI Records and an EMI Publishing company. There are also independent music publishers that are not associated with independent record companies, for example PeerMusic or Bucks Music.

Your lawyer, accountant and manager can all refer you to publishers they think will be suitable for your style of songwriting.

WHAT DOES A PUBLISHER DO?

Have you ever wondered why we call them publishers? So have I. As far as I can work out it comes from the early days of the organised music business when music was published in the form of sheet music in the same way as a book is published. Nowadays, of course, sheet music forms only a tiny part of the income that a songwriter and a publisher can make. These days the major income comes from the use of songs on sound recordings (mechanicals) or with TV, film or other moving images (synchronisation). If the Internet develops in the way we think it will, the rights in a song may well be far more valuable than a physical sound recording like a CD or a cassette (see Chapter 7).

They have three main roles. Firstly, they issue licences to people who want to use your music. Secondly, they collect in the income from those licences. Thirdly, they actively look for ways to use your music – for example, putting it in an advert or on a film soundtrack. The first of these roles is largely done in conjunction with the collecting societies (see Chapter 15) except in the area of new media, such as the Internet, where they are still feeling their way. Some publishers are better than others in doing the second and third roles. Obviously, you need to be satisfied that they can do a reasonable job of collecting in the money for you. Whether you need them to be good at the last role will depend on the type of songwriter you are. Although I doubt many songwriters would turn down additional ways of making money if a publisher brought it to them.

So that people know whom to come to when they want to ask to use a song, and so as to track the money and collect it properly, the publisher has to register the songs with all the usual collecting societies around the world. Sometimes this is just filling in a form. In other countries they have to also send them a tape and a written copy of the words and music, called a lead sheet.

If your music publisher is one of the big four publishers then they will have their own companies in each of the major countries in the world. One or two of the independent publishers, most notably PeerMusic, have their own companies worldwide too. Most of the independent and smaller publishers don't have the resources to set up overseas companies. They appoint local publishers in the country concerned to look after their interests there. This is called sub-publishing.

Publishers will also occasionally do some of the things that were traditionally only done by record companies. They will provide studio time for you to record demos. Some act almost like record companies, putting records out in limited editions as a way to attract record company interest. There are even some that will provide financial support for you when you're out on the road promoting your records or provide extra funds for promotion or press coverage. Most of these sums are recoupable from your publishing income as and when it comes through. The main reason they would do this is not so as to be identical with a record company. They do it to give you a bit of a boost, a head start or to top-up funding provided or not by your record company. Their main role is as set out above – licensing use of music, collecting in the money and protecting the rights in your songs.

WHAT ARE MUSIC PUBLISHING RIGHTS?

Before you can have any rights in a literary or musical work[1] (i.e. in lyrics or music) you have to establish that the words and music are original and that they have been recorded in some way. This could be sheet music, with the words and music written down, or a demo of someone singing the words and music.[2]

1 Section 3(1) CDPA.
2 Section 3(2) CDPA.

HOW DO YOU PROVE THAT YOU HAVE COPYRIGHT IN A WORK?

There are a number of recognised ways of doing this.

You could put the sheet music or demo tape in a safe deposit box with your name and the date on which you wrote it on it and get a receipt.

You could send it to your lawyer and ask him to write back to confirm when he received it from you. Some lawyers aren't happy about doing this. They don't want trouble later if they lose the tape in among the one hundred and one others in their office. Also they can't really confirm something that they have no direct knowledge of. They do not know you wrote it or when you wrote it. They can only say that you sent a tape to them on a particular day.

The most popular way is to put the sheet music/tape/disc in an envelope addressed to yourself, which you then post to yourself by registered/recorded mail so you have a receipt and you then keep it unopened in a safe place. The postmark and the fact that it is still sealed up means that you have proof that that tape, sheet music or whatever must have existed some time before the postmark date. So if someone copies the song illegally a couple of years later, you have evidence that your version was written before theirs.

WHO OWNS THESE RIGHTS?

The first owner of the copyright in a musical or literary work is, quite simply, the person who creates an original work and records it in a tangible form.[3]

Of course it's possible for there to be more than one writer or composer.[4] These are called co-writers. One person might write the words and the other the music or the co-writers might all work on both elements.

Famous examples of successful co-writing partnerships are Elton John and Bernie Taupin, Andrew Lloyd Webber and Tim Rice and, more recently, Robbie Williams and Guy Chambers. The song is co-owned. It's perfectly possible for two separate publishers to control parts of the same song; for example, Robbie Williams's current works are published by EMI Music Publishing Limited while Guy Chambers's are published by BMG Music Publishing (UK) Limited.

Where there are co-writers it's very important there is a record of who owns what part of the music or lyrics. When you finish a new song and give it to your publisher they fill in a form on your behalf called a Joint Registration Form. This is the form needed to record the details about the song, which is then sent to MCPS/PRS (see Chapter 15). The form has to give the title of the song, who wrote it and in what shares and if there are any restrictions on what can be done with it. If you don't have a publisher and you are a member of PRS or MCPS or both, you should complete and file that form yourself. The publishing agreement will say that all songs are assumed to be written in equal shares by all co-writers unless the publisher is told something different when the work is delivered. The whole question of who wrote what can be the cause of major arguments between co-writers including members of the same band. This can be the case even where not all members of a band contribute to the writing. Those members that do write resent those that don't. You definitely ought to sort these

3 Section 9(1) CDPA.
4 Section 10(1) CDPA.

issues out at an early stage before you've made any money and it becomes a real issue (see Chapter 11).

- A recent, well-publicised case involving a dispute between band members is that involving the former members of Spandau Ballet.[5]

Spandau Ballet was formed in 1979 and made up of the two Kemp brothers, Martin and Gary, and Tony Hadley, John Keeble and Steve Norman. They were part of the New Romantic movement and after turning down a record deal with Island Records they set up their own label, which they eventually licensed to Chrysalis Records. Their first single, 'To Cut A Long Story Short', went Top 5 in the UK. They released a couple more singles before having a Top 3 hit with 'Chant Number 1'. They employed a number of producers including that Mr Trevor Horn again. They released six albums plus a Greatest Hits compilation. The last album, *Heart Like A Sky*, was released in 1989. Ten years later they were in court arguing over song royalties. In the mid-1980s the Kemp brothers, Martin and Gary, took up acting and appeared together as the Kray Twins in the film *The Krays*. Martin Kemp is currently appearing as bad boy Steve in *EastEnders* and was not involved in this case.

Everyone agreed that Gary Kemp had written the lyrics to all the songs. The dispute was over who composed the music. Gary Kemp's company received all the publishing income from the songs. He volunteered to give half of this money to the other band members but stopped this arrangement in 1987. The other band members sued, saying that it was a legally binding agreement to pay this money. They also argued that if this wasn't a binding agreement then they were entitled to the money anyway because they were co-authors of the songs and therefore co-owners of the copyright. They said they had contributed enough to the music to make them joint authors. The judge decided that there was no binding legal agreement. Gary Kemp was sole author of all the music save for a song called 'Glow'. The judge also confirmed that to be a joint owner you have to have contributed to the song's creation, not to its interpretation. So if a drummer just adds a little drum loop that doesn't make any material difference to the song, that will not qualify for a claim that he has co-written that song.

DURATION OF COPYRIGHT

As we've already seen, the copyright in a musical or literary work lasts for 70 years from the end of the calendar year in which the author dies.[6] If a song has been co-written, the rights last until 70 years from the end of the calendar year in which the last surviving co-writer dies.[7]

WHAT RIGHTS COME WITH OWNERSHIP OF COPYRIGHT?

The copyright owner of a literary or musical work (i.e. a song) has rights very similar to the recording copyright rights we saw in the last chapter. The main rights are the right to authorise the reproduction of a musical or literary work with or without visual images (the

5 *Hadley & others* v. *Kemp & Another*, 1999 Chancery Division.
6 Section 12(2) CDPA.
7 Section 12(8) CDPA.

mechanical and synchronisation rights I mentioned above); the right to authorise distribution of the work;[8] the right to rent or lend the work to the public;[9] the right to authorise public performance of the work or its inclusion in a cable broadcast service[10] and the right to make an adaptation of the work or to do any of the above in relation to an adaptation.[11]

WHERE DOES THE MONEY COME FROM?

MECHANICAL LICENCES AND ROYALTIES

A song can be used in many different ways.

The biggest source of income for most songwriters is the issue of a licence to record a performance of a song. For example, if a record company wants to record a performance of your song it has to ask permission from you or your publisher or the person who administers your songs. This may seem a bit strange. You have written a song that your band wants to record. It seems odd to have to ask permission from someone else to record your band performing it. But remember that different people are going to control the rights in the sound recording and the rights in the song. There are separate copyrights here and the same people will probably not control them both. The record company has to pay a licence fee to the owner of the rights in the song. Originally, when a recording was reproduced it was literally done mechanically, using mechanical piano-rolls originally. So the licence to reproduce the song on a sound recording is called a mechanical licence. The amount of fee, the mechanical royalty, is either fixed by negotiation between representatives of the record and publishing companies in the country concerned or by law.

The present licensing system in the UK was the result of a referral to the Copyright Tribunal in 1992. The record and publishing companies couldn't agree on what was a proper licence fee. The 1988 Copyright Act says that the remedy in these situations is to refer the dispute to the Copyright Tribunal. The scheme approved by the Copyright Tribunal is operated by the Mechanical Copyright Protection Society Limited (MCPS) on behalf of publishers. The current licence fee is 8.5% of the dealer price of the record or approximately 70–80p per CD album depending on the dealer price. The MCPS can only license the mechanical reproduction of a song if it's a straight 'cover', i.e. if you intend to faithfully reproduce the original version by someone other than the original performers. If it's not a faithful reproduction then the MCPS can't issue a licence and you have to get permission of the original writers or their publishers.

Until recently, mechanical reproduction took the form of physical product such as a vinyl record, a cassette tape or a CD. It now extends to new formats such as DAT, DCC and Mini-disc. Many new methods of reproduction are being developed via the Internet. Some of these still take a tangible physical form, for example, downloading a computer file containing music on to an MP3 or similar player. In other cases there is not a physical end product; the

8 Section 16(1) (b) and Section 18 CDPA.
9 Section 16(1) (c) and (d) and Sections 19 and 20 CDPA.
10 Section 16(1) (e) and Section 21 CDPA.
11 Section 21 CDPA.

downloaded material is retained on the hard drive of the computer. There is still a reproduction involved in the process. There is also a lot of readjustment that music business personnel have to make to bring their thinking on the traditional methods of using copyrights in line with the new technologies.

At the end of 1999 the MCPS issued guidelines for the rate to be paid for digital download of music off the Internet.[12] Many record companies have already complained that it is too much and have said that they will effectively ignore the guidelines by going direct to the publisher. While it is very encouraging that the MCPS has set rates for what publishers should be charging for these downloads it remains to be seen if that is the rate the record companies will agree to pay.[13]

The MCPS also publishes guidelines for the licensing of other uses such as CD-ROMs, music in toys and in computer games. Some but not all publishers have given authority to MCPS to grant licences for these types of uses on their behalf. But because not all have, you have to check with MCPS for each song you want to use. An awful lot is still left to individuals to negotiate. What you will probably end up paying or receiving, depending on which side you are on, may be less than the MCPS guidelines.

CONTROLLED COMPOSITIONS

Although in this book I'm mostly dealing with UK copyright and licensing schemes, the situation in the US is important as it can have a huge impact on publishing income coming from the United States.

The situation in the US is very different from that in the UK. In the UK we have a licensing scheme and a fixed rate that has to be paid for a licence. In the US the law sets a fixed rate (7.1 cents a track) for the right to reproduce a song on a record. But you have to realise that in the US the record industry has an awful lot more power than the publishers. The record industry lobbied the legislators and got a clause included in the law that allows a different rate to be set if the record companies want to. Well, surprise surprise, the record companies have set a different rate. And is it higher? What do you think? The almost universal position in the US is that the record companies will only pay 75% of the fixed rate. This is referred to as a 'controlled compositions' or 'reduced mechanical royalty' clause. Obviously you can only agree to this reduced rate if you are the owner or controller of the song. You can't speak for anyone else. The problem is that you will be under considerable pressure to agree this 75% rate. This means that you are losing a quarter of your US publishing income from the reproduction of your songs on records. If you already have a publishing deal then you won't be allowed to agree to this without your publisher's agreement. Your publisher should fight on your and their behalf to get improvements on this rate. If you have a lot of bargaining power you can get a 100% rate. If you have medium bargaining power you can get them to agree to increase the 75% rate to 85% and then to 100% based on sales of a given number of records.

12 The proposed rate is 10 pence per download for up to 5 minutes of music and 2 pence per minute thereafter.

13 There are, of course, also questions of whether this rate applies only for uses in the UK and that will be difficult to police given the global nature of the Internet. See also Chapter 7.

On a couple of occasions the UK record industry has tried to introduce a similar system here. So far they have not succeeded but we remain ever vigilant. I'd like to be able to put a sensible argument here on behalf of record companies as to why they do this with these US mechanical royalties. But for the life of me I can't think of a justification. The US laws have given the opportunity to do it and they've taken advantage of it. End of story.

Most US record companies try to further reduce their liability to pay full mechanical royalties by limiting the number of tracks on a record that they will pay royalties on. This is usually no more than ten or eleven. So if you have twelve tracks on your album you will not get a mechanical royalty in the US on at least one or two of those tracks.

These 'controlled compositions' clauses cause a lot of problems in every record deal negotiation. There are some improvements that your lawyer can try and get for you but this is often the most keenly fought clause in the whole recording contract. A lot of money is at stake for both sides.

SYNCHRONISATION LICENCES AND ROYALTIES

If you're a songwriter who writes mostly music for films, adverts or computer games then your main source of income may not be mechanical royalties but fees from the issue of licences to use your music with moving visual images. This licence is called a synchronisation licence because it gives the right to synchronise music with visual images. The publisher also licenses and collects income from these licences. The fee for this use is called the synchronisation fee.

We can all think of artists who have broken into the big time via an advert or indeed where a flagging career has been boosted by a track used in a particularly good ad campaign or in a film. Beck and Smoke City both broke the charts via Levis ads, and what about Wet, Wet, Wet and 'Love Is All Around Us' in the film *Four Weddings and a Funeral*? For the right music an advertising company will pay a lot of money – £100,000 or more as a synchronisation fee for the right work is not unheard of. I should just say, though, before you all rush to get your music into adverts or films, that many advertising companies pay a lot less than this. Many also commission writers to write songs that sound like, but aren't, famous songs. Some songwriters make a career of writing jingles for adverts or in composing sound-alike songs. For some this is their main source of income. Others do it as a way to fund them writing their masterwork – that film soundtrack or concerto they otherwise wouldn't have the money to do.

In some countries there is a fixed rate for synchronisation licences. In most cases, though, it has to be fixed on a case-by-case basis. So this again is an area where your publisher can get a good deal for you.

If you want to put one of your songs in a promotional video for one of your singles then your publisher will probably give you a free synchronisation licence. If there is any chance that it will earn income commercially then they will want a separate fee.

If there is a synchronisation fee payable there needs to be an agreement between the publisher and you as to how they are going to split that money. Will some or all of it go towards recouping any earlier advances? Will some or all of it be paid to you or kept by the publisher? Obviously from the publisher's point of view they would like to keep their publisher's share of this income. For example, if you were on a 75:25 split of royalties in your favour, the publisher would want to keep 25% of the fee for himself. As to the remaining 75%, it's obviously in your publisher's best interests to use it to help recoup the advances they've made to you. You may not be in desperate need of cash and may decide that it would be sensible to agree to do that. On the other hand, you might view it as some badly needed cash and argue with the publisher for at least some of it to be paid through to you. The publishing deal may spell out what is to happen or may say that it is up for negotiation on a case-by-case basis.

The situation may change if you are commissioned to write some music or a song for a specific project such as a film soundtrack. Publishing agreements will often say that even though they may have an exclusive arrangement with you, you can do these deals and keep the commission fee provided the synchronisation fee is paid through to them. Now it doesn't take much intelligence to work out that as a songwriter you might want to increase the commission fee and decrease the synchronisation fee. The PRS rules also now require the publisher to use all his reasonable efforts to find additional uses for a piece of music or song written specially for a film. So they have to try and get it recorded or used in some other way.

The MCPS has a mandate from most but not all of its members to grant synchronisation licences. Here again, however, there are difficulties in relation to new-media uses such as the Internet. Because many publishers have retained the right to licence use of music with visual images, and because most uses on the Internet involve visual images, this means in effect that anyone wanting to use the music on the Internet will still probably have to deal directly with the publishers.

PERFORMING RIGHTS

We've looked so far at two main sources of publishing income – the mechanical licence and the synchronisation licence. The third main source of income is the right to publicly perform a song. Public performance doesn't just mean live concerts – it includes the playing of a music in shops, restaurants and clubs; in fact anywhere that music is played in public.

Most writers who have had some success become members of the Performing Right Society Limited (PRS) or one of its overseas affiliates. The PRS is the only UK performing right society for the administration of the right to perform a work in public and it is responsible for the collection of income generated by the public performance of the music. The income comes largely from blanket licences taken out by broadcasters, shops, pubs and so on, as we will see below. When you become a member of the PRS, the rules say that you have to assign your performing rights in your songs to the PRS. The PRS could have taken a licence of these rights or have been appointed as your agent, but it prefers to take an assignment. If you end your membership, the performing rights are returned to you or to whomever you direct. In fact the performing rights in your songs that they look after are more than just public performance. The 'performing rights' controlled by the PRS are the right to publicly perform a work, the right to broadcast it and to include it in a cable broadcast service and the right to authorise others to do any or all of the above. So every time your song is played on television, radio, cable or satellite you will receive (eventually) some income from that use of your song.

The PRS monitors use of music on TV and radio programmes by means of cue sheets. These are lists of music played on each programme, which the station producers complete after each show. The PRS has a random sampling policy for live shows. They couldn't possibly cover all live gigs but do monitor the main venues and they keep the type of venues monitored under review.

So that there doesn't have to be a separate licence every time a song is played in public, the PRS has entered into licences with most of the broadcasters. They have done the same with major places of entertainment such as clubs and restaurant chains. These are called 'blanket licences' because they cover all songs controlled by the PRS. If you have a blanket licence you don't have to worry about whether you can play a particular song provided you have paid the annual licence fee negotiated with PRS.

Using cue sheets or samplings the PRS gets a good idea of what music has been performed and calculates the amount due under the various blanket licences. The shares due to the songwriter members of PRS are paid out at regular intervals (four times a year) after the PRS has deducted its fee for doing the administration. The PRS rules require that at least six-twelfths (i.e. 50%) of the performing income is paid to the songwriter direct. It can't be used by the publisher to recoup any advances. This can be a very valuable source of income for an impoverished songwriter who is unrecouped and can't expect any royalties or further advances from his publisher for some time. The other 50% can be paid to a publisher nominated by you as having the right to publish your songs. This 'publisher's share' can be divided between you and publisher. If they do share any of it with you, that share usually goes first towards recouping any outstanding balance on your account with your publisher. If you don't have a publisher, you can collect 100% of the income yourself. Unlike music publishers, the PRS is not there to go out and get your song played or performed for you. That is still mainly the job of your music publisher. PRS is there to make sure that public places playing records do so under a proper licence scheme so that you can have a chance of earning some money from this use of your songs. If it weren't there then each publisher would have to enter into separate arrangements with each broadcaster, shop, restaurant and so on. This does not make economic sense so the music publishers, who are also members of the PRS, are happy to allow the PRS to do this job for them. Provided, that is, that they don't charge too much for doing the job – there are periodical renegotiations of the fee.

PRINT

Although not as relevant these days, your publisher also has the right to issue licences to someone else for a song to be reproduced in printed form as sheet music or to do it themselves. Print income from sales of sheet music is not a large source of income for a popular music writer. For classical composers, however, it can be a very lucrative source of income. Included in this print category is the hire out charge the publisher makes to orchestras wishing to have access to the 'parts' of the work, i.e. the sections written for the different instruments in the orchestra. Fees of £20–30,000 for the hire out of parts for a large orchestral or operatic piece are common.

RECORD DEAL BEFORE PUBLISHING?

Having a publisher already on board when you are negotiating a 'controlled compositions' clause in a record deal can be a great help. It used to be the case that you did your record deal first and got a publishing deal later. Nowadays the publisher fills many of the same roles as a record company in finding you the right co-writers, publishers or even recording and releasing limited edition single records. The decision therefore becomes much more of a personal one. For some it's important that they have got a deal, any deal. So if the publishers come courting first they will do that deal first. Others stick to the tried and true method of getting a record deal first and then hoping that that deal and the success of their first release will push the bidding up for their publishing rights. This is a dangerous game – if the first release doesn't prove to be a success, the publishing offers may dry up. You may be a writer who wants to hang on to your publishing rights for as long as you can, in which case you're going to be concerned to get a record deal that will give you enough by way of personal advances to live on for a reasonable period of time without having to go looking for money from a publisher.

If you don't have to do a publishing deal you can become self-published. This way you fully control the copyright in your songs and how they are used. How do you do this? Usually by becoming a member of the various collecting societies like MCPS and PRS. The collection societies fulfil a lot of the administrative functions of a publisher but a self-published songwriter still has to do a lot of work himself. The collection societies don't automatically notify foreign societies of their interest in a particular song. The songwriter will have to track down where the music is being used and check if the right amount of money has been paid.

Most creative people are not known for being organised enough to do this nor will they necessarily have the resources. This is one of the reasons that most new writers look for some form of support from a publishing company. If you're a more established songwriter you may be more comfortable with this kind of arrangement or will appoint someone to administer it for you. Below I'm going to look at the three main types of publishing agreement and at some of the pros and cons of each. One of them will be the right one for you and once you've worked out which it is you can make your pitch to get it.

TYPES OF PUBLISHING DEAL

If you decide that being your own publisher isn't an option for you then there are three basic types of music publishing agreement that you can do which can provide outside support for you. The administration deal, the sub-publishing deal and the fully exclusive songwriting deal. Within the category of exclusive publishing deals there is a sub-category where you just assign your rights in a single song. This is called the single song assignment. The rules on restraint of trade also apply to the single song assignment. So the comments I make about what is or is not reasonable in an exclusive publishing contract will also apply to the exclusive single song assignment.

THE ADMINISTRATION DEAL

Administration deals are popular if you are a songwriter who has a small but potentially lucrative catalogue or collection of songs. It may not be worthwhile for you to join the collection societies and be self-published. You may not have the necessary time, energy or organisational abilities to go tracking down the income yourself. You may prefer to employ someone to do it for you.

These types of deals also appeal to established songwriters. They may not need a publisher to try to exploit their songs. They may be disillusioned with exclusive publishing deals or want to own their copyrights. They may not need upfront advances against income and may relish the increased control that they would have if there were no publisher breathing down their necks. The same rules apply to these assignments as they do with sound recordings so the comments I made in Chapter 3 still apply here.

The administrator doesn't usually take an assignment of any interest in the copyright but is granted a licence for a period of time. If an administrator asks to take an assignment of your rights outright, I would be very suspicious and would need to be convinced that there was a very good business reason to do it. If you assign your rights then you aren't in a position of control. There isn't very much of a difference with an exclusive publishing deal, yet you are likely to see only small or no upfront advances. So what's the advantage? If it's for a licence term then the term can vary greatly from one year upwards. A three- to five-year licence term is common. Many are for much longer. I have recently concluded one that was for the life of copyright. I was still comfortable to do it because the deal overall worked for that client and at least if it was a licence and things went wrong then he wouldn't have to worry about getting his copyrights back as he had held on to them.

As the name suggests, the administrator administers the songs for you. You hand over the job of registering your songs with the various societies and of licensing others to use your songs. Of course they also deal with the collection of the income from these licences and prepare accounts for you showing how much you've earned. It's up to you and the terms of the contract whether you give your administrator the freedom to issue whatever licences he thinks right for the songs or you can insist that he has to come back to you for permission each time. This could prove a bit of a pain for you, and for him, so you may want to say that the commonplace licences like the right for your band to record your songs can be issued without coming back to you but if someone wants to use your songs in an advert or a film then you want to know about it first. As I said before, don't put too many restrictions on what licences your administrator can grant if you want to maximise what you can earn from your songs. By all means put a stop to something that you have a real problem with, for example, if you're a vegan you may quite rightly not want your work used in adverts for beefburgers. But think carefully before you block all uses of your songs in adverts because you're cutting off a potentially very valuable source of income.

The administrator could be an individual, perhaps an ex-musician or songwriter himself, or it could be a company that specialises just in administration. On the other hand, it could be a music publisher who does administration deals as well as signing up songwriters to exclusive deals. Most of the major publishers and the bigger independent publishers will do administration deals in the right circumstances.

The administrator will usually charge 10–15% of your gross income as their fee. You wouldn't usually expect an administrator to pay any advances. You will be paid only when your administrator has collected in some money. It's therefore very important to know how often the administrator will pay you. They should pay you at least every three months. It's also important to check out their reputation for efficient collection of money, particularly outside the UK. The administrator may be very good in the UK but overseas he may not have the necessary resources or contacts. In which case it is likely that all he will do is to collect what comes through collection societies overseas that are affiliated to the MCPS and PRS. If this is the case then you have to ask yourself whether it's worth it because you can get this income yourself through direct membership of MCPS and PRS. You ought to be getting some kind of added value by having the administrator on board. It may be as little as taking the load off you but it wouldn't be unreasonable to ask the administrator to try to track down unpaid licence fees or royalties on your behalf – and if he has a worldwide deal he shouldn't just limit his activities to the UK.

You often do an administration deal when you aren't too concerned about getting other uses for your songs. If you know people will either not want to put your songs in a film or advert or if they do you are so well known you don't have to sell yourself then you won't worry about someone going out and actively looking for these extra uses. What I'm getting at is that an administrator will look after the administration side but won't be out there pitching your songs to advertising agencies or film companies.

THE SUB-PUBLISHING DEAL

The sub-publishing deal is a mixture of an administration deal and an exclusive publishing agreement. The owner of the copyrights sub-licenses some or all of these rights to a publisher. The original owner usually keeps the copyright so it's normally a licence rather than an assignment of rights. These types of deals come up in two very different circumstances.

You may be an established songwriter or are a songwriter who wants to own or control your copyright but you may want something more than a pure administration deal. If so, a sub-publishing deal may suit. You may not need an advance or you might be prepared to do without an advance in return for control of your copyright. That isn't to say that a sub-publisher won't pay any advance at all. They may pay modest sums in advances but they may not be as big as you would get under an exclusive publishing deal. Why? Because the sub-publishers don't get as much ownership or control from a sub-publishing deal as they would from an exclusive songwriting deal. You choose what song copyrights go through the deal and, depending on the deal, you may be free to have some of your work published by someone else.

If you do need someone to go and search out deals for you then you won't get that from an administrator. So a sub-publishing deal may work for you. You get someone actively looking for other ways of earning money from your songs and possibly spending some of their money to try to help that happen.

You might set up your own limited company to hold the existing copyrights and the copyright in any new works you write. This company then sub-publishes some or all of the rights to a publisher. In some cases the publisher will want an assignment of the copyright.[14] As you know, my advice is to avoid this if you can – but if you don't have much choice then try to get them to agree that this is only for a limited period of time. This period is called 'the Rights Period' or 'the Retention Period'. The shorter you can make it, the better for you in terms of control of your copyrights. But bear in mind that the shorter the period of time that the sub-publishers control your copyrights, the less opportunities they have to make money from your songs, and this might be reflected in the type of deal they offer. If you do get a publisher to agree a licence term then this could be as short as a year but is more likely to be for at least three and possibly up to five years.

The sub-publishing deal also appeals to smaller publishers, ones that don't have their own established systems overseas. Instead of the cost of setting up their own companies in each of the main overseas countries, such publishers do sub-publishing deals in those countries. They keep the rights they have but grant the overseas publisher the right to use some or all of those rights in their country for a period of time.

Whichever type of deal we're talking about, the sub-publisher needs to have the right to register the songs, to license some or all of the main publishing rights, such as mechanical and synchronisation rights, and to collect in the income.

The sub-publishing contract will set out the extent to which the songwriter or small publisher has the right to grant licences to exploit the publishing rights. Don't be surprised if the sub-publisher presses for overall control and only wants to have to get your approval on certain very specific matters. You may have approval over alterations to the songs or over the grant of licences to include them in adverts for products that you might disapprove of. If you tie the sub-publisher's hands too much then they can't easily get further uses for the songs. You are employing a sub-publisher and paying them a large fee to be pro-active on your behalf so you need to balance the need for creative control against commercial realities.

How much you have to pay a sub-publisher will depend on a number of factors like how famous or successful you are, your bargaining power, how much the sub-publisher wants to control your catalogue of songs (whether for market share or income or to have the kudos of having you on their books), and how much you're expecting them to do. It's likely to be more than you would pay under an administration deal but probably a little less than under a fully exclusive songwriting agreement. A sub-publishing fee of 15–20% of the gross income received is common. If you expect a big advance then that may increase to 25% to compensate for the additional risk the sub-publishers are taking. They have paid out some

14 Often this is in order to get 'market share', which is the measure of how many copyrights a publisher controls either in terms of numbers or, more often, in terms of how much income they generate. Market share is watched by the money markets and the analysts and is also keenly contested by the publishers themselves as a measure of how well they are doing.

money to you on the strength of what they know about you and your potential. If you don't live up to that then that's the sub-publisher's risk. The contract doesn't usually allow them to demand that money back.

What does a sub-publisher do?

Your sub-publisher should provide the same basic services as under an administration deal, including registering the songs, granting licences, collecting income and accounting to you on a regular basis. It's important to check whether there'll be a delay in getting your money in from overseas.

Some larger publishers can account to you and pay you what you are due in the same accounting period that they receive the monies from overseas. For example, the sub-publisher grants a mechanical licence to reproduce your song on a record in the US. The record sales take place in the period between March and June 1999. The US record company will probably pay the mechanical royalty in the next three months so it will be in the sub-publisher's account by the end of September 1999. You may have a deal with the sub-publisher that says you are paid in September for income received in the period up to the end of June. In the scenario I have given, the income won't have been in until after the end of June. If the deal you have is that you will get paid in the same accounting period, you will get it in September. If it's not then you will get it at the next accounting date, which would normally be March 2000. This is a six-month delay which, when you're first expecting your money from overseas, can seem a very long time to wait. If prompt payment and cashflow are important to you (and let's face it, they are to most of us) then you need to check this out carefully. Needless to say, the sub-publishers are the ones earning interest on the money sitting in their bank accounts for six months, not you.

In addition to the basic administration services, the sub-publisher should give you something more for the extra money they're getting. This could be an advance but the sub-publisher should also be more pro-active, going out and looking for other uses for the songs, suggesting co-writers, finding film projects or adverts and so on.

If you are a smaller publishing company appointing a sub-publisher overseas, you should be expecting them to act as if they were a branch of your company overseas. They should have the same philosophy as you. I know this sounds a bit new age but it's important. You may have a reputation in the UK for signing up indie songwriters. Your overseas sub-publishers should also love the same type of music otherwise they won't know what to do with it or how to work with it.

If you're a songwriter with your own publishing company you may not notice any difference between what sub-publishers do and what you would expect from an exclusive publishing agreement. The sub-publisher will usually expect exclusive rights to sub-publish your songs and will charge a similar fee to an exclusive publisher. The crucial difference is that you retain the copyright in your songs and have much more control. Some songwriters set up their own publishing company solely for tax reasons and in such cases, although it's technically a sub-publishing agreement, it is to all intents and purposes the same as an exclusive publishing agreement.

THE SINGLE SONG ASSIGNMENT

The single song assignment is a bit of a halfway house. You don't do an exclusive publishing agreement. You are free to publish individual songs yourself or through a variety of different publishers. Unlike under a sub-publishing agreement, you assign the rights in a song to a publisher; you don't license them. The assignment could be for the life of copyright or it could be for a shorter Rights or Retention Period. You may receive an advance but it is likely to be small. The publishers are likely to get a fee of about 20–25% of the gross income received.

Deals such as these would be attractive to a songwriter who only writes a small number of songs on an irregular basis or who wants to keep his options open. The publisher still gets the rights they need in the particular song and market-share in that song. Because the publisher controls the copyright in the song, it is in their interests to get as many other uses for the work as possible. The publisher will also carry out all the usual administrative functions and should account to you regularly. The same comments that I made above about accounting delays apply here. The song assignment will decide how much control you have over how your song is used. Because it's a one-off, you may not have as much control as with an exclusive deal for all your songs but if you have enough bargaining power you should certainly be able to prevent major changes to your words or music and have some control over the use of your song in films or adverts.

EXCLUSIVE PUBLISHING AGREEMENT

If none of the above options appeal or are on offer then there is the exclusive publishing agreement. For most pop songwriters this is the Holy Grail. Getting an established publisher behind them means that they've arrived, that someone else has faith in their work and is prepared to put money and commitment behind that conviction.

RESTRAINT OF TRADE

As we saw in Chapter 3, whenever there is an exclusive arrangement containing restrictions on what you can and cannot do there is an assumption that it is in restraint of trade. We also saw that the leading case in this area, *Schroeder* v. *Macaulay*, established that this doctrine also applied to exclusive record and publishing contracts. We know that the contract was found to be an unreasonable restraint of trade and, as such, was unenforceable but so far I haven't gone into any details as to what in the contract was found to be unreasonable. It was a publishing contract so I felt it was better dealt with here.

- *A. Schroeder Music Publishing Co. Limited* v. *Macaulay*.[15]

The particular parts of the contract that led the court to decide that is was unenforceable were that it was an exclusive arrangement, it required absolute commitment from Macaulay but

15 [1974] 1 WLR 1308.

there was no corresponding commitment on the part of the publishers to do anything with the songs. They could accept them and tuck the copies away in a drawer or put them on a shelf and forget about them. The term was for five years but Schroeder could extend it for a further five years if more than £5,000 worth of royalties had been earned in the first five years. This wasn't a lot of money even then. Macaulay had had to assign the copyright for the life of copyright. Even though in those days this was 50 years after the end of the year in which he died, not 70 years, it was still a long period of time to have a publisher controlling the copyright in his songs exclusively and without having any obligation to do anything with them. The advance that he received was very low. It was £50 with further payments of £50 as each earlier advance was recouped. This was almost like putting him on a wage but with no guarantee of when he'd receive his next paycheque. The court felt that, taken as a whole, the contract was an unreasonable restraint of trade.

As a result of this and later cases there has been a change in music publishing contracts. The length of the term is now limited and there is a maximum backstop – usually no more than 3 years per contract period. There is also usually a requirement that the publisher has to do something with the songs. For example, the contract will often say that if the publisher hasn't granted a mechanical or synchronisation licence for a song, or there hasn't been sheet music printed of it or it hasn't been performed in public within, say, a year or two of the song being delivered, then you have the right to ask the publisher to do something with it. If nothing happens within another three to six months then you usually get the copyright in the song back.

WHAT IS IN A TYPICAL PUBLISHING CONTRACT?

EXCLUSIVITY

If you sign an exclusive publishing deal then you are usually agreeing that the publisher will own and control all your output as a songwriter during the term of that contract. In return for that exclusivity you can expect a commitment from the publishing company to do something with your songs. You can also usually expect that your publisher will be reasonably pro-active on your behalf.

Even though it is an exclusive deal you can sometimes have exceptions to this. As I explained above, the exclusivity may not apply where you are commissioned to write a song or some music specifically for a film. The film company will usually want to own the copyright in that piece of music or song. Your exclusive publisher may agree that these commissioned works are excluded from your publishing deal. This could be agreed at the time the contract is done as a blanket exception or your publisher could agree to consider specific requests on a case-by-case basis.

If you are regularly commissioned to write music for films then they aren't going to want to automatically exclude all these from your agreement. By not automatically agreeing that the film company can own the copyright, your publisher may gain some bargaining power with the film company to get a better deal. As the terms of the contract should say that you benefit one way or another from income from these deals, it should be in your interests for them to argue on your behalf.

Occasionally a publisher will agree that the songs you write for a particular project are excluded from the deal. For example, you might write some songs for a largely uncommercial project that the publishers aren't interested in. Songs written for this project could be excluded from the deal. If you have a lot of bargaining power, you could insist that songs you write for another commercial project must be excluded from the deal. Just bear in mind that the more songs you don't give your publisher control of, the more it is likely to reduce the deal terms they're prepared to offer you.

RIGHTS GRANTED

The publisher will expect to have assigned to them the copyright in all your songs already in existence that no one else has the right to publish. The assignment is usually of all rights in those works, subject to the performing rights that you may have already assigned to the PRS.

If you've done a publishing deal before, another company may still have the right to act as publisher of those songs. If the Rights or Retention Period runs out while your new publishing deal is still running, the new publisher will expect to get the right to publish those songs too. If you don't think they should then you need to argue for this at the time the new publishing deal is done.

It is possible to grant a publisher some but not all of the rights of a copyright owner. I am currently trying to hold back rights to exploit music online from a few publishers but it's true to say that they feel very uncomfortable about it. In other deals I've done I've given them the right to issue mechanical licences but not synchronisation licences. Obviously you can do this if you have the necessary bargaining power but there's no point in doing it unless you can do something with the rights you've kept back. Remember also that the more rights you hold back, the more likely it is that you will get a worse deal from the publishing company.

TERRITORY

The rights that you assign could be for a particular country or worldwide. We saw in Chapter 3 that it was reasonably common to have one deal for one country, such as the US, and another deal for the rest of the world. Split-territory deals are not so common in publishing contracts. Depending on who the publishers are and what their overseas set-up is like, they may have sub-publishing deals in some countries (see above). As a songwriter you should find out what the situation is overseas. You need to know that the sub-publishers are good, efficient companies and that there won't be any accounting delays.

RIGHTS PERIOD

You could assign rights for the life of copyright or for a shorter Rights or Retention Period, which runs from the end of the term of the publishing contract. This period can vary considerably from anything as short as two to three years to more than twenty years.

The Retention Period often gets shorter when there is a more positive economic climate and if there is a lot of competition to sign good songwriters. A few years ago I could get Retention Periods from some of the major music publishers as short as five years. This was when there were loads of good songwriters and a lot of money around. Publishers were going for short-term publisher's market share and weren't as concerned about hanging on to copyrights for any length of time. Many of the copyrights were for dance music songs and I guess they gambled that most of these would have a short life span. Now there is less money around, songwriters are expected to prove their worth over a longer period of time and it's difficult to get Retention Periods of less than ten years unless you've got a lot of bargaining power.

TERM

The term of a UK music-publishing contract is usually shorter than that of a record contract. It's quite common to find a music-publishing contract with an initial period of one year and then options in the music publisher's favour for a further two or three option periods. Each contract period is usually for a minimum of twelve months but can be longer depending on how long it takes you to fulfil the Minimum Commitment requirements that a publisher has for each contract period. For similar reasons to those given for record contracts, the options are in the publisher's favour, not yours. The publisher has too much invested to allow you to just walk out the door when you want to.

Rolling contracts

Some publishers are in favour of a different way of working out the term of the publishing contract. Songwriters often like this way too because it gives them certainty upfront. What happens is that, instead of a term made up of a number of optional contract periods, the publisher fixes the term upfront and says it will run for, say, three or five years with no options. That fixed period may be extended until you have fulfilled the Minimum Commitment. Sometimes, but not often, there is no Minimum Commitment; the publishers just publish anything you do in the fixed term. This is a big risk for the publishers to take. You may take the advance payable on signing the deal and then not write another thing. To offer this kind of deal the publishers have to know you very well and be convinced that you are going to continue to write good songs. For a songwriter, this is not only a great show of faith from your publisher – it's also a relief. You don't have to worry about fulfilling the Minimum Commitment or of delivering songs to order.

With a rolling term you get a single advance when you sign the deal and this is recouped from your earnings over the term. When the initial advance has been wholly or partly recouped you are paid a further advance. This is called a rolling advance. Publishers won't usually pay you an advance in the last twelve months of the fixed term because they won't have enough time to recoup it before the deal runs out. When you work out how recouped you are, to see if you should get a further advance, you should try to get the publisher to take into account some of the income that has been earned from your songs but which hasn't yet come through to their or your account in the UK. This is 'pipeline income' that we came across in the min-max formula in record contracts.

MINIMUM COMMITMENT

There are a number of different types of Minimum Commitment. The simplest is where you are just required to write a minimum number of songs. If you co-write, your share of all the co-written works must add up to an equivalent number of whole songs. For example, if the Minimum Commitment is to write five new songs and you always only write the lyrics, so only control 50% of each song, then you will have to write ten half-songs to add up to the five whole ones. This type of commitment works best for a pure songwriter who writes for others and doesn't perform and record his own material.

There may be an additional requirement that in order to count towards the Minimum Commitment the song must be exploited in some way; for example, it must be commercially released as an A-side of a single or as an album track. This puts a greater burden on you if you are a pure songwriter who can't easily control whether anyone else will want to record your songs. The publisher usually insists on this when they want to be certain there will be some form of exploitation, and hopefully some income, before it commits to any more advances or decides whether to exercise an option to extend the term.

There may be a requirement that you have to write a minimum number of the songs on an album. That percentage varies depending on the songwriter and the style of music. For a band, the requirement is usually that you have to write at least 60–70% of the songs on your own album. There is also usually a requirement that that album has to be commercially released. This sort of arrangement works better for a songwriter who also performs and records his own material.

A much less common commitment is one that you get when you have a songwriter who records some of his own material, writes to commissions from others or writes for a number of different styles of music, for example, film, TV, classical and popular. The Minimum Commitment could be a number of 'points' with a different value being given to each type of usage, genre, format and so on. For example, two points for a ballet commission, five for a track on a popular music album, with the total points required per contract period of, say, thirty points. The publisher is only likely to agree to this sort of commitment where you are already established in a number of these areas.

ADVANCES

It's usual under an exclusive publishing agreement for the publisher to pay advances. As we saw with record contracts (see Chapter 3), this is a pre-payment of your share of the gross income from the use of your songs. It's not a loan; it's not repayable to the publishing company if you never earn enough from the songs it controls to cover the amount of the advance. It isn't usually returnable by you but if you take the money and run, never delivering a single song, your publisher may get a bit upset and they are likely to ask for their money back.

What size advance can you expect? It will change with particular circumstances. Your bargaining power, the number of co-writers there are and how much is your own material and how much is sampled from others will all help to determine the figure. It will also depend on how much the publishers think they are likely to earn from your songs on average. If the record deal has already been done, the publishers may take their lead from what they know of the level of that deal. If that was a particularly 'hot' deal, the publishers will know that they probably have to increase the overall terms of their offer. There are also semi-scientific financial models that help publishers decide how much they can realistically risk. Some publishers rely on these models while others work on more of a gut-instinct or a combination of the two. You also have to factor in market forces. If a publisher really wants to sign you up – whether to increase the profile of the company, for market share or just because the A&R man wants it – then that publisher will pay whatever it takes.

The higher the advance, the more the publisher will expect from you in return and the larger percentage of the income that the publisher will keep as their fee. The publisher will be more reluctant to give you a higher than average royalty if they have had to pay out a high advance – £50–75,000 for a writer for 80% or more of the songs on an album isn't unreasonable. Much higher figures can be expected if there is 'hype' or if you have a proven track record. If the publishers know that there is already some income out there from your catalogue waiting to be collected, or that you have a song on the next album to be released by a chart-topping act, they are more likely to risk paying higher advances.

The publishing deal is likely to recoup a lot faster than the record deal. Why is this? Well, with a publishing deal you only have to recoup the personal advances and maybe a bit of money in demo costs or tour support – there aren't the additional recoupable costs like recording costs, video costs and tour support. Also, the publisher pays through to you a much larger percentage of the income earned for the use of your songs than most record companies do with the income from sales of your records.

ROYALTIES

The publishing advance is recouped from your royalty earnings after first taking off the publisher's fee. For an exclusive publishing deal this will usually be about 20–25% of the gross income.

Before we move on to consider royalties in any more detail, I have to explain to you the two ways that you can calculate the percentage that you receive. The percentage can be calculated 'at source' or on 'receipts'.

'At source' means that there have been no deductions made by anyone (after the collection societies and the VAT man and payments to any arranger or translator) from the gross income earned from your songs. For example, your publisher may have sub-publishers or their own companies overseas. These people have to be paid somehow and they could be paid out of the money that the publishers get paid, their 20– 25%. Or they could be paid off the top, off the gross before the income is paid through to you. 'Receipts' means its after any such 'cut'.

Let me give you an example: ff100 is earned in France from sales of recordings of your song. If you are on a 'source' deal, nothing gets deducted off that ff100 by the sub-publisher in France before it is paid through to your publisher in the UK. The UK publisher would then deduct his 25% (assuming the VAT and taxman have already done their worst) and pay through ff75 to you. If you were on a 'receipts' deal then the sub-publisher in France would first take his cut of, say, 15% (ff15), leaving ff85 to be sent through to your publisher in the UK. He then takes his 25% of that £85, leaving you with just ff63.

As a songwriter you should try to get an 'at source' deal. But your publisher may not have any choice. The deals done with their sub-publishers may mean they have to do it on a receipts basis in order to make any money out of use of your songs overseas. If you are offered a 'receipts' deal, the very least you should do is to try to limit the amount the sub-publishers can take off the 'at source' income. For example, you might want to say in the contract that the sub-publishers can't deduct any more than 15–20%. In the *Elton John* v. *Dick James* case, the sub-publishers were spread all over the world and many were associated with Dick James and his UK companies. There was no limit on what these sub-publishers could take off the top as their cut. As Elton was on a 'receipts' deal, he found himself in a situation where the sub-publisher took cuts of 50% or more, leaving small amounts to come into the UK where a further percentage fee was deducted by Dick James – leaving very little over for Elton.

SYNCHRONISATION AND COVER ROYALTIES

Sometimes the publishers justify taking a larger piece of the pie by saying that, in order to do certain work for you, they need the incentive of getting more of a fee. Part of me says that this is a rip-off and that getting 20–25% of your income should be enough for most purposes. The reality is that the business has accepted that publishers will get a larger fee for these types of work and it is hard to buck against the trend unless you have a great deal of bargaining power. What areas am I talking about? The two usual areas where publishers take a larger fee are synchronisation licences and covers.

I described a synchronisation licence earlier (see page 80). For reasons that are obscure to me, publishers seem to think that they should get a larger fee for going out and finding a film or TV project that your work would be suitable for. And there's me thinking that's what you were paying for in the first place. Silly me. No, they need a further incentive. They usually look to get about another 5%, so if you were paying your publisher a fee on mechanical royalties of 25% then you would see that increase to 30% for synchronisation royalties.

If you find that the publisher won't move on this point, the best thing is to make sure that they don't get this increased percentage on projects that you or someone other than the publisher introduces. For example, if one of your mates from drama school brings a film project to you, you wouldn't expect the publisher to take a bigger fee because they didn't go out and find that work.

The same sort of rules should apply to a cover. As you know, a cover is a recording of a song done by someone other than the songwriter. So, for example, if Sinead O'Connor later records a track first recorded by U2, Sinead's version would be the cover. Once again the publisher will probably want an increased fee for finding other artists keen to cover your works. The answer, once again, is to make sure that something doesn't count as a cover unless the publisher has actually done something positive to get it. For example, if you bumped into an artist at an awards show and he was raving about what he thought he could do with your song, and he goes on to cover that song, it hasn't happened because of anything the publisher has done. The publisher shouldn't get an increased fee for that cover.

You have to be particularly careful if you are a songwriter who doesn't perform your own songs. If you aren't careful you'll find that you are paying the higher fee for most of what you are doing because the recording will always be by someone other than the person who wrote it – you. Everything will be a cover. In these cases I always push for all recordings to be treated in the same way and not as covers. The publishers are often very reluctant to do this, saying that getting anyone to record a song requires effort, that it's harder if the songwriter isn't the performing artist. You have to stand your ground on this. If you are a songwriter you will be paying a publisher to find ways to use your songs. You shouldn't expect them to increase their fee just because you aren't going to record your own songs.

PERFORMING INCOME

The PRS rules require that at least six-twelfths (50%) of the performing income has to go to the writer/composer. This is called 'the writer's share'. The other six-twelfths is called 'the publisher's share'. Depending on the deal you have, the publisher will either say that they intend to keep the whole of the publisher's share or they will agree to share some of it with you. The difference is that you get to keep the writer's share and don't have to put it towards recoupment of your advances. Your share of the publisher's share will go towards recoupment of any unrecouped advance.

When you're dealing with contracts for the use of music in a film or TV programme it is still common for the publisher to insist on keeping the entire publisher's share and not putting any of it towards recoupment. TV and film publishing deals have lagged behind popular music deals where it is usual for the publisher to share up to 50% of the publisher's share with the songwriter.

ACCOUNTING

The publishing company will usually account to you every six months. You will be sent a statement of what use has been made of your songs in the previous six months and how much income has been received. It should show the percentage that they have kept as their fee and the amount that has been credited to your account. Your share of income will go first to recoup advances. After that, your publisher should send a cheque with the statement for the royalties due to you. Even if the account isn't recouped you or your representatives should check these accounting statements to see if they seem right, that the correct fee has been deducted. If, for example, you know that your music was used in an advert in the last six months but there is no mention of income from this in the statement, you should ask your publisher to explain. It also pays for you to audit the books of the publisher company from time to time. You don't want to be doing this every five minutes but you may want to run a check after you've had a particularly successful time. You'll probably also want to think about doing an audit when the deal comes to an end, as that is going to be your last practical chance to check up on your publisher. Because it can be very expensive to carry out an audit (£5,000 plus is not unusual), you only want to do it when you think there's a reasonable chance of getting something back from it. If the audit shows up serious errors in your favour you should expect them to reimburse you the main costs of doing the audit as well as paying you whatever sums the audit has shown are due to you.

You shouldn't take your time over raising any concerns you might have about an accounting statement because the publishing contract will probably put a time limit on you raising objections. Usually if a statement hasn't been challenged for three years, sometimes less, then it is said to have been accepted and no objection can be raised to it after that time.

WHAT CAN YOU EXPECT FROM A PUBLISHER UNDER AN EXCLUSIVE PUBLISHING AGREEMENT?

We have already seen that there is a presumption that an exclusive songwriting agreement is in restraint of trade and it is up to the publisher to show that the contract, taken as a whole, is reasonable to protect their interests and fair to the songwriter. As we saw in *Schroeder v. Macaulay*, a publishing contract should require the publisher to do something with your songs that they control and if they don't manage to do so within a reasonable period of time then you should be able to get those songs back. The publisher has to ensure that they do what they can to get the songs used, to maximise the income from all uses and to make sure that the songs are properly registered and that income is properly collected and accounted through to the songwriter.

Your publisher should also take steps to protect your songs from unauthorised uses. Sampling of songs is rife and it is up to them to either prevent such uses by court action or, if you and your publisher are prepared to allow the sample use, to ensure a proper amount is paid in compensation (see Chapter 13).

• Open-ended contracts are likely to be seen as unfairly restrictive, as we see in the case of Holly Johnson and Perfect Songs Limited.[16]

This case came to court at the same time as the related case involving Johnson's record contract (see page 57). Both the record and publishing companies were trying to get an injunction to bind Holly Johnson to the contracts, even though the band he was a member of, Frankie Goes To Hollywood, had disbanded. Holly Johnson argued that both agreements were unenforceable as being an unreasonable restraint of his trade.

When the court looked at the contract it found that is was potentially a very long contract, that it was exclusive but there hadn't been equal bargaining power when it was entered into. It found that the restrictions in the contract weren't reasonable and declared that the publishing agreement was unenforceable. The judge was concerned that Holly Johnson and his fellow band members hadn't had any choice in whether they did the publishing deal. It was offered as a package with the record deal. There was also no obligation on the publisher to do anything with the songs. There was no reassignment of the rights in the songs if the publisher failed to exploit them in any way. The judge also thought that it was unfair that Perfect Songs had full control over what happened to the songs once they were delivered. The songwriters had little or no

16 *Perfect Songs Limited* v. *Johnson and others* [1993] E.M.L.R 61.

creative control. The court considered what financial benefits the songwriters got out of the deal and found that the 35% fee retained by the publisher was too much.

• Another case that has had an effect on the form of publishing contracts is the Stone Roses publishing dispute.[17]

The Stone Roses were a Manchester band that had a hit with an album called *The Stone Roses*, released in 1989. They were signed to the Silvertone label, part of the Zomba Group. The members of the Stone Roses were also offered a package deal. They couldn't do the record deal without also signing the publishing deal. As we saw in the case of Armatrading and Stone, it is very important that the songwriter gets independent advice from his own lawyer, someone who is familiar with the music business and its contracts. In this Stone Roses case, the songwriters had their own lawyer but he was not experienced in music contracts and made hardly any changes to the terms of the contract. There was no equality of bargaining power. The agreement was an exclusive one and the rights were assigned for the life of copyright. There was a limited obligation on the publisher to do something with the songs under their control. After five years the Stone Roses could ask for the rights back in any of their songs that hadn't been exploited. The first contract period was linked to that of the record deal. The court found that the first contract period of the record deal was capable of being extended indefinitely. As the two were linked, this meant that the publishing agreement was similarly open-ended and as such unreasonable. The court also found that the advances weren't reasonable and objected to the lack of artistic or creative control by the songwriters. Because Zomba had obtained an injunction preventing the band from recording for anyone else, they couldn't bring any more product out until the case was over, when they signed a big deal with US label Geffen. The band did release another album in 1995 called, appropriately enough, *The Second Coming* but split up shortly afterwards.

As a result of these and similar cases, it is now common to have clauses in the publishing agreement making it clear that the publishers have to do something with the rights they have. Also that the songwriter should have some say on what happens to the songs once they're delivered. It is usually to say that no major changes to the music or any change to the lyrics can be made without the writer's approval. The criticism of the 65:35 split has led to the average publishing royalty rising to 70% in the songwriter's favour, with the publisher keeping no more that 30%.

MORAL RIGHTS AND CREATIVE CONTROL

A songwriter may have strong views on what he wants or does not want to happen to his songs. For example, a songwriter may believe passionately that no one should be allowed to alter the words or music without his approval. As we saw above, the Holly Johnson and Stone Roses cases have led to creative controls being included in most publishing deals. That doesn't usually extend to straight translations. Those are taken to be a logical part of

17 *Zomba* v. *Mountfield and others* [1993] E.M.L.R 152.

the exploitation process. But if in the translation the translator wanted to give the lyrics a different meaning, and you objected to this, you should be entitled to prevent this happening. Obviously I'm not talking about minor changes but major ones that change the meaning of what you've written significantly. This contractual control overlaps with a songwriter's moral rights (see Chapter 12). Where you are able to hang on to your moral rights you should do so. The reality is that because our copyright laws, while acknowledging the rights, allow you to waive them, all publishers have put clauses in their contracts requiring you to waive these rights. What we lawyers now do is to put contract clauses in to give you the same or similar rights to what you would have got from using your moral rights. You might ask why we bother with this farce. Why don't we acknowledge that the songwriter has certain rights to object to what is morally being done to his songs? Well, the essential difference is that the moral rights usually go a bit wider than what you get under your contract and a moral right is capable of being enforced by you even if your publishers don't want to take any action.

A songwriter may want to reserve a song for himself or his band to record and won't want another artist applying for and getting a mechanical licence to record that song first. The publisher will usually agree to not issue a first mechanical licence to another artist where the songwriter wants to reserve it, but will usually require that there is a time limit of, say, six months on this. If it hasn't been recorded in that time then the restriction is lifted.

Finally, of course, the songwriter will want to ensure he is properly credited.

WHAT TYPE OF DEAL SHOULD YOU DO?

How do you decide which deal is best for you? To some extent this may be out of your control. You may not be offered anything other than an exclusive publishing agreement. Or you may not be able to afford to keep control of your copyrights. You may be able to afford to do so but haven't got the organisational talents necessary to make sure that your works are properly protected and the income collected. In these cases the exclusive songwriter agreement is for you. But if you aren't fussed about an advance and you do want to control your copyrights, you may want to go for either a sub-publishing or an administration deal, depending on the amount of activity you require from your publisher.

CONCLUSIONS

- Decide what type of deal would ideally suit you.

- Decide if you need an advance and, if so, how big an advance – this will help you decide whether to go for a sub-publishing or an administration deal.

- You should try to do deals where your share of the income is calculated 'at source' but if you have to have a 'receipts' deal then make sure you put a limit on what the overseas sub-publishers can deduct in their fees.

- If you are receiving more that 70% of the gross fees you are doing well.
- Look at the Minimum Commitment. Is it realistic? Can you achieve it within a reasonable period of time?
- If you're a songwriter but don't also record your own works, try not to agree to a Minimum Commitment that means your songs have to be exploited in some way as this will be outside your control.
- Again if you don't record your own works, hold out for no reduction in the amount of royalty you receive on 'covers'.
- Make sure there is no delay in you receiving your money from overseas.

5: **GETTING A RECORD MADE**

INTRODUCTION

Just to make life easier for myself, I'm going to assume that you've signed a record deal and that the funding for making your record will come from the record company either as a separate recording budget fund or as an all-inclusive advance (see Chapter 3). At the end of the chapter I'm going to look at other ways of making a record, for example where you are funding the making of the record yourself and at new sources of funding.

PRODUCTION DEALS VERSUS DIRECT SIGNINGS

But before I go into the process of recording a record, I need to look at two different ways of structuring a record deal. This has an impact on how the process is run and supervised.

PRODUCTION DEALS

It's easy to confuse production with the record producer's role, which I deal with below. A production deal is one where someone (whether it's an individual, a partnership or a company) acts as a middleman between the record company and the artist. This middleman is the production company.

Sometimes a smaller label or someone who doesn't want a role as a manager finds a talented artist. They may know they haven't got the necessary funds to make the record or, if they can afford to make it, they haven't got the necessary clout to get decent manufacturing, distribution, marketing or promotion. The label or individual could sign up the artist and then start to look for a company with greater resources to fund the recording, manufacture and so on. In effect they are selling on the rights they have to the artist's services either by a licence of rights or an assignment of them.

In either case there is a contract between the production company and the artist called a production deal.

WHAT IS A PRODUCTION DEAL?

The contract may look very like a record deal. The production company could sign the artist up for an album with options to make further albums. The number of options may be less than in a straight record deal, perhaps two options instead of four or five. The money available will usually be less than a straight exclusive record deal with an established larger record company and in some ways might resemble a development deal. The deal will probably be structured as a 'net receipts' deal as opposed to one where you are paid a royalty on record sales. It will also probably say somewhere in the contract that the intention is to try to get another company involved with greater resources. The production company will want to agree that if that third party company wants more options then you will agree to that.

It is a little difficult to agree upfront what sort of deal will be done with the other company. I usually try to get a situation where the artist gets the opportunity to be involved in the negotiations with the third party. After all, the third party need to know you are 'on side' so should want to co-operate with you. If the bigger record company are going to pay advances to the production company, you will want to know that you will get a decent share of that. Also, if you are on a 'net receipts' deal, you'll need to know that the royalty that is being paid is high enough when it's split between you and the production company. For example, if you are on a 50:50 net receipts deal and the royalty is 18% then you'll be on a 9% royalty as will your production company. Maybe your percentage should be higher – 70% or 75%. If you are the production company you should work out what's a good deal for you and should be looking at getting a clear profit of a 3–4% royalty.

WHAT'S IN IT FOR THE OTHER RECORD COMPANY?

The bigger company have the advantage of having someone else find and develop a new artist. By the time the project is brought to them they can hear what it's going to sound like. Some of the risk has been taken away. If they are licensing a finished record from a production company, they know exactly what they are getting. There's also a middleman to deal with the artist – you become someone else's problem. The downside of this for the recording company is lack of control. They need to be confident that the production company can deliver the goods. They are more likely to go with someone who already has a track record.

WHAT'S IN IT FOR THE PRODUCTION COMPANY?

The production company have a much closer involvement with the artist. They have the thrill of discovering an artist early and of developing them. It gets another company to take the risk on manufacture, distribution and marketing costs. But at that stage, of course, it will lose control. If the bigger company then fails, all the production company's work will have been wasted. For the production company it's essential they choose a bigger company with a good marketing department or that the contract with the bigger company allows them to insist on outside press and marketing people being brought in if necessary. If it works, the production company gets their costs and expenses repaid, the financial risk on the manufacture, distribution and marketing taken off their hands and a decent royalty into the bargain.

WHAT'S IN IT FOR THE ARTIST?

If you get a production company interested in you then it's a step up on the ladder. If they know what they're doing, you have a second chance later of getting the bigger company involved. You should also have greater artistic and creative freedom unless you sign to a production team who are control freaks. The downside for you if you don't get the deal right is that you could end up sharing a larger than necessary piece of the pie with the production company. You are also one stage removed from the record company that is promoting your record so it is that much harder to get your views heard.

FINDING A STUDIO

Whether you're signed direct or via a production company one thing you'll have to do is to find a suitable recording studio. It could be as simple as the 'studio' in your back bedroom or as complex as a full-blown commercial studio. Before you decide on a studio you should look at several. It should have the equipment you'll need already installed. If it has to be hired in it will add to your recording costs. You should listen to material produced in those studios and, if you can, talk to other artists who have used them. You should also talk to an in-house engineer or producer. How enthusiastic are they about the place and how it's run? If you have a record producer in mind or a favourite engineer, ask them what they think of the various studios on your shortlist.

You also need to think about where it is. Is it easy to get equipment in or out? Is it secure? We've seen stories in the press of the latest recordings by Oasis, and others, being 'leaked' from the studio. You don't want to risk that happening. Does the studio keep tapes safe and secure and who is responsible for this?

A studio can either be one that you go to day to day or a residential one where you stay in accommodation at or near the recording studio. Your own personal arrangements might decide which is better for you. If you have a young baby or are recently married you might want to be at home regularly. Or perhaps, thinking about a new baby, it might be a good reason to get as far away as possible. Some bands respond best when they are immersed in the project in a residential studio. For others the idea of spending 24 hours a day, 7 days a week with the other band members is their idea of hell.

STUDIO PACKAGE DEALS

The recording studio may block out a whole period of time for you; for example, 7 days, 24 hours a day. The studio is yours for the whole of that time. These arrangements are sometimes called 'lockout' deals. Other deals are for a fixed eight- or ten-hour day. If you overrun you may either find that the studio has been hired out to someone else or that there are heavy financial penalties. Some studios will give you discounts on their usual rate if you record at times when the studio would not normally be in use, for example in the early hours of the morning. This is called down time. It's fine if you're on a very tight budget or if you just want to put down some demo tracks. However, if you're planning to use down time to record your whole album, you are putting very great limitations on yourself. It's mentally and physically tough recording an album without adding to it by constantly recording at two in the morning.

Some studios will offer you a package deal that includes mixing and mastering of the finished recordings. There are two things to bear in mind here. First, the studio must have the technical capabilities to do a good job and, second, the price offered should represent good value.

Your A&R man or production company representative is going to be an important source of information for where you choose to record. These people also have a vital role to play in giving you feedback on how the recording is going. It is far too easy to lock yourself away in a studio and become isolated from reality. You will need feedback and constructive criticism. The A&R man won't be sitting at your shoulder all the way through the recordings but he will want to visit the studio regularly during the recording process. Don't surround yourself with yes men, you'll need people who can be objective and whose opinion and judgement you respect.

Once you've chosen your studio you need to haggle on a price – or your manager, production company or A&R man will do it for you. Before you book the time make sure that any people you want to help with the recording, such as a producer, engineer or session musicians, are available. If you really want to work with a particular person then you may have to adjust your recording schedule to work around them. If they live outside the UK they may need a permit to work here. This can take time and it has to be factored into the recording timetable.

Another key factor in the choice of the studio is whether you can afford it. Studio costs and fees to a producer usually make up the bulk of the recording costs. You'll have to recoup these so it is important that you keep an eye on them.

THE RECORDING BUDGET

When you were pitching for your record deal you may well have done a 'back of an envelope' calculation of how much it would cost you to record (see Chapter 3). Now you're going to have to do a much more detailed one. You and your manager are going to have to work out how long you think you are going to take to record the album, how many days of studio time and what that will cost at the studio of your choice. You need to know how much your producer of choice will charge and how long a mixer will take to mix it and what he is likely to charge. If there are session vocalists or musicians who will need to be there for all or part of the recording time then you need to know how much they will charge per day or session. There are minimum rates set by bodies like the Musicians' Union and Equity (see Chapter 15) but good people may want more than the minimum rate. If special equipment is required then you need to work out how much this will cost to hire and if it's more cost-effective to buy it. It may be a piece of equipment that you'll need to have later when you're out on the road promoting the album. You may have an equipment budget as part of your deal or the cost may be built into the recording budget. Another possibility is that you'll have to buy the equipment out of your personal advance.

Don't forget rehearsal time. You don't want to spend expensive studio time rehearsing the songs until you're ready to record them. Do all of this before you set foot in the studio. Whether you do this in a professional rehearsal room or in a room over the local chip shop (which is what one of my clients did) will depend on your budget.

Once you've thought of everything you might possibly need, add 10% to it. This is called a contingency. It's to cover extra costs when you spend another day in the studio or on mixing or when you have to hire in equipment because yours or the studio's isn't up to the job.

If you have a recording fund deal then your total budget should not exceed about 60% of the total advance to give you enough to live on. If you have a deal where you have an advance plus a recording budget, you'll have to keep within the maximum set by the record company and you'll have to take your finished outline budget to them for approval. Bear in mind that most record contracts say that, if you overrun the agreed budget without first getting clearance from the record company, you will be liable for the extra expense. It'll be deducted from your royalties and possibly also from any further advances due to you under the deal.

MASTERING COSTS

These are a grey area. They are the costs that are involved in getting the final mixed recordings into a state ready to be made into records. The record contract will say whether these costs are to be included in the recording budget or not. Mastering can cost several thousand pounds so it is important to know when setting your financial budget.

THE PRODUCER

The role of the producer has been described as 'getting the dynamics and emotion of the music on tape'. The producer makes your material come alive. It is possible for you to produce yourself and many successful artists do. By the same token, most artists, particularly when they are starting out, might find it difficult to get the necessary distance in order to hear how the music will sound to an outsider. The producer can be your external critic.

Because you are going to be working closely together, you need to have similar musical tastes and influences. You have to like working with them and respect them. You have to have a common vision of how the music should sound.

As you can imagine, finding the right producer is very important. It's because some artists find it very difficult to find a producer who understands what they are trying to do that they produce themselves. Then, it may be that the mixer can act as the necessary external critic.

Your A&R man can be very helpful in pointing you in the direction of possible producers. He can do a lot of the filtering process. He may play your demo to a series of different producers to see who is interested. He may invite producers to come to your gigs to get a feel for how you sound. Some vocalists need a little help in the studio in keeping in tune. Good producers will realise that when they hear you play live.

WHAT DOES A PRODUCER GET PAID?

Fee or Advance

Unless they are doing you a favour and cutting a special deal with you, the producer will usually expect to be paid a fee per track that they produce. This could be a pure fee, which is not recouped. It could be an advance against the producer's royalty or it could be part non-recoupable fees and part advances. Good producers can charge £3,000-plus per track and many of those will expect half of it to be a non-recoupable fee. Whether they get that will depend on the negotiation.

Royalty

The producer may just work for a fee but more often they'll expect to receive a royalty calculated in the same way as your record royalty is calculated. A good producer may insist on a royalty of 4% of the dealer price or 3% of the retail price. They may ask for escalations in the royalty if you sell more than a given amount.

RECOUPMENT OF COSTS

Another big bone of contention is whether the producer receives his royalty as soon as it has recouped any advance he has received, or if he has to also wait until his royalty, together with your royalty, has also recouped the recording costs on the tracks he has produced. If he agrees to the latter, the producer may say that once that's achieved, his royalty is calculated as if he'd been paid from record one after recouping his advance. This is difficult to follow so let me give you an example.

A producer is on a 3% royalty and he has received £30,000 in advances. The recording costs on the tracks he worked on were £200,000. Your royalty together with his 3% is 12%. Say each record sold makes you £1.25. You'd have to sell £230k ÷ £1.25 = 184,000 copies of the record for the advance to be regarded as recouped. Say the producer's 3% royalty earns him 31p. To recoup his £30,000 advance, he'd have to sell £30k ÷ 0.31 = 96,774 copies. If he is on a deal where he's paid retrospectively he'd then get paid on a number of copies sold between 96,774 and 184,000 copies i.e. 87,226 × 0.31 = another £27,040. If you sell 96,775 so that the producer recoups his advance, but you don't sell more than 184,000, you don't recoup the recording costs and your producer gets no more royalties. So the producer is taking a risk – but if it pays off he gets a windfall.

In the US, producers are almost invariably expected to have to wait until all recording costs have been recouped. Very rarely do US record companies accept that payment should then be retroactive. In the UK, however, it's much more common to have retroactive deals or indeed some deals where the producers don't have to wait until *any* recording costs have been recouped – they are paid their royalty as soon as they have recouped their advance. This is very risky for an artist. You can only really do it if your record company agree to advance you the cash to pay the producer. You are unlikely to be recouped as you have all the recording costs, video costs and so on to recoup first. This pushes you further into debt so you're only going to want to agree to this if it is the only way you're going to be able to do the deal, to get that particular producer.

WHO DOES THE CONTRACT?

This is another key difference between UK and US producer deals. In the UK it is usually the record or production company that will do the deal with the producer. They will issue the contract and negotiate the terms. In your record contract it should say whether or not the record company have to get your approval of the commercial terms. At the very least you should have approval of the royalty, because it will usually come out of your royalty, and of the advance, because it will usually be a recoupable recording cost.

In the US it is the artist who issues the contract and negotiates the deal with the producer – or the artist's lawyer. This is, of course, more expensive but does give the artist more control over the terms. It also means that the contract is not with the record company but between artist and producer. If the artist doesn't pay, the producer can only sue the artist, who may not have the money. In the UK the contract would be between the record company and the producer so if anything goes wrong the record producer sues the record company, not the artist. This leaves the producer in a more secure position than if he'd had to rely on the artist. It is because the US record companies don't want to get involved that they keep out of this. US companies will usually do the royalty calculation for you and, if you ask them to, they will pay part of the royalties direct to the producer. This isn't the same as saying they are responsible for payment. They make it clear they are doing it as a favour.

REMIX ROYALTY REDUCTION

Because the royalty to the producer usually comes out of the artist's royalty, it is in the artist's interests to make sure the royalty doesn't eat too far into his royalty. A good record mixer may also want to be paid a royalty. What I try to do is to get the record producer to agree that if the mixer is on a 1% royalty then the producer's royalty is reduced by 1%. Some producers are happy to do this – or at least they agree to it. Others are adamant that, if they've done a good job of production, they shouldn't see any reduction in their royalty just because the record company or artist decides to bring in another person to mix the records. If this becomes a real sticking point it's sometimes possible to get the record company to add in a bit more of a royalty for the mixer, for example another 0.5%.

CREDITS

The producer will usually want to receive a credit on the packaging and on the record. I haven't yet seen any producers arguing about what happens when the recording is digitally delivered online but I'm sure that's only a matter of time.

Sometimes a 'name' producer will insist on having the right to remove their name from the packaging if their work is remixed and they don't like or wish to be associated with the end result.

STANDARD OF WORK

Whether it's you or your record company that's doing the contract, you will want to know that the work the producer does will be of a good standard. You will probably stagger payments to the producer so that the final instalments aren't paid until recordings of the necessary standard have been delivered. So what is that standard? Well, just as we saw with record contracts, there is usually an argument as to whether all the producer has to do is to deliver technically satisfactory recordings or if they have to deliver recordings that are commercially acceptable. This is of course a very subjective test and the producer may well argue that they have no say in what the artist chooses to record so it's not their fault if the finished recording is not commercial. A common compromise is to say that it must be a first-class technical production and of at least the same high standard as previous productions that the producer has done.

RIGHTS

The producer is usually required as part of their contract to assign any and all copyrights they have in the sound recordings to the artist (US deals) or to the record or production company (UK deals). The recordings may have been made in a studio owned by the producer. In that case there is a possibility that the producer could be said to have made the arrangements for the recording to be made. If so, the producer could claim to be the first owner of copyright.[1] To ensure that the producer can't make such claims, the record company will want to make sure that they take an assignment of any copyright the producer may have.

In the US they deal with it slightly differently. There the contracts will say that for the purposes of copyright the producer is employed by the artist. Under US copyright laws the employer (artist) owns the copyright in anything an employee (producer) creates in the course of their employment.

The producer may perform on the recordings. He may play an instrument or programme a keyboard. He may therefore have the same rights as any other performer.[2] In which case the record company will want to know that the producer has given all the necessary consents to their performances being used. The contract will usually require them to confirm that. It will also usually say that the fee or advance that the producer is paid includes any fees for their performances.

As a pure performer, the producer will not have any moral rights (see Chapter 12) but producers will usually insist on being credited. If they have made any original creative contribution to the writing or composing of the music or the words then they may have rights as a co-author of that song.[3] As long as you, the artist, are happy to accept that this is the case and can agree the level of that collaboration then this is not usually a problem. But as the producer's share may well be published by someone other than your publishers, you will need to know that a mechanical licence will be available on standard industry terms so that you can include their share of that song on the recording. If you have had to agree to reduced mechanical royalties in the US and Canada (the so-called Controlled Compositions clauses) then, so as to lessen any impact on you, you should make sure the producer accepts the same reductions. If they are a big enough name they may refuse to do that, so you will need to bear this in mind. If the producer co-writes a number of the songs on the album then this could affect your ability to fulfil your Minimum Commitment requirements that you may have in your publishing deal. So you need to also take this into account when agreeing what percentage share is allocated to the producer. Most producers don't co-write the songs but

1 Section 9(2) (aa) CDPA and Chapter 3.
2 See Section 191A ff CDPA for performer's rights and Chapter 3 for more details on what these rights are.
3 See Section 9(2) (3) CDPA on authorship of words and music and section 10 on co-authorship. See also Chapter 4.

if they do they will have moral rights in their work. The contract will usually require the producer to waive any moral rights they may have.

If the producer hasn't co-written any of the songs, or even if they have contributed but don't wish to claim any share, the contract will usually require them to warrant (guarantee) that that is the case.

PRODUCER'S DUTIES

In addition to making sure that the production is of the required standard it's also the job of the producer to try to keep the recording costs within the budget and to let the artist/record company know if it's likely to run over budget. The contract might make the producer responsible for any overrun on the budget that is their fault.

They are responsible for getting all session musicians to complete the necessary consent forms, buying out their rights and getting all the necessary performers' consents. They have to deliver these signed forms to the record company with details of who played what on each recording. They also have to keep all recording tapes safe and deliver them up to the record company when asked to do so. This includes all outttakes (i.e. recordings that didn't end up in the final mix on the record).

- One case in which these 'outtakes' then found their way on to a commercially released record involved Bruce Springsteen.[4]

Bruce Springsteen had had agreements early in his career with Flute. Those agreements had been declared to be void from the outset. As we saw in other cases, such as *Elton John* v. *Reed*, this was in itself unusual because most courts will not declare agreements to be void (i.e. as if they'd never been entered into), only voidable (i.e. could be set aside as to future rights). Because the recording and publishing agreements were said to be void, Springsteen argued that he was the owner of the copyright in all previous recordings including any outtakes or other unreleased material. He didn't produce any evidence in court to back up his claim that all copyrights had been reassigned to him but the court accepted that in all probability this had happened after the court ruling on the validity of the agreements. As we have already seen, reassignments do not have to be in writing[5] but it is advisable to do so in order to be able to prove ownership if you need to. Having accepted that he was the owner of the sound recording copyright, the court decided he was within his rights to claim that CDs containing outtakes of his recordings released by Flute were an infringement. It also found that Masquerade Music Limited, which imported CDs containing further Springsteen recordings, was also liable for secondary infringement.[6]

Although a record company is unlikely to risk upsetting you by releasing records containing outtakes while you're still under contract with them, they may not have any such qualms after the end of the contract. Your producer will have been obliged to hand those

4 *Springsteen* v. *Flute International Limited and Others* [1998] Chancery Division.
5 Section 90 CDPA.
6 See Sections 22–26 CDPA and Chapter14.

outtakes over to the record company so your agreement with the record company should cover what can or can't be done with them.

MIXING

This is the stage between production (i.e. the recording and capturing of the essence of the song) and mastering (when it is made ready for duplication).

The mixer selects from all the various recordings he has of a song those that will be mixed together to make up the final version. He also chooses which parts to emphasise or not, for example a guitar part or a vocal might be brought into more prominence.

The mix might be done by the producer. In fact the first mix often is. As they have been close to the recording process throughout, you'd think they would be best placed for the job. They may well be, but there are very particular talents in mixing and sometimes a fresh 'ear' can hear things that the producer and the artist can't.

There are also mixers who take the finished, fully mixed recording and play around with it – maybe adding a different rhythm or bringing in elements either sampled from the recordings or from other recordings. These are called *re*mixes. When samples are being introduced you have to be very careful that all necessary rights have been cleared and that the mixer has permission to include them (see Chapter 13). Remixes are often done to create a different sound for radio or for use in clubs.

MIX CONTRACTS

The contracts for mixers and remixers are very similar and follow the same format as producer contracts (see above).

FEES AND ADVANCES

A mixer or remixer will usually only receive a fee for their work. This can be as much as £10,000-plus for one track to be remixed by a big-name DJ. These are non-recoupable.

Big-name mixers can sometimes demand an advance that is partly non-recoupable and partly on account of royalties. The same comments apply here as with producer deals.

ROYALTIES

If a mixer has enough clout, he can ask for and get a royalty of 0.5–1%. This is usually calculated in the same way as the artist's royalty. As we saw with producer deals, the artist has to work out if there is going to be sufficient left after producers and mixers have received royalties to make it worthwhile.

The same issues also come up here as to who does the contract, whether the mixer gets his royalty only after all mix costs have been recouped and what standard of work is expected from him.

RIGHTS

As with producer deals, the record company will usually require the mixer to assign any sound recording copyright to the record company. There has been an increase in the last couple of years in remixers arguing for the right to retain a separate sound recording copyright in their mix. It is possible, if they've added enough original elements or have re-recorded the track as part of the remix process, to create a separate sound recording copyright. I think if I were the artist I would be nervous about some mixers owning a version of my track and I'd want to have restrictions on what they can do with it. If they want to just put it on one of their own record compilations then that might be all right. If I were the record company that had paid for the remixes I think I'd want to own them and perhaps license rights back to them for their compilation.

The mixers aren't usually performers but most mix contracts will require them to give all necessary consents to use any performances they might make.

Mixers also don't usually contribute to the creative writing of the song. Some remixers may claim that they have added enough original elements to create a new work. This may be true, depending on what they've done, but more likely they'll be said to have done a new arrangement of it. They can submit that arrangement to PRS and if PRS accepts it is an arrangement they can receive an adjudication of the performance income. This eats into the writer's performing income and most publishers will expect that whole percentage to come out of the writer's share. Because they aren't claiming co-authorship they wouldn't get to share in mechanical royalties, only performance income. If you are in any doubt as to whether they should be allowed to do this then your contract should ask them to confirm they have no interest in the underlying song at all. It will also usually require them to waive any moral rights.

PRODUCERS AND EXCLUSIVE DEALS

A development that is gaining ground at the moment involves a producer, who is also an artist, who is currently signed to an exclusive recording agreement as an artist. As we know, exclusive recording agreements usually allow you to do performances on other people's records provided you aren't featured. This may not be enough for someone to get as involved in another project as they'd like. So they act as producers, not artists, and sign producer deals that tie them exclusively as producers of an act. The deal looks very like a record deal and you have to be very careful not to put yourself in breach of your record contract. The record contract may also put restrictions on whether you can be on artwork for covers, in videos and so on, which could seriously restrict what you can do with the other project. If you were at all in doubt, it would be better to clear this project with your exclusive record company – even if you do end up sharing some of your royalties with them. Record companies are understandably very upset when artists they've signed exclusively and invested a lot of money in go off and help sell records for another record company.

MASTERING

This is part of the post-production process. Your recordings have been produced and mixed to your satisfaction and that of your record company.

The next stage before the recording goes to be manufactured into records is mastering. It straddles recording and manufacturing. It isn't just a mechanical process of ensuring all the right digital notes are in the right places. It's the means to give it a final 'tweaking' before the record is released. A good mastering person can make the sound more punchy, warm, full or louder. They can bring out details not already obvious. Mastering is a separate process from the mix and needs a different set of ears. Some bands swear by a particular person mastering their records in much the same way as film directors have their favourite editors. The mastering process helps the recording sound great no matter what medium it is manufactured in – CD, tape, vinyl or whatever it is played on.

I'm sure you can think of albums that sound fantastic on CD but really 'woolly' on the tape version. Or ones that sound fantastic played over headphones on your CD Walkman but which sound awful on the car CD player. This could be a problem of the mix but it's just as likely that someone has skimped on the mastering process.

When mastering a recording, equalising and compression of the sounds gives a consistency from track to track. Have you ever found yourself constantly having to adjust the volume between tracks on a compilation? It's either earth-shatteringly loud or so quiet that you're straining to hear the words. That's an example of bad mastering. Radio really brings out the difference as the radio process itself compresses the material. If a recording hasn't been properly mastered it can sound thin and weak.

You've spent a small fortune on making the recording so don't spoil it for a few thousand pounds in mastering costs.

The person doing the mastering is engaged to do the job by the record or production company. They either provide the mastering suite and equipment or the company hires and pays for one. They are paid a fee for their work. The record company usually pays it and, depending on the contract, will either treat it as a recoupable recording cost or as a non-recoupable manufacturing cost.

DELIVERY REQUIREMENTS

There are a number of things that you have to deliver to your record company before you can be said to have completed your side of the recording process.

As well as the finished, fully mixed and edited recordings, you will also have to deliver up all outtakes and all copies of the recordings. You may have to deliver finished recordings of additional tracks to act as B-sides or second tracks on singles. You will also have to deliver up all signed session forms and clearances for any samples that you've used in the recording.

You'll have to deliver a list of all the tracks on the album in the order in which they appear (called a track-listing). You'll probably also have to give them what is called 'label copy', which is all the information that has to appear on the label and packaging of the record. This includes things like who performed on each track, who wrote each track and who publishes those writers. If you've agreed to give credits to producers and mixers or a name check to the studio then you have to also give those details to the record company. This is also when you get to say thanks to all your mates, your mum 'and everyone else who knows me'. But don't go overboard or there won't be room enough for your name. However, if particular people have been helpful or supportive then by all means say thanks.

The contract will be very specific about what you have to deliver and to whom. It will also be quite technical about the form in which it requires you to deliver the recordings. It's very important that you do deliver all that is required of you. If you don't then you'll find all sorts of things don't happen. You don't get an instalment of your advances due on delivery. You don't start the manufacturing process and you don't start time running for when the record company has to release the record.

You should try to get written confirmation from the record company that you've delivered. It should be from the person identified in the contract as the person to whom delivery has to be made, for example the senior vice-president of A&R.

If you can't get that then you may have what is called a 'deemed acceptance' clause in your contract; that is, if you deliver to the right person all the things you're meant to and they don't tell you they haven't accepted the record within a give period of time (about 30 days usually) then they are said to have accepted it and can't get out of it.

If you haven't got that then you may have to just look at the circumstances. If you delivered all you had to by 26 March 1999 and they paid you the delivery advance on 5 April and mastered the album on 12 April then it is reasonable to assume that they'd accepted that delivery had taken place by 12 April at the latest, and arguably by 5 April.

ARTWORK

One key thing that usually has to be delivered is the artwork for the cover of the album. Without the artwork the record can't be released so it may be reasonable to assume (depending on the contract and individual circumstances) that delivery hasn't taken place until the record company has the finished artwork.

It usually wants the artwork delivered to it in a specific format, which these days is usually electronically, online or on disc.

Some talented bands do the artwork themselves. Some leave it to the record company's art department. Most hire someone else to do a design to their brief or specification.

If you are doing it yourself make sure you can do it to the required professional standard. If you're relying on the record company to do it try to make sure you have final approval. If you're bringing in someone else make sure they have a good, professional reputation for their work. Look at covers you admire, see who designed them. Interview a few designers and ask to see examples of their work. Do you get the feeling they understand what you want and what, if any, message you're trying to convey? Remember that if a potential customer doesn't know who you are, they may be attracted to pick up your CD over all the others by the striking artwork on the cover. You could use art students and do it on the cheap but then you could end up spending a lot of time supervising the work and would have been better off going with a professional in the first place.

If you have a logo (see Chapter 8) make sure it's on the artwork. This is all part of making the package look inviting and identifiably part of your image. You have to use it to rise above the masses; indeed, these days, striking artwork and logos repeated on your website not only make the association easier – it also helps to brand you and to make your work stand out above the crowd.

Once you've decided on a designer, you need to agree terms with them. You need a straightforward contract setting out what they are going to do, by when and for how much. If they're VAT registered they'll need to send you a VAT invoice before you pay them VAT on top. You may want to make payment in two instalments; one when they start work and the other when they deliver finished work that is satisfactory.

If photographs are to be used you need to agree who is going to be responsible for supplying those and at whose expense. The record company will usually organise and pay for a photo-shoot, but it may not necessarily be with the top-name photographer you'd like to use.

You need an agreement with the designer, photographers and so on that confirms you are the owner of the copyright in the photographs and any design rights in the artwork and graphics. There should be an assignment to you of any copyright or design rights they might have acquired. Ideally you should have the right to do what you want with those designs, photographs and so on. However, in the last couple of years designers and photographers have grown wise to the fact that they can earn more money if you have to go back to them for permission to reuse their work. For example, they may now agree to license the artwork or photo to you for your album cover only. If you want to use it on a poster, T-shirt or other merchandise, or as a backdrop on your live stage shows, then you'll have to come back to the photographer or designer for further permission. If they give it – and there's no reason why they have to – then they will probably want another fee for it.

The cost of commissioning someone to originate artwork could be limitless, depending on who you use, but record companies don't usually want to pay more than about £1,500. The record company doesn't usually have any rights to use the artwork in any form of merchandise other than sales of the album, so they will only be interested in getting album cover rights. If you think you'll want it for other purposes you'll probably have to pay for those yourself.

Whether you commission the designer or the record company it is usually the record company that pays for and has rights to it – albeit only for limited activities. The cost is usually non-recoupable and the record company will usually give you the right to use the artwork for other purposes – if it has those rights – if you repay to the company 50% of the origination costs.

● The value that attaches to a distinctive artwork design was highlighted by the application for an injunction made by Creation Records (Oasis' record label) against the publishers of various newspapers, including the *Sun*, in 1997.[7]

7 *Creation Records Limited* v. *News Group Limited*, EMLR 444 1997 16.

Oasis were going to release another album in the autumn of 1997 and decided that the photograph for it should be taken at a country hotel. Noel Gallagher, the lead guitarist and deviser of the band's artwork, had a particular idea in mind, a kind of homage to The Beatles and their cover of *Sergeant Pepper*. The hotel swimming pool was drained and a number of different objects were delivered to the hotel, including a white Rolls Royce. This was lowered into the pool at an angle and Noel then supervised how the other objects were to be placed. A professional photographer took a number of photos from various angles so that the band had a choice of different images in different lights. Oasis thought it was essential that the plans for the photography were kept secret and only a few people were allowed in on the secret.

Inevitably word leaked out and a couple of newspaper photographers turned up including one freelancer from the *Sun*. He got some photos, one of which was published a few days later in the *Sun*. It was very similar to the one chosen for the album cover but had been shot from a different angle. The *Sun* offered copies of the photo for sale to readers in a poster form. Although other newspapers also published photos it seems none were very clear and none were offering posters of them for sale.

Creation got an immediate injunction restraining the *Sun* from publishing any more photos or from offering copies for sale. The judge then had to decide if that injunction should continue.

Creation Records were arguing that the freelance *Sun* photographer had infringed their copyright or had breached confidence.

The argument that the way the scene was put together attracted a copyright as a dramatic work was rejected by the judge. He also rejected the argument that the *scene* was a work of artistic craftsmanship, a sculpture or a collage. A film set could be said to be a work of artistic craftsmanship, but the judge decided that this was just an assembly of disparate objects without the necessary element of craftsmanship.

Creation and Oasis might have been thought to be on stronger ground in arguing that there was copyright in it as an artistic work of collage – being a collection of unrelated things. Their barrister argued that it should be put in the same category as the infamous Carl André bricks displayed at the Tate Gallery or Gilbert and George's living sculptures. The judge declined to follow that line of argument, as the assembly of objects didn't have the same degree of permanence – it was going to be dismantled after a few hours. This is a very restrictive view of what would be entitled to copyright protection.

The judge did find that there was copyright in the photograph but the *Sun* didn't copy that original – the freelancer took his own photograph of the same scene. Which was why Creation was trying to establish some kind of copyright in the scene.

So, having failed on all their ingenious copyright articles, Creation's barristers then argued that the freelance photographer had breached confidentiality. On this ground they had more luck. The judge did decide that any reasonable person would have assumed that in viewing the scene they were getting confidential information and so the freelance photographer was obliged not to photograph the scene. The *Sun* had admitted their photographer had to get around a security cordon to get the film out so they must have known it was intended to be confidential.

On balance the judge decided Oasis/Creation had more to lose if the *Sun* were to continue to be allowed to sell posters and continued the injunction on the basis of breach of confidence. If he hadn't, potentially huge sales of posters and other merchandise by the band and their label would have been lost.

Once your artwork is delivered you should then be in a position to press for a release date for the album. This will depend on a huge number of factors, which I'll deal with in the next chapter, but once a provisional date has been set then the manufacturing process can begin and the whole marketing department should swing into action.

CONCLUSIONS

- Choose your studios well. Decide if they'll be residential or not.
- Set a reasonable recording budget and stick to it.
- Get the best producer and mixer you can afford.
- Don't skimp on mastering costs but keep an eye on remix costs as these can get very high.
- Check you've complied with the delivery requirements in your contract.
- Try to get copyright ownership of the artwork.

6: MANUFACTURE, DISTRIBUTION AND MARKETING

INTRODUCTION

Until about two years ago there was no serious viable alternative to the tried and tested method of distribution. You finished your record, it was mastered and 'cut' (i.e. literally cut into the vinyl) or digitally mastered (i.e. put in digital form in a computer programme from which digital records such as CDs and DATS could be made). The only discussion or change here was digital versus analogue manufacturing methods. Once you had your physical CD, tape, vinyl record or whatever, you packaged it up and it was distributed to the record stores on the back of a van.

This traditional method still accounts for more than 95% of record sales. It is, however, predicted that in the next five years there will be substantial growth in online sales and online distribution. The 'clicks and mortar' versus the 'bricks and mortar' argument. I deal with these issues in a little more detail below but you'll also see some of the potential impact of this revolution in Chapter 7.

MANUFACTURING

First, let's deal with traditional forms of manufacture.

For at least the foreseeable future the compact disc is going to be around; cassette tape sales are declining but the prediction of the death of vinyl was premature. It survives (albeit in a niche market) beloved by DJs and specialist collectors. New physical formats are also breaking through such as the mini-disc. It was launched in the early 1990s but singularly failed to impress. But it refused to lie down. Gradually more product became available in this format; it was very portable, the sound quality is good and, significantly, the price of players fell below £150 for the first time in 1999, putting them on everyone's Christmas list.

Social commentators argue that people will always want the experience of going into retail stores, of handling the product, enjoying the social interaction – if you can count being jostled in a queue for ten minutes as enjoyable social interaction. Retail stores are not going to disappear but they may evolve. Their margins are very tight and, with their high-rent high street locations, they will feel the pressure of the Internet unless they evolve into more efficient places that people like to visit, where the experience is pleasant and where the customer can get what they want. There are already a number of stores that are now putting on trials of in-store machines where you can select your CD or series of tracks that are stored digitally on a central computer server. The customer's selection is downloaded, together with appropriate artwork, and 'burned' on to a CD. The artwork is printed off and the customer has their very own CD to take away. At the moment, single tracks can take up to 10 minutes to download. As the technology improves so this may become viable for whole albums. What this might lead to is that no record will ever go out of stock or be deleted; as it will be stored digitally and reproduced on demand, it won't take up valuable space in warehouses and can be available within minutes.

So, assuming that your record is going to be reproduced in a physical form, say as a CD, how do you go about this?

If you've paid for the recording yourself or via a production company then you won't have a record company to organise the manufacturing for you. You are going to have to go to specialist CD manufacturers and shop around for a deal. Lists of manufacturers can be found in the *Music Week Directory*. Before you decide on a manufacturer you would be well advised to gather together as much information on what's available as you can.

What service does each company provide? Is it a full-service company, which will produce a production master from which to reproduce the CDs, or will you have to find a company to make a production master for you and deliver that, together with film or discs for the artwork, to the manufacturer? If so, would it be cheaper, easier and quicker if you looked for a full-service company?

You will need to check the small print very carefully. What hidden costs are there? Do they charge you to deliver finished records to you?

What other services can they provide? Can they offer a distribution service or any marketing services like sales teams? If they do, is it better to use them for these services or to look for separate companies to provide them?

Look at the quality of their work. Ask to see samples. Do they do everything in-house or is it farmed out? Who else do they work for? If they've got a number of majors on their books, what kind or priority will you get? If Virgin come along with a new George Michael release will your record get pushed aside even if it is climbing up the charts and demand is rising?

Once you've narrowed down your choice you have to look at how quickly they can turn things around. They may have a minimum production run (say 5,000 copies). Is that all right for you or were you looking for a more modest 500 copies?

Once you've decided on your manufacturer you'll need to agree a price, the number of units to be produced and a time for delivery. You ought to try to keep some of their fee back until you see things are running according to plan – but if they are a small, unknown company they are likely to want cash upfront. Even so – keep an eye on things. Check the quality of the sound and of the artwork. Is the running order correct without any gaps in the songs? Have all the names been spelled correctly and correct credits given? If anything is wrong pull them up on it immediately. Don't wait until they've finished the run.

You also have to be sure that they can continue to manufacture repeat orders as your first batch, hopefully, sells out. You need to keep close contact between your distributor and your manufacturer so that you can put your repeat order in as soon as your distributor tells you that stocks are dwindling. This need for close co-operation is one of the reasons why some people prefer to keep production and distribution with the same company.

P&D DEALS

As you can probably guess, 'P' stands for production (i.e. manufacture) and 'D' for distribution. A P&D deal is one that combines both of these services in one contract with one company. Companies that offer P&D deals can often also offer marketing services, such as a telephone sales team (telesales) or a strike force (a specialised team targeting record stores to take your records). Whether you want to go for these additional services will depend on your overall marketing plan and on the price and reliability of the service.

You should ask the same questions of P&D companies as you would of a straight manufacturer.

In addition, you'll have to ask another series of questions about their distribution operation. Who do they supply records to? Is it just the small specialist stores or can they get into the major retail chain stores?

MAJORS VERSUS INDIES

Until recently, all the big five major record companies had their own distribution facilities. Mergers in the last couple of years have resulted in some of those facilities being combined. The remaining majors are also considering saving costs by pooling their operations. Without an efficient distribution system all your talents and efforts in making the record, and the marketing people's work in getting you noticed, will mean nothing if the distribution company doesn't have the records in the stores for the public to buy.

All distributors have to balance this efficiency with a speedy response. If they can't meet demand quickly then your records won't be available, the customers won't be able to buy them and you won't get your chart position. Missing a week in the charts can be fatal.

The majors tend to manufacture their records locally and then ship them to a centralised depot, usually somewhere in Europe, and from there to local distribution centres in different countries. It doesn't take much thought to see how savings could be made by pooling the local distribution centres.

In 1998 Sony and Warner merged their distribution interests in the UK in a newly modernised distribution centre in Aylesbury.

As well as dealing with their own artists' records, some of the majors act as separate distribution companies for other companies' records and other products, such as books and mobile phones. BMG has been very pro-active in this area.

The distributors also have to bear in mind the need to reduce costs of distribution of physical product, such as CDs, so as to be able to compete with online distribution. They will also need to have warehousing space to be able to handle the product that will be ordered online but still distributed in physical form.

Very small distribution companies are likely to either use specialist distributors or use the facilities of one of the majors. Other, bigger independent distribution companies, such as Pinnacle and Vital, are big enough to have their own warehousing and distribution set-ups. Contact details are in the section on Useful Addresses.

In the late 1990s it was thought to be a good marketing ploy for some 'credible' artists to be seen to be released on independently distributed labels. These distributors had their own chart and the artist could maintain the fiction that they hadn't sold out to the majors. As the music business continues to move away from indie to more commercial pop music, this need for an independent distributor may fade away.

If you aren't signed to a major, or you can't get a deal with a major distribution company, you may not have any chance but to go to the independent distributors. The independents may also decide to create strategic alliances within the independent sector to deal with the online threat and to help them maintain a reasonable profit margin.

You also need to be aware that some smaller distributors pass on the job of actual distribution to another company. You should ask if that's what your chosen distributor does and, if they do, you should try to find out how reliable and financially stable that other company is. As we'll see below, there are some things you can do to protect yourself by retaining ownership of the records until you've been paid.

CATALOGUE OR SINGLE ITEM DISTRIBUTION DEAL

You could do a deal for all the records you're likely to produce in the next year or so. These are called 'catalogue deals' and would be suitable for a small record label or production company. Maybe for a company that was going to license in rights to records by other artists. Catalogue deals can also be suitable for an artist who has decided that he doesn't want or need the facilities of a record company and wants to distribute his own recordings.

You could, however, just give distribution rights to a single track to a distribution company.[1] You might choose this route if you are just seeing this release as a stepping stone to getting a record company interested in you. Just bear in mind, though, that if the distributor is only dealing with one track for you, you won't have much bargaining power and will have to push hard to ensure that you get the priority you need.

EXCLUSIVE VERSUS NON-EXCLUSIVE

Catalogue distribution deals are likely to be exclusive but there may be one or two exceptions to the exclusivity. For example, you could have the right to put tracks on compilations to be distributed by another distributor or a major record company. Or you could have the right to distribute small quantities of the records yourself to one or two specialist outlets.

Non-exclusive distribution deals are less common but might be used if you wanted to use one specialised distributor to target certain specialised outlets but keep the right to also put your work with a more mainstream distributor.

TERM

This is really only relevant for exclusive catalogue deals.

1 Section 18 CDPA.

The distributor would deal with all your product over a period of time. This could be open-ended, continuing until one or other of you gives notice, usually three months at least. Or the term could be a fixed period of, say, one year, with the distributor having the option to extend the term for another year. Or the term could be for one year with further one-year extensions unless you give notice before the end of that time that you don't want it to carry on. You have to be careful with this one because, unless you're very good at remembering when to give notice, you might miss the relevant 'window' and find yourself locked in to another twelve months.

Obviously, a flexible term and agreement is important if you think you might want to move your label and catalogue to a bigger distributor or a major. It could also be very important if you aren't sure how good the distributor is. On the other hand, the distributor might have greater commitment to you, and be more inclined to give you priority, if they know you're going to be with them for a pre-determined minimum period of time.

TERRITORY

The distribution deal could be a worldwide one but is more likely to be for a limited number of countries, for example just for the UK or the UK and Europe. If you're a UK artist or label looking to distribute your records beyond Europe, for example to the US, then you're much more likely to do it through licensing the rights to another record company with their own distribution set-up (see Chapter 3). It is possible to have deals where you ship finished records to them and they distribute them, but this is less common.

There's a problem with distribution deals for just one country, for example the UK, which concerns imports or, more particularly, parallel imports.

What are these? Let's take an example. You have the rights to distribute a particular dance track in the UK. Another record company has the rights to distribute the record in France. If the record is released in France first, the French record company could export the records into the UK where they risk taking your market from under you. But that's not allowed I hear you say. They have only French distribution rights. Ah yes, that's right, but then there is the tricky principle of a common marketplace throughout the EU, which is meant to encourage the free movement of goods. So, within the EU, it's illegal for you to outlaw parallel imports. You can tell the UK distributor that they're not to actively try to get orders from outside the UK but it's very difficult to police it. How do you know who approached who?

It's easier, in theory, to prevent parallel imports coming in from outside the UK. For example, if you were giving one UK distributor European distribution rights and licensed the rights to a record company in the US for North America, your contract with the US record company could specify that they aren't to ship records outside North America. The problem is that there are specialised exporting companies that also act as genuine domestic distributors. The US record label could legitimately sell records to such a company and then deny any knowledge or responsibility if that company then exports the records to the UK.

This is why there is a lot of pressure to ensure that a record is released simultaneously in as many countries as possible or to ensure that there is something special about the release. For example, Japan, which suffers badly from cheap imports, often insists that its releases have extra 'bonus' tracks to make the records attractive to the domestic market.

There is also pressure on price levels within the EU. The idea is that if the dealer prices are the same throughout the EU there is less demand for imports brought in cheaper than the domestic product.

There are, of course, new issues facing distributors as a result of the growing market in buying records online. The Internet is a global marketplace and one of the main challenges is to try to find new ways of dealing with the fact that it is one big territory. Suppose you had a distribution deal with one company in the UK and another with a company in the US. Your licence deal with each would have to say either that it was open house on export sales and both could offer records for sale on their websites, for purchase anywhere in the world, or that territory is limited to the US/UK and they aren't to solicit offers or fulfil orders from each other's country. For example, your email address is UK registered and you go online to try to buy a CD that you know has been released in the US but isn't yet on sale in the UK. If you went to a US website to try to buy the CD it should come up as saying that they will not accept orders for distribution outside the US. While this can be frustrating, it is one way of dealing with the territorial issue. Obviously, if you had done a worldwide distribution deal with one company then that would not be necessary.

Downloads off the Internet are another challenge to traditional distribution deals. If you store a recording in digital form on the Internet there is no need for you to have large warehouses; the recording is made available to the consumer in the form of a computer file on demand. If there weren't a worldwide distribution deal in place then the same restrictions would have to be in place to stop a company accepting orders from customers outside its territory. Record companies and music publishers are now investing large amounts into systems called rights management systems that will police where a file is being downloaded to ensure that payment is being made and which would also enable them to track whether a distributor was breaking the terms of their distribution licence (see Chapter 7).

RIGHTS GRANTED

If you're doing a P&D deal you'll be required to give the distributor the right to reproduce the sound recording[2] and the right to distribute and sell those copies.[3]

PRICE

The distributor will take a fee off the top of the price it gets paid. So, for example, if the distributor gets paid £7.49 for each record sold, they take a percentage of that for their fee.

The percentage can vary a great deal depending on how many additional services they provide, such as a telesales service or a strike force dedicated to pushing your records. It can be as high as 28–30% of the dealer price if you are unknown or only have one track to push. The best deals for you would be 15–18%, which would be when you are a successful

2 Section 17 CDPA.
3 Section 18 CDPA.

independent company with a high turnover of successful product. Sometimes the percentage the distributor takes can go down as your turnover increases. An average amount for a distributor to deduct would be 20–23%.

The distributor will also usually have a discount policy. This is a sliding scale of discounts on the dealer price that have to be given to the various retail outlets. For example, major national chains like Woolworths or Virgin Megastores would be able to command a discount on the price because they order in bulk and generally pay on time.

In early 2000 the Virgin boss, Sir Richard Branson, got into a heated dispute with the major record companies by refusing to pay them on the Christmas sales through his stores. His argument was that he was trying to force a debate and a resolution of the issue of online discounts. Sir Richard thought that the record companies were undercutting the traditional bricks and mortar stores with their online pricing. This was a relatively early stage in the debate to take such a firm line as even the best statistics suggest only 5% of records are purchased online at the moment. But it is a measure of the concern that the traditional retailers feel over the growth of online sales.

PAYMENT TERMS

The distributor will often pay half of what you're due within 30 days of receiving the payment and the balance within 60 days. So if they got paid for a record sold on 28 February 2000 you'd get half your money by the end of March and the rest by the end of April.

The distributor will probably keep back some of the money as reserve against records that are returned. They usually have a fixed policy on this but sometimes will negotiate the level of reserves with you. The reserve on singles is generally higher than for albums unless the album has been advertised on television. Retail stores may take 100 copies of your record but on a sale-or-return basis. So although the distributors have sent out 100 copies they don't know how many have actually been sold and will not include these copies as sales until they have been paid.

The distributor will not generally take responsibility for bad debts. They won't usually pay you before they get paid. Some will but that can lead to big problems. For example, you do a P&D deal with a local distributor and they agree to pay you on the number of records they actually send out, less a reserve against returns. They ship out 1,000 copies of your record to the stores and pay you on 750 copies, keeping back a 25% reserve. Months later the stores return not 250 but 500 copies; they are then out of pocket by 250 copies. Even worse for you is a case where you do a deal with a local distributor and they pay you on what they get paid on. They then do a deal with a bigger distribution company and ship your records to that bigger company. The bigger company sells your record but for whatever reason fails to pay the local distributor who then can't pay you. Your records have been sold but you can't get paid.

RETENTION OF TITLE

A way of protecting yourself when you are in a chain of deals like this is to retain your title (your ownership) of the records until you've been paid. Retention of title documents do have to be very carefully drafted in order to have a chance of working. Assuming the end company has gone bust, the liquidators of the company will want to hold on to whatever stocks (i.e. your records) that they can. They will want to sell them to raise money for the creditors of the company so they'd like to get around your retention of title if they can legitimately do so. So get specialised legal advice on this.

ADVANCES

Before I leave this section I just want to touch on the question of advances. Will a distributor give you an advance? Yes, he might if you've got a good track record for finding hit records or have a catalogue that has a regular turnover. The advances for small independent labels or individual artists are not likely to be high – possibly only a few thousand pounds, although I have seen advances of £20,000-plus for suitable catalogues. As with most advances, they aren't usually returnable if you don't sell enough records for them to recoup their advance.

THE FUTURE OF DISTRIBUTION

We've already seen the greater pooling of resources between major record companies. The mergers of the major record companies themselves are a sign of fundamental changes in the way music will be distributed. AOL and Time Warner are seeking to combine AOL's customers and Time Warner's content and cable companies and Warner is presently seeking clearance to merge their music interests with those of EMI to acquire yet more content. There is talk of BMG being in talks with Sony on combining their music interests. MCA and Polygram have already merged and re-emerged as Universal owned by Seagram. All major companies are working out online strategies and making strategic alliances with telecommunication and technology companies. All this is because they think they need to be in the best position to ward off the challenges of the Internet and also to enable them to be in the best position to take advantage of the benefits in cost savings that online distribution can bring.

It's all very well the statisticians and pundits telling us that 95% of record sales will still be of physical copies in the next five to eight years. The fact is that if even a small percentage of sales is online, that can affect the profit margins of the bricks and mortar retailers. If these are mail order online sales, warehouses will still be required but the levelling down of prices online will pinch profit margins still further. If sales are no longer of physical product but actual online distribution then pressing and manufacturing plants will suffer, and we'll also have to deal with the problems of piracy that come with online distribution.

MARKETING

You're making progress. Now you've got a record, it's been mastered and copies manufactured and you've found a company to distribute it.

The next crucial step is to let the public know about you and your record. This marketing process has many elements to it and in fact it is an ongoing process. As soon as you've got something to sell – a record, live performance, merchandising, yourselves – you need to let people know about it. In the online world this is often referred to as 'getting yourself heard above the noise'.

ARTWORK

Getting the right artwork for the record is crucial – it could form part of the whole campaign. It could be used as the backdrop to a poster campaign and be put on T-shirts and other merchandise (see Chapter 8).

PHOTOGRAPHS AND BIOGRAPHIES

The artwork may be a photograph of the band or other graphic designs. In any event you're going to need to have some decent photographs. They'll be needed for information packs, for the press, for letting overseas licensees or associated companies abroad know what you look like. Get the best photographer you can afford or your record company will pay for. The costs the record company pays aren't usually recoupable or repayable by you unless you want to use the photographs for merchandising, when they may expect you to repay half the costs.

The record contract will usually give you approval over the photographs that are used. It will also usually give you approval of the official biography that they put together on you. This is a bit like your life history – how your life so far is presented to the outside world. If you're sensitive about any part of your past, or of giving your true age, it'll be useful to have approval.

If you give the record company photographs or biographical details they'll assume you've approved them, so make sure you're happy with them.

IN-HOUSE OR EXTERNAL MARKETING

Bigger record companies will mostly have in-house marketing and press departments. These are staffed by dedicated marketing and press people, one or more of who will be allocated to marketing you. You need to be happy that these people understand the gameplan and, preferably, that they love your music. At the very least they should like it because otherwise they won't sound convincing when they try to sell you to the press, radio, TV and so on.

If your marketing is to be done in-house it will normally be paid for by the record company on a non-recoupable basis.

The position changes if you're with a smaller company without their own in-house marketing departments or when you just can't get on with the in-house people and insist on using outside specialists. These costs are usually partly or wholly recoupable from your record income.

Whether it's being done in-house or with a number of outside specialists, the whole campaign has to be co-ordinated.

The sales force and any special strike force have to be primed with artwork, photographs, biographies and campaign details. Promotion packs have to be sent out to any exporters, to clubs, DJs and to some retail outlets.

The fact that your record is being released has to be notified to the music press, the chart compilers and MCPS/PRS to get the relevant mechanical licence and details registered for the public performances. Each release has to have its own catalogue number. One label I acted for, called Produce Records, had a successful act called The Farm and their catalogue identity was MILK 1, 2, 3, etc.

Each release also has to have a barcode to enable it to be scanned through checkouts in the stores.

If you're going to do special promotional items, these have to be designed and put out for manufacture well in advance. There have been some very innovative and plain cute gimmicks produced. For example, EMI handed out lemon-shaped squeezy toys to promote a single by Pocket Size called 'Squashy Lemon Squeezy'. One sits on my desk and is a great stress release toy.

If there's to be an advertising campaign, the adverts will have to be designed and approved well in advance so that they are ready for distribution at the same time as the promotional packs, posters, promotional items and so on.

The strike or sales force goes into action several weeks before the release date, trying to get orders from the retail shops. These are called the 'pre-sales'. Everyone is interested in getting these figures as they are a good indicator of how well a particular record is being received. It will help determine the chart position, it tells the marketing people how much more work they have to do and pre-sales can give you some information to pass on to your manufacturer and distributor to help them assess how many more copies will be needed. Also in what areas of the country it's selling best, as the distributor may need to make more copies available in those areas. The aim is to get the campaign to run as a seamless whole.

You'll be needed to do interviews until you're bored of the sound of your own voice. Your press people should be setting up reviews of your records and any live dates that you're doing to promote the record. You may be doing personal appearances and may be performing a couple of numbers either live or mimed to a backing track.

TV ADVERTISING

Part of the marketing campaign might be to advertise your records on television. This is an expensive business. A basic television campaign in four ITV regions can easily cost between £60,000 and £100,000. The record company is only going to want to spend this money if they think they will earn it back in extra record sales. To keep their risk to a minimum, the record company will try to recoup some or all of these costs, either as a further advance or by reducing the royalty payable to you. How this works is that the record company reduces by 50% the royalty they would otherwise have had to pay you on sales of your records until they have recouped 50% or more of the costs of the TV ad campaign.

We lawyers try to get you the right of approval over whether an advert is made but we have to fight for this as record companies know if you get the right of approval you will only give your approval if you get a better deal on recoupment, which means that they don't recoup so much of the cost. If we can't get you approval we try to limit the ways in which your income is affected, either by restricting the reduction to sales in the country where the campaign is run or limiting the time over which they can recoup the costs from reduced royalties, or both.

Don't rule out the idea of a television campaign without carefully looking at the proposals. A good, targeted campaign could be what it takes to lift your record into the Top 20 albums chart, which could make all the difference to you being a megastar or just an artist who once had a record out.

TV & RADIO PLUGGERS

It's absolutely crucial to the success of a record that it gets exposure on radio and TV. Unless your records get decent radio plays, they are unlikely to go into the charts. A Top 20 chart position can get your record on to programmes like the *Pepsi Chart Show* and included on multi-artist compilations.

The problem is that the people who decide on what's played on Radio 1, Capital Radio, Heart FM and so on are becoming more conservative; fewer records are being chosen for the playlists (the lists of records the DJs are required to play). They tend towards the commercial pop end of the market and even artists of 27 years of age are thought to be too old!

The TV and radio pluggers could be employed in-house by the record company but can often be outside agencies that specialise in this work.

WHAT DO YOU PAY EXTERNAL MARKETING AND PRESS PEOPLE?

There are many different ways of paying for external marketing and press work. Remember, if you aren't using in-house people, some or all of these costs will be down to you one way or another.

Retainers

Press people are often on retainers. These are regular, monthly payments which are made to keep them as your press agent, constantly having an eye to press opportunities for you. When you aren't actively doing any promotion, for instance when you're in the studio recording the next album, the level of retainer could be quite small. It would then increase when press/promotion activities rise around the time of release of the record.

Bonuses

If someone is on a retainer or a fixed fee, they may be paid a bonus for achieving certain targets. For example, a press officer could get paid a bonus for every front page/cover he gets that features you.

A plugger might get a bonus if your record goes into the Top 30, 20, 10 or whatever.

Fixed Fees

Marketing and press people could be on a fixed fee, possibly with bonuses linked to success.

Royalties
Press and pluggers could be on a retainer or a fixed fee with bonuses or possibly the incentive of a small royalty (0.5–1%) on each record sold. Good pluggers, and those in great demand (usually the same ones), can insist on 'points', i.e. a royalty. If you want the best, you may have to pay this. It will either come out of your artist's royalty or be paid by the record company or a bit of both.

WHERE DO YOU FIND THEM?
The usual ways – word of mouth, those companies already on a retainer arrangement with your record company, those companies known to your manager as doing a good job in this area of music. The *Music Week Directory* carries a list of press and promotions companies but it would be a good idea to get a recommendation from someone in the business before you choose one.

DO THEY WANT A CONTRACT?
If they're on a fixed fee they'll probably just invoice you for the fee when the work is done. If you've agreed they'll undertake something out of the ordinary, or you're putting them on a retainer, you'll probably want a simple contract. If they're being paid a royalty then you'll definitely need a contract setting out how that royalty will be calculated and when it will be paid. The simplest thing is to do this on the same basis as you get your royalties under your record deal.

VIDEOGRAMS

Promotional videograms are an essential part of the marketing process. A good video can get your record played on TV music stations such as MTV, which is all-powerful. There are also Breakfast TV and Saturday morning TV programmes that look to play videos as well as all the cable and satellite channels.

However, videos are very expensive to make and there's no point in making one if your record doesn't get radio plays or TV airtime. It'll be a waste of money. The video has to fit in with the overall marketing plan. You'll end up paying some or all of the costs so be careful you don't overspend or make a video unnecessarily.

The creative elements such as what the story is going to be (the storyboard), who's going to produce and direct it and when and where it's to be shot will probably be agreed between you and your record company. Depending on your contract, you may have a final say on some of these things and the record company on others.

RIGHTS
The record company will usually expect to own all rights in any audio-visual recordings of your performances.

If you have a lot of bargaining power you can limit the rights you give them to audio-visual rights on recordings you make for them under the record deal. Most major record companies won't give you this as they want to know that any recordings of your live set cannot be put out as a competing record or video. You might have to agree that you won't do that with any recordings of your performances without their approval.

LONG-FORM VIDEO

This might be a compilation of your best promotional videos or it might be a specially made 30-minutes-plus video, maybe of you out on the road touring, or live performances inter-cut with interviews and so on.

The record company may have the exclusive right to do this or they may have the first option to bid for the right to make one or the right to match an offer that someone else may have made to make one.

The cost of making a long-form video is usually mutually agreed between you and the record company and a separate account is set up. You usually get to dictate, or at least approve, all the creative aspects of the long-form video.

The royalty rate will be similar or slightly higher than that for promotional videos. There may be an advance payable for the long-form or the record company may have had to match any offer made by a third party. The advance and the costs should only be recoupable from the royalties on this long-form video. Income from records or any commercial use of promotional videos should not be used to recoup these costs.

DVDs

This is the latest development. Digital Versatile Discs. As the name suggests, these are physical discs that contain not only music but also many other elements – visuals, interviews, video games and a whole lot more. The possibilities are endless. The danger is that quality suffers when the pressure is on to put as many elements as possible on to these discs. However, after having a difficult time getting off the ground, Christmas 1999 saw players finally gain ground in the home entertainment market. Indeed, some statistics suggest that DVD is gaining market share at a faster rate than compact discs did when they were first marketed in the 1980s. The search is now on for good content. I also think demand will rise in the next year or so as the new generation of video game consoles, such as Sony PlayStation 2, are also equipped with DVD players.[4]

EPQs

This is the name given to electronic press packages. That is, pre-recorded interviews, photos and biographies together with promotional clips of your latest single release that are put together by your in-house or external press officer. These take the form of videotapes at the

4 As a measure of how the manufacturers realise they now have to take a global view of their business, they recently formed the International Optical Disc Replicators Association (IODRA). The IODRA has a number of the leading manufacturers among its membership and seems intent on acting as a forum for debate on issues that are of concern internationally, such as piracy (see Chapter 14).

moment (though CD Roms and DVDs are starting to be seen) and they are sent out to reviewers, press reporters, DJs, radio station controllers and so on as an additional means to promote you. Most new record contracts contain a clause that says that the record company can put one of these together and that you'll co-operate with them. In future it is likely that these will take the form of online computer files that are emailed around. There seems to be no reason why you wouldn't want to agree to the compiling of an EPQ but you might want some creative control and you will need to agree whether some or all of the costs can be recouped.

CONCLUSIONS

- Decide on whether you need separate manufacturing and distribution deals.
- Check the returns and discounts policies of your distributor.
- Try to retain ownership of your records until you've been paid.
- Get your marketing campaign organised well in advance.
- Agree whether your press and plugging is to be done in-house or by outside agencies.
- If outsiders are doing it, try to get the record company to agree that only 50% of the cost is recoupable.
- Get approval of any photos and biographies.
- Get approval, if you can, of any television advertising campaigns for your records, particularly if your royalty will be reduced.

7: **NEW MEDIA / E-COMMERCE**

INTRODUCTION

There is only one certainty in this area of the business: by the time you read this, much will have changed. The whole area is developing so quickly that it's difficult to keep up. But keep up we must, as this is a phenomenon that is not going to go away. When I started writing this chapter, AOL and Time Warner had announced their merger. By the time I was halfway through it the news had broken of the proposed merger of EMI and Warner Music, thus ushering in probably yet another period of uncertainty in the music business.

This whole area of exploiting rights online and e-commerce is a rapidly changing and expanding new market place. It opens up a number of new distribution and marketing opportunities for artists and labels. It also opens up the whole issue of whether content is truly king, as some say, or if it's a case of creativity being sold short or devalued by the telecommunications industry, whose main business is not music or film.

As well as providing a number of potential new sources of income it may bring potentially far-reaching changes to society, to how we view the music industry, to the retail experience. It's also giving us lawyers a number of legal issues to sort out. Some of these I'll deal with below. For those of us who've spent years dealing with essentially the same legal/intellectual property issues, this is a great new challenge. There are only so many 86-page record contracts you can look at without going seriously insane. Many people are wary of the Internet or say that its influences are overstated. I think the Internet should be viewed as an opportunity, not a threat. It may or may not revolutionise the music business but at the very least it will shake up our ideas and give us another outlet for the music.

REPRODUCTION AND DISTRIBUTION

Let's look first at how the Internet has brought us new ways to reproduce and distribute music. As we saw in Chapters 5 and 6, until very recently the only way of doing things was to make recordings of an artist's performances (now mostly in digital form) which were then mastered and distributed as physical copies, tapes, CDs and so on. Indeed, only a few years ago, the last threat to the music business was seen to be video games. Then the music business embraced that and started producing music for these games. We were then still dealing with a physical form of distribution. The phenomenal growth of the Internet, as a source of information on artists and as a means of making music available in downloadable form, has led to us thinking more and more that non-physical means are the way forward, that the traditional forms of tape or CD will be replaced by computer programmes and downloading of computer files containing music. Maybe the true revolution will only come when that music is available through our home entertainment systems in our living rooms through the remote control. This is still some way away; the traditional record label isn't dead yet, but it's going to have to evolve rapidly in order to keep up with these changes.

New forms of reproduction are already with us. The process of digitising sound recordings and then compressing them using technologies, such as those associated with the MP3 format,[1] makes it possible to distribute a near-CD-quality digital sound recording online. Depending on the equipment, it takes about ten to fifteen minutes to download a single track on to your PC. It still takes an unacceptably long time to download an album, 45–60 minutes on average, but as compression technology[2] and bandwidth[3] improve so the quality will also improve and the download time will shorten considerably. At the moment no one wants to tie up a computer and, more importantly, an expensive telephone line for the time it takes to download a whole album. It still isn't a friendly consumer experience and until it is quick, user-friendly and reasonably priced it won't take off commercially. For the time being, therefore, it remains a reasonably small market. As telephone charges are cut[4] and technology improves to the extent that an album can be downloaded in, say, ten minutes, the market for this material is going to explode (assuming the price is right). Companies such as BT and Telia (a Swedish company) are putting in a lot of time and resources into improving bandwidth through your phone lines (in the case of BT) and through the technique of 'streaming' a broadcast of an artist's performance (in the case of Telia). There are, of course, many other telecommunications and IT companies throughout the world working on this problem too. The greater the bandwidth that can be made available, the better the quality is likely to be and the less time it will take for things to download on to your computer. At the moment it is the cable companies that are delivering a large part of the available bandwidth because normal (or even the currently available high-speed) phone lines can't do the job – yet. The time is rapidly approaching when they can.

A new form of distribution is also already with us. Once the computer file containing the music is on your hard drive, you can use MP3 players, such as the Diamond Audio Rio or the new RIOport 500, to download music on to the player. Already available are portable devices, such as Sony's Memory Stick, which allow you to transfer your downloaded music to a portable player, office or in-car audio system. Once music becomes truly portable, and these devices drop to a realistic price, consumers are likely to go for them in the same way as they did with the Walkman, the CD Walkman and, more recently, the mini-disc.

There is a lot of music available now for digital download, but this is mostly not from big-name artists. The number of famous artists making their music available online is small but growing. Sony has started to embrace this form of distribution. There are, understandably, concerns about making available online a new album from a successful artist, as piracy is rife and it's not possible to make much money from it at the moment. I think that will change and consumers will start downloading music in large enough numbers to make it commercial. At the moment, however, it's still largely seen as an extra way to promote an artist. Gradually we are seeing record companies doing deals with companies to digitise their

1 MP3 = MPEG 1 layer 3 compression technology.
2 MP4 is already with us and telecommunications companies are busy developing other compression formats.
3 Bandwidth is the 'pipe' down which the digital signals are sent to PCs.
4 British Telecom now has 'all-in' packages where, for a monthly subscription, customers can have unlimited Internet access.

back catalogue and to make this available online. As this happens, so the number of downloads is likely to increase and eventually reach a critical mass that will make this a commercially viable new platform for music. Before that can happen, though, we'll also have to get the piracy issue sorted and the means of proper accounting established, as well as proper payment to the artist.

Companies are also looking at different ways of making music available as downloads. There are some that do 'timed' downloads, i.e. ones that can only be played once or for a short time – say 30 days – before they become inaccessible unless you pay an additional fee. These are often used as promotional 'tasters': you listen to extracts from an artist's new album for a limited period of time and, if you like the sound of it, you can then purchase the whole album for a further fee. The album will then either be sent to you in the form of a computer file or as a physical CD by mail.

As I said earlier, as I sat down to write this chapter Time Warner announced its merger with America Online (AOL). Why was this such a revolutionary, and yet at the same time obvious, move? Time Warner has the content through its various music, film and TV companies and bandwidth through the cable companies it owns. AOL brings to the deal its vast customer base and access to enormous numbers of potential purchasers of this content with a brand name that has consumer trust and loyalty. When it was announced, some analysts started talking about this being the deal that finally burst the over-inflated bubble of Internet stock prices. Warner Music announced almost immediately that it intended to merge with EMI. Indeed, in February/March 2000 there was a 'reassessment' in stockmarket terms of the value of Internet companies, and stocks of new technology companies did plummet in value. Many have since recovered their price.

One of the main concerns we have about the availability of music online is that of piracy. You can attach an MP3 file containing music to the email facility of your PC. This means it can be sent to everyone in your email address book. It's also possible to 'rip' a track off a CD using readily available software. The digital form of the track can then be uploaded on to a computer. Once it's on there it can be downloaded as an MP3 file and sent by email to hundreds if not thousands of other people. Even a brief search of the Internet right now will turn up thousands of MP3 websites, many of which are illegal or pirate sites. The record companies had the option of trying to stop these websites, or of trying to ensure the use of music is properly policed and payment is made. The music business will have to try to replace the money obtained from the sale of the physical CD with the equivalent for online delivery of the same music. You can argue over the semantics of whether or not this activity is a mechanical reproduction but this remains the underlying issue.

- The Recording Industry Association of America (RIAA), which represents many US record companies, took action to try to stop online piracy. RIAA was concerned at the proliferation of unauthorised MP3 files containing unlawful copies of music and brought an action in the US against Diamond Audio[5] seeking an injunction to prevent sales of the portable Rio MP3 player.

5 *Recording Industry Association of America Inc.* v. *Diamond Multimedia Systems Inc.* 1999 (unreported).

RIAA lost the case on appeal. The International Federation for the Protection of Intellectual Property (see Chapter 15) began a similar action in the UK but abandoned it after failing to get an injunction preventing the MP3 players from being imported.

By July 1999 RIAA was saying that they had decided that it wasn't practically possible to shut down all the pirates and that instead they were going to concentrate on getting security devices implanted in the music files to prevent illegal copying and to make the pricing structure for getting music online right. The US is more advanced than we are in having laws in place to cover this area. The 1998 US Digital Millennium Copyright Act makes it unlawful to seek to circumvent any such security or rights management systems. This particular part of the Act actually comes into force in October 2000. RIAA believe that these measures, coupled with the availability of quality music by big name artists, would mean that consumers would go to the legitimate sites for their music, not to the pirates. Let's hope they're right because otherwise a whole generation of computer users is going to get used to the idea of not paying for music.

- In January 2000, RIAA brought an action in the US against MP3.com.

  MP3.com is making available consumer choice compilations, which they send to the customer in a physical form (i.e. a CD). The consumer selects their own favourites from the catalogue on offer. As an added service to the customers, they have apparently been keeping a copy of the customer's compilation online so that the customer can also listen to it on their PC and presumably also download it on to a portable player. RIAA argued that this breaches the terms of MP3.com's licence to reproduce this music. In May 2000 a US federal judge ruled that this *was* a breach of copyright because MP3.com didn't own the music and hadn't got permission from the owners. MP3.com said it would appeal, but shortly afterwards announced that it had reached an accord with BMI (a collecting society for publishers and songwriters in the US) to use the huge catalogue of songs it controls. MP3.com seems to be coming in to the legitimate arena.

- The RIAA case against Diamond Audio can be compared with a court action brought in the UK in 1988 by CBS against Amstrad.[6]

  CBS tried to prevent Amstrad from selling machines that allowed tape-to-tape recording on the basis that this would encourage consumers to make multiple copies of a recording and thereby deprive the artist/record company/music publisher of income. The case went to the House of Lords. It was rejected on the ground that there was no liability on a manufacturer of a device which was capable of being used for unlawful purposes if the device was also capable of being used lawfully and where the manufacturer neither had control over the use of the device after sale nor was actively encouraging unlawful use. Because Amstrad didn't market the machine as allowing you to make illegal copies, and because it was lawful to make a copy for your own personal use, Amstrad were allowed to continue selling the machines.

6 *CBS Songs* v. *Amstrad Consumer Electronics* [1988] 2 All ER 484.

LAWFUL VERSUS UNLAWFUL WEBSITES

As well as the many pirate MP3 websites on the Internet there are also many legal MP3 files up there. The copyright owners of the music may want the material to be available free of charge. They may be using the website as a promotional tool, as a means of bringing a new artist to your attention.

- In an attempt to try to control the content of a website, a court in Germany brought a criminal case against the general manager of CompuServe in Germany for unlawfully allowing pornographic material to be available on a website hosted by CompuServe.[7] He was convicted in May 1998 on the basis that, as controller of the Internet service provider (ISP), he was responsible for the content of the websites using that ISP. Naturally, this was of concern to those people who ran ISPs, who were now afraid that they might be laying themselves open to a criminal charge. They said that it was impossible to monitor the content of all the websites on their ISP. In practice what they will usually agree to do is to close down a website if a lawyer or a court has told them officially that the site they are hosting contains pornographic or other unlawful material – including illegal MP3s. In late 1999 the Appeal Court overturned Mr Somm's conviction and so we will have to wait until there is a clearer line from the EU on this issue.

RIAA brought another legal action against a company called Napster, claiming that Napster aids large-scale copyright infringement by making it easy to share unlicensed music. Napster was set up by a young musician, Shaun Fanning. He developed software that enabled users to find other computers with MP3 files, link them directly to one another, and share music files with one another without paying the copyright owners. The software was made available free from the Napster website, which also supplies a directory of available songs, making searching easy. RIAA's action was followed by several more from artists such as Metallica and Dr. Dre. Napster filed a defence that it could not be held liable for any illegal material sent over its server (a so-called 'safe harbour'). In May 2000 a federal judge in California ruled that this defence was not available. The case continues.

IF YOU CAN'T BEAT THEM, JOIN THEM

As I mentioned earlier, most record companies have decided that it's a futile exercise to try to police all the websites on the Internet or to try to stop these illegal uses entirely. The focus has shifted to rights management and protection systems.

SDMI

Record companies, in partnership with IT companies, are now looking at ways to try to control the use of music online by introducing various security measures. The record

7 *Bavaria* v. *Somm* 1998 (unreported).

companies appear to have accepted that they can't do much about CDs that are already in existence. These 'legacy CDs' as they call them are already out there and there isn't much that can be done to prevent unlawful copying. This isn't to suggest that the record companies have given up the whole battle against piracy. There is still a huge fight going on to prevent illegal, pirate copies of tapes and CDs largely being made in countries such as China and the Far East where they don't subscribe to the accepted principles of protection of copyright and performer's rights. However, on the question of Internet/MP3-type files, they've got together with a number of commercial partners from the communications and technology sectors to develop an open standard to rival the MP3 that will be incorporated into players and into digital music files. This is known as the Secure Digital Music Initiative (SDMI), which was launched by the IFPI in December 1998 and thus presented their first approved standard in 1999. This standard is initially for portable players but is meant to be adaptable to all types of players. Players that incorporate the SDMI portable standard are supposed to reach the market in the US in the spring of 2000 although the record industry doesn't think that it will have online music content incorporating the standard available before the summer of 2000.

The SDMI standard works on the basis that the players contain encryption technologies that will enable them to recognise and only play legitimate computer files. A technique called watermarking[8] will enable the tracking of legal files. There is already in existence a system of permanent and temporary passwords on computer files, which will allow only one copy to be made of a file and played on a legitimate MP3-type player. This then destroys the temporary password. If you then try to copy it again, the copy won't play because the player can only find one of the required two passwords. The permanent password is the means by which the systems track that it's a legitimate copy. It is of course always possible to find ways around these protections. Software already exists to circumvent many of the password technologies. The law makers are aware of this and both the Millennium Copyright Act in the US and the proposed EU Directive on Copyright and Related Rights in the Information Society make it illegal to seek to circumvent these rights management or protection systems. The Directive is one of a series of laws that are being enacted to clarify the legal position on copyright and performers' rights in the information/e-commerce society and to seek to make digital/online commerce as secure as possible without stifling trade and creativity.[9]

These are, of course, global rather than territorial issues. There would be no point in the EU or the UK bringing in a law on digital reproduction if you could get around it by making illegal material available on an ISP based in the US. The solution has to be an international one.

8 Watermarking is essentially a system whereby a file is marked (in the same way as bank notes have a watermark to show they are legitimate), which enables them to be recognised as a legal copy and to trace the copy back to its source.

9 Other initiatives include the EU Directive on certain legal aspects of Electronic Commerce in the Internal Market; the proposed Digital Signatures Directive and the UK's own Electronic Communications Bill published in July 1999. The last two seek to make commercial transactions online more secure through the use of digital signatures or other encryption techniques. The EU Copyright Directive also proposes implementing the 1996 Berne Protocol to the WIPO treaty, which is an attempt to bring the laws on copyright into the digital era internationally.

EUROPEAN INITIATIVES

It's also vital that laws are in place that can be applied to the digital era. In order to clarify the copyright situation the EU Directive on Copyright in the Information Society, which has just been adopted and must be brought into force in EU member states, will confirm that the right to prevent a work being reproduced without permission will extend to non-physical means (i.e. online). The distribution right and the right to prevent communication of a copyright work to the public will also be extended to online distribution or communication.

The music business was particularly concerned that the new laws allowed a copyright owner to prevent reproduction of a work by means of temporary copies. For example, if someone turns on a computer and logs on to a website containing music, they may choose not to actually download any music tracks to listen to later but just listen to a live concert by a favourite artist (a webcast). Even so, they are reproducing that work, if only while they are logged on to that website. Copyright owners were concerned that this would undermine their rights completely, unless temporary copies were forbidden without the consent of the copyright owner. What *is* to be allowed is the right to make 'ephemeral copies' such as those that are created when an email message is transferred from one ISP via another to the end recipient. The implementation of this directive into UK law will make it much more certain whether or not a copyright infringement is taking place as a lot of the grey area will have been removed.

THE FUTURE

No-one in the music business can afford to ignore the Internet. It is possible to decide that it's not for you right now but the ostrich mentality of ignoring the whole area of Internet/ e-commerce will only work in the short term. Companies will have to decide sooner rather than later whether to go the whole way and permit full download of music ('clicks and mortar') or just to allow the consumer to preview the music online before buying it via mail order or through the 'bricks and mortar' traditional retail store.

The Jupiter Communications Plug-In Conference in July 1999 predicted that for the next five years 95% of sales would still be of physical copies of records. Some analysts believe that this is too conservative and that online distribution will become much more significant much earlier than that. The five-year projection seems to be based on how long it took for CDs to establish themselves as the dominant carrier. If that is the case then when you look at the exponential growth of online commerce you can see why some believe it will happen much sooner.

However, you can understand why the record companies don't yet want to alienate their traditional commercial partners – the retail stores. HMV made the headlines in September 1999 by declaring that it would refuse to stock new material and back catalogues of any artist whose work is first made available online. This was a perhaps understandable reaction to the decision by David Bowie to make his new album available not only as a downloadable file online but also exclusively available to online mail order customers two weeks before it was physically available in the retail stores.

Of course, an artist with an established 'brand' name such as David Bowie is always going to attract attention and publicity when they do something like this. For the less well-known artist there is still a question of how he gets his material heard above the 'noise'. The record companies believe that they will have a valuable role to play with their traditional marketing skills. They claim that the majority of their investment in a new artist is in marketing and that the Internet and online distribution will not change that.

Record companies are gradually embracing the idea of downloading tracks or albums wholesale. Some of the major record companies are hedging their bets by investing in companies that make the systems which enable music to be made available online in downloadable form. Many are experimenting with such things as temporary or 'timed out' downloads.

Also proving popular, at least in the short term, are 'custom CDs'. The customer decides from a catalogue of available recordings which ones they want on their CD. These are then burned on to a CD and dispatched to their home. Some companies, such as MP3.com, see this as an important market; others, such as Emusic.com, have announced that they are getting out of that market and concentrating on downloads.

Buying CDs over the Internet through user-friendly companies such as Amazon is seen as an extension of traditional mail order. The CD is sent within a day or two of the order being placed online. The advantage of this method of shopping is that it is often cheaper than the retail store even after allowing for post and packaging. One of the consequences of the global nature of online shopping may be the levelling out of prices in all major markets. One potential downside is that this may lead to all these CDs being manufactured in the country where the ISP is located, for example the US, as opposed to in the local area if it were bought in a local record company store. Some companies, such as Globalfullfillment.com, say they hope to avoid this by trying to source the physical CDs locally wherever they can.

Online shopping is interesting in that in so many ways it is mirroring the 'bricks and mortar' equivalents. Companies such as Yahoo! and AOL, whose business it is to group (or aggregate) companies together through website links, are apparently charging companies such as Amazon significant amounts in 'rent' each year to buy a prominent space in their online shopping malls.

The retail stores are fighting back. They argue that the customer will still want the social experience of meeting friends in a shopping centre and buying records in a record store. To counteract the commercial challenges of the Internet, retail stores are experimenting with providing booths in stores where the customer can select their favourite music from a database. Their personal selection is then burned on to a CD and made available to them as a physical copy in 10–12 minutes. That time will get shorter as technology improves. Artwork for the CD can also be printed off on the spot and the customer goes away with their own compilation CD in a proper case. The advantage to the retail record store is that they no longer have to stock an artist's entire catalogue on site or in their expensive warehouse facilities. As the music is stored digitally it can be reproduced as many times as you want from a computer file on demand.

THE WAY FORWARD FOR ARTISTS AND LABELS

What does this all mean to you, the artist, and to smaller record labels? For unsigned artists it will provide a new way to get your music to the public with low upfront costs. A website can be set up for a few hundred pounds and if you don't mind making your music available for free you can store it on downloadable MP3 files.

The same applies to small record labels. The initial investment is much lower and, provided they can promote their website well, they stand to make more profit than if they go through a traditional distribution deal (see Chapter 6). That said, most record companies are making very little money from music online. It's being used to promote either an artist or some other service that the website is offering. We have to be very careful that we don't devalue music and that it's available in its own right and at a fair price.

The Internet is perfect for artists or record labels specialising in a niche market. With a good website, regularly up-dated (daily if possible but at least once a week), you can target your fans, which is much more effective than a general mailshot. Artists such as Todd Rundgren have done this very successfully and Alanis Morissette's last album was sold online in a joint venture with one of the Internet companies.

With appropriate marketing it's also possible to be a virtual record label, an e-label, existing only online. At the moment the biggest growth area of my business is Internet start-up companies. They are coming in at the rate of about three a week and they are all looking to use music in one way or another. Exciting times.

The majority of new artists will, however, still need the kind of financial support that a major record label can give. They may need A&R guidance, support for touring and a big budget to spend on marketing. More established artists, who don't need creative guidance or tour support, might look to other companies outside the traditional record labels for their marketing support. Already Microsoft is looking at investing in new recordings by established artists. AOL has clearly seen the advantages to acquiring catalogue. It's a logical extension for these sorts of companies whose forte is aggregating and marketing.

WHAT ARE THE ADVANTAGES FOR THE ARTIST?

Record companies should have lower overheads if they store material digitally for online distribution. At present these savings are not being passed on to the artists. The major record companies are now arguing that the manufacturing, packaging, and distribution costs account for only 10% of the actual costs. So that destroys their traditional argument for the artificially high packaging deductions. They now argue that their biggest cost is marketing, which won't go down by using online distribution. You might say that that's a very convenient argument. Also one to watch is the replacement of the packaging charge (which clearly can't exist in online distribution) with a charge for the fulfilment costs (i.e. the overhead costs of maintaining a secure credit card system, customer support and so on).

PRICING MODELS

At the moment most major record companies are continuing with the royalty-based system of calculating payments to the artist. Some are seeking a 'break' (i.e. a reduction) in the basic royalty to cover the research and development (R&D) costs of developing the Internet. Well, that may have worked for Sony and Phillips (Polygram) who did have R&D costs in the development of the CD but it certainly doesn't work with online distribution.

At the moment many companies are still following the principles they apply to physical mail order to online mail order. They are looking to pay a reduced royalty of 50% of the otherwise applicable royalty. However, one I saw recently is applying a royalty rate equal to that of a single record and so probably nearer 75% of the full royalty rate.

Many companies are looking at paying artists a percentage of net receipts. Anyone offered this type of deal should check what is being deducted from the gross income and should always try to get 50% or more of the profits.

Some companies are experimenting with other price models. There is the 'pay per play' system where a customer pays to be able to play a track for a fixed number of times.

Others are looking at subscription price bases where a consumer gains access to the catalogue of a particular record label on payment of a monthly or annual subscription. Many think that this will be the way forward. You pay a monthly subscription just as you would for your cable or satellite television services and for that you can have unlimited access to music. Naturally the challenge for us lawyers will be to see how we can ensure a fair balance between what the record company or the website company gets to keep and how much is paid through to the artist.

PUBLISHING INCOME

So far I've looked mainly at income from the sound recordings. There should, of course, also be a payment for the right to reproduce the underlying song. At the moment it's possible to get a licence to broadcast online music controlled by the PRS for a fixed fee per annum. The PRS is also looking at introducing blanket licences for material other than live broadcasts, with fees to be agreed on a case by case basis. At present it's very difficult to legitimately license many online uses. Without a blanket licence scheme the service provider has to get a separate licence for every use direct from the copyright owner and this is unworkable in practice.

In September 1999 the MCPS announced that they were recommending a digital download fee of ten pence per download for five minutes of music with an extra two pence per two minutes thereafter. The record companies were unhappy because it will cost them more than the physical format equivalent, but MCPs are now offering blanket licenses at this rate.

Collection societies are trying to be flexible in their attitude to this new medium and are trying to strike a balance between encouraging a new source of income and obtaining a fair return for the use of their members' copyrights. The trouble is that it is taking too long to get these systems in place and in the meantime people are having these very creative ideas but are unable to deliver them legally because the licensing system isn't there.

All these arrangements will probably be subject to frequent review until the new medium matures into an established method of selling music. Also international deals are only in place in principle at the moment between the various collecting societies to enable a one-stop service. If you are broadcasting a webcast in both the UK and the US it still isn't clear if you have to get two licences, one for each country. This is in danger of stifling trade and has to be addressed by the music business internationally.

ACCOUNTING SYSTEMS AND TAX

So far I've touched on questions of security and how payment is being made for copying, distributing and communicating music to the public. What about collecting the money? At the moment various companies are looking at tracking systems for accounting worldwide but no internationally acceptable system is yet in place.

The whole question of how e-commerce is to be taxed is also fraught with difficulties, which are, thankfully, outside the scope of this book. If you intend to venture into online distribution then you should take specialist tax advice as well as consulting a specialist lawyer.

MORAL RIGHTS

Another issue, which may gain in importance with digital copying or distribution online, is that of moral rights (see Chapter 12). If a song or a recording can be digitised then it can also be digitally manipulated, possibly by the end consumer or by the record company. Some artists are very sensitive about their work being altered in any way and for these artists we lawyers have to be careful to try to protect the integrity of that work as far as we can. One of the ways is, of course, through the assertion of moral rights. These rights are often waived or excluded in contracts and it is therefore important in this area to make sure any moral rights that are waived are replaced as far as possible by contractual protections.

MARKETING ISSUES

Digital technology is opening up new means of distribution and new challenges of pricing and protection. It also raises new issues on how to market an artist.

The Internet and the ever-growing use of email and ownership of email addresses means that it is now easier than ever to gather data and information on who your fans are and what attracts them to a particular artist.

It costs relatively little to acquire a domain name. Software is also available to help design a website. There are many hints available on the Internet itself; some sites have free downloadable designs or images. Remember, though, that when using images/designs supplied by someone else, you need to be sure that the copyright owner is willing for you to use them free of charge. You should check for any limitations on what they can be used for. These restrictions will often be in the 'small print' at the front of a computer programme or on the home page of a website, which most people click on but never read.

WEBSITE DESIGN RIGHTS AND COPYRIGHT

An artist may decide to employ someone to design his website. The website is likely to be made up of many different elements, all of which could be the subject of copyright or other legal protection.

The website will have words which, if original, could be a literary work with its own literary copyright.[10]

The website will no doubt have visual images or graphics. These could be still photographs, moving images or film. Each of these could have its own copyright.[11]

The website will be made up of a number of computer programmes. Computer programmes are also protected by copyright.[12]

The site may well also contain music. If it is the artist's own music and lyrics, which he owns, then he doesn't have to worry about getting permission to use it. If it's someone else's work then permission has to be obtained from the owners of the copyright in the music and the lyrics and, unless the artist owns it himself, also from any owner of the separate sound-recording copyright (see Chapters 3 and 4).

The designer will have copyright in the original design drawings. He may also have a design right.[13]

In this area of the music business there's an increasing tendency to register a patent in a particular aspect of a website or an innovative use of computer or compression technology. Patents are outside the scope of this book but if you feel you've created something that could be capable of patent protection then you should take advice from a specialist patent lawyer.

When commissioning someone else to design a website, you have to make sure that all rights have been cleared for use in the site design, that you have all the rights you need to do what you want with the website. You also need to find out whether these rights have been 'bought-out' for a one-off payment or if there is an ongoing obligation to pay for the use. It's possible that in order to use the music or a sound recording you'll have to pay a royalty or further fee.

If the person commissioned to design the website is your employee then you will own the copyright in their original work[14] but the other rights may still have to be cleared.

If you ask someone who is not employed by you to design the website, you must make sure that you take an assignment from them of all rights in the website. You could make this

10 Sections 1(1) (a), 3(1), 1(1)(b) and 5(1) CDPA.
11 Sections 1(1) (a), 4(1) (a) and (2) CDPA.
12 Sections 1(1) (a) and 3(1) CDPA.
13 Sections 1(1) (a), 4(1) (a) and Part III CDPA.
14 Section 11 (2) CDPA.

a condition of the commission fee or it could be the subject of a separate fee or, occasionally, a royalty. The designer may grant the right to use the work only on the website and not, for example, to print design elements from the website and sell them separately as posters or otherwise as part of a merchandising campaign (see Chapter 8). These additional uses could be the subject of a separate fee.

Assignments of copyright should be confirmed in writing.[15] A written agreement also establishes what rights you have and on what terms. It should contain a confirmation from the designer that he has all the necessary rights from third parties for the use of any or all elements of the design.

HOSTING AGREEMENTS

Once you have the website, you need to find a way to make it available to others via the Internet.

You could become your own ISP. You set yourself up with the necessary Internet capacity to launch your own site and could also provide that service to others. This isn't, however, the way that most artists get their website on the Internet. More usually you arrange to have the website 'hosted' by another ISP. Anyone going down this route should have an agreement with the host ISP setting out the kind of service that will be provided and at what cost. These agreements are called hosting agreements.

If you are trying to establish yourself as having a website to which your fans and potential customers return over and over again then you need to know that the host will supply a reliable service. We all know of systems where the hardware on the server 'goes down' on a regular basis. These sites get a reputation as being unreliable and people are less likely to go back to them. Fans or potential fans won't bother to go to a website that's never available or which is difficult to use. The first is the fault of the server, the second that of the designer. Both are your problem.

The hosting agreement should insist that the server would be functioning properly at least 95% of the time. It should provide compensation if the server is 'down' more than an agreed percentage of the time or for more than a maximum agreed number of hours a day.

If the website is to be used to sell merchandise online, you'll need to know that any credit card payment facility is 100% secure. The ISP should guarantee this in the hosting agreement.

The ISP should also be able to supply a reasonable amount of 'back office' support to process orders, keep the databases up to date and provide technical support. These facilities are also sometimes referred to as fulfilment centres.

The ISP should agree in the hosting agreement to provide regular, detailed information on the number of 'hits' (i.e. visits that are being made to the website). This is the information you need to establish who your fans are and who is likely to want to buy records, merchandise, concert tickets and so on.

15 Section 90 (3) CDPA.

The website becomes your one-stop shop window on the world. Its design and reliability will say a lot about you. A good website will enable you to target your likely market with greater precision.

OWNERSHIP OF DOMAIN NAMES

It is important that you retain control over the website and of the domain name (the address) that leads people to the website.

The band name is a key element in the branding of the band (see Chapter 8). Successful branding means that you not only get to sell more records but also merchandise, membership of your fan club and tickets to your concerts.

Obviously, the record company has an interest in sales of your records. As we saw in Chapter 3, the record company are likely to be either owner of the copyright in the sound recordings or at least an exclusive licensee of the copyright with similar rights to those of a record company with exclusive sound recording rights.[16] It therefore makes sense for you to co-operate with your record label and their ISP. The website could be linked to other websites by artists on the same record label, and vice versa, or with the label's own main site. It makes sense to co-ordinate efforts.

What is more objectionable, however, is the move by some record companies to *own* your domain name. The trend was probably first publicised by Sony but extended to other record companies.

What's the problem with this? Well, would you ever think of searching for information on a favourite artist by using the name of their record company? Unlikely. Far more likely is that you'd use the band's name. If you wanted to find the Manic Street Preachers' website you would search under their name, not Sony's, wouldn't you?

The record companies are aware of this and some want to cash in on the 'branding'. They also have a vested interest in acquiring the database of names and email addresses of fans visiting particular websites. If a consumer is a fan of, say, Steps or Billie, the record company or marketing company could try to sell them material by other pop artists.

There are of course data protection issues in all of this. If you are putting together data on people electronically, you have to register with the Data Protection Register. You can't do what you want with the data you collect. You have to get permission to use it for a purpose other than that for which it was collected. You will have seen magazine adverts for a particular product. If you send off for that product you'll be asked to fill in a form with your details. The product owner may want to try to sell you other products that they have in their range or to sell their list of customers and their product preferences to another company. They can't do this without your permission. There is often a box on the form that you have to tick if you *don't* want your information to be used in this way. This 'negative' consent technique is lawful and is being adapted for online use, although the Data Protection Registrar is apparently in favour of you having to tick a box if you *do* want more information

16 Section 180 CDPA.

– not the other way around. You will often find a box that has to be checked or unchecked to block your information being used in other ways. If you're compiling a database and you don't comply with the rules on passing on information then you can be fined.

The Data Protection legislation has just been updated and extended to information held in hard copy form as well as electronically. The Data Protection Act 1998 came into force on 1 March 2000. The Act also implements the Database Directive.[17] A key tenet of the Directive is that information held on an individual should not be sent to a country that doesn't have adequate protection in place to keep personal information confidential. The EU has, somewhat controversially, declared that the United States doesn't have sufficient protections in place. Negotiations are continuing.

If, however, these data protection hurdles are overcome then a database of consumer profiles and information is a valuable asset. If you own your domain name then, subject to anything to the contrary in the hosting agreement, you will own the data collected in relation to that website.

Sony have included in their standard contracts wording that gives them ownership of the artist's name as a domain name. The clause reads as follows:

> *Sony and its licensees shall have the exclusive right, throughout the world, and shall have the exclusive right to authorise other persons, to create, maintain and host any and all Websites relating to the artist and to register and use the name '[artist name].com' and any Resource Locators (or URLS); addresses, or domain names for each Website created by Sony in respect of the artist.*[18]

This means that any artist who signs a contract with Sony with this clause in it won't be able to set up his own website or register his name as a domain name independent of Sony.

Arguments that Sony use in their defence of this clause are that it's an extension of their marketing efforts, that they always work with the artist and that it's open to negotiation.

I can see an argument for this while the record label has an exclusive deal with an artist. Even then I'm concerned that they're using the artist's 'brand' to further the record company's own interests outside their traditional sources of income. Why should the record label own your outlet for merchandising or concert tickets?

However, the wording goes on to say: 'All such Websites and all rights thereto and devised therefrom shall be Sony's property throughout the territory *and in perpetuity* [my emphasis].'

What justification can there be for this? Why should Sony own your name as a domain name forever? What if Sony ends their contract with you after one album? Why should they go on owning the domain name and the website forever? The reasons are, of course, because they fear losing control over what is likely to become a valuable marketing tool and also because it is already a new means of distribution and revenue. Will we see a new trend

17 European Union Directive on the Legal Protection of Databases.
18 Source: CNET News.com (Beth Lipton) 15/9/99.

in sales of databases of fans by an artist's former label to his new one? Will there be a transfer market in artist domain names?

Of course Sony maintains that they will always negotiate questions of ownership with the artist. What happens if you part company with your record label on less than friendly terms? What chance then of getting a favourable hearing to your request for transfer to you of your own domain name?

The solution, of course, is not to give the record company the rights in the first place. This is, however, easier said than done. Just imagine the scenario. You have been working for months towards a record deal. The contract is there and the advance cheque is dangling before your eyes. How many artists/managers are going to make this a priority issue?

Partly as a result of the bad publicity it got from taking this line, Sony made it known at the annual music business convention in Cannes in January 2000 that they would be amenable to *not* owning the name forever. They also said that they weren't interested in any of the income earned from the website other than from sales of records or downloads. Let's see what happens in practice.

Of course, I hope that a mixture of education and experience will mean that artists become aware of the importance of this issue. In the short term, however, is there any other way that you can more easily resist this requirement from the record company that they own your domain name?

You could make it more difficult for the record company by registering the domain name yourself first. Then the record company are asking you to give up something you already have and value. That is always more difficult.

If you follow my advice on branding (Chapter 8), you may apply to register your name and logo as a trade mark. If the record label then tries to make you give them the rights in the name, you have a strong weapon with which to fight them off.

HOW DO YOU MAKE IT STICKY?

One of the big challenges of marketing online is to make sure that fans come to a particular website and, once they've found it, come back to it over and over again. Phrases are bandied about as to how you get more 'eyeballs' (visitors) and whether the website is 'sticky'. The design of the website is, of course, crucial. It should be eye-catching and user-friendly. The text used in it should be designed so that it features prominently in the lists of websites that come up when key phrases are used to search for information using one of the search engines such as MSN, Yahoo! or Excite. This is an art form in itself and specialist web designers should be used.

The website should be regularly updated. There has been an increase in the number of people going under the slightly sinister title of 'webmaster'. The ISP host should be able to provide regular access to a webmaster who can help to put the latest news online.

The website should be easy to view. The key information should be available without having to go through several 'click through' layers. It should all be on the home page – the first page a visitor to the website sees.

The website should be different – it should have something that will raise it above the general 'noise' online. It's all very well if you're David Bowie or Prince making your records available online. Just by saying you are doing it, your name (or brand) is well known enough to guarantee you press interest. However, if you are Joe Bloggs trying to get noticed then you have to be more innovative.

BEING DIFFERENT

In October 1999 I got sent my first e-demo. The band put together a package that consisted of a brief biography of the band members and a sample of their latest demo. It was simple and to the point. It also had the advantage of being the first one I, and perhaps many others in the UK music business, had received. If for no other reason, that made it memorable.

In a few years the majority of new demos may be delivered to record companies in this way. If this becomes the norm then the artist will have to think of a more novel way. At that point it may be that a CD along with some photos and a printed biography will seem so different that it will get attention.

REACHING THE FAN BASE

The Internet is a great means of reaching your fan base. Someone, jokingly, said to me that in future, bands might call themselves the equivalent of Elvis.com to make themselves supremely marketable in this new medium. Well, it has already happened. In autumn 1999 the band Marillion released an album called *Marillion.com*, which is apparently the same name as their website/domain name.

The Internet can give you a profile of your fans, of where they live and what about you and your website interests them in particular. This may in fact surprise you and make you change your marketing plans. If you're doing a countrywide tour you could email your known fans in each town that you are visiting to drum up support and ticket sales beforehand. You could use the local fans to spread the word for you among their e-pals. They will probably be delighted by the personal involvement with you.

THE INTERNET AS A NEW SOURCE OF REVENUE

As well as having a great potential for marketing, the domain name and website can be the means to new sources of income.

There are companies, such as Yahoo! and MSN, that act as 'aggregators'. Through them and their linked systems the consumer has a one-stop website to access all sorts of information, whether to do with leisure activities such as hotels, holidays and flights or books, music and business information. Because they are a magnet for Internet browsers, the aggregators have identified that they can make money from selling advertising space on their pages in the form of 'banner' advertising which appears when someone logs on to their website. They sell this advertising space in the same way that space in newspapers or advertising breaks on television is sold. It may be that a service you are providing (e.g. a webcast) is going to attract a customer to one of these aggregators' sites. The aggregator is using the fact that a customer can receive the webcast to attract other advertisers to that website. You can negotiate to receive a share of that advertising revenue.

The aggregator's site will also be the place where the database is collected. If the webcast is broadcast on that site then the database of 'hits' or 'eyeballs' will include your fans. You should therefore try to get access to that database for your own marketing purposes. If you can't get them to agree that you own or co-own it you should at least try to control what is done with it. If the aggregator wants to try to sell all or part of it to another company you should have some say in that and if there is money to be made on the transaction you should have some of it.

As I mentioned at the beginning of this chapter, I think that the Internet is a great opportunity for us. It may not take over the traditional outlets for music overnight but it is already providing a source of other ways to market an artist and in time will also give an artist another way of making their music commercially available.

CONCLUSIONS

- Artists should try to own their own domain name.

- The Internet is a very valuable marketing tool.

- If you commission someone to design your website make sure they give you ownership of all the various elements of it.

- There is no standard set as yet for what artists should receive in income from online sales of sound recordings. This means the whole question is open to negotiation on a case-by-case basis.

- MP3 files are a valuable source of promotion if you bear in mind that at the moment you are unlikely to collect any income from anyone downloading that music.

8: **BRANDING**

INTRODUCTION

In this and the following chapter I'm going to look at the whole area of branding, first by looking at merchandising deals, at how you get a trade mark and at the benefits of building up a reputation in your name, and then, in the next chapter, by looking at sponsorship deals. Branding is the way in which you use your name, logo and reputation to build up a particular image in the public mind.

You may think that this is not relevant for an artist just starting out in the business. It's true that new artists are going to be more concerned about getting that first record deal than worrying about their brand. However, you only have to look at many of the boy and girl bands – and some of the more successful young US artists such as Britney Spears – to be able to see that putting a bit of thought into branding, even at its simplest level, can pay big dividends. It can be as simple as getting a good, memorable name and registering it as a domain name. With those two small and cheap steps you have already started to establish a brand.

Branding is big business and is likely to become bigger with the growth of online activities on the Internet. At its most straightforward it is the building up of your name and reputation, which will help you sell more records and concert tickets. At a more sophisticated level you can use your name and reputation, and your public image, to help sell other things, and not necessarily ones that involve music. Artists such as The Spice Girls used their names, likenesses and the 'girl power' image to sell everything from crisps to soft drinks and sweets.

This idea of branding isn't anything new. All successful companies have invested a lot of money in the company name and logo and in establishing name recognition for their products. Think of Heinz, Sainsbury's, Coca-Cola or McDonald's. Companies such as Virgin have turned branding into an art form. The Virgin name is now associated with everything from planes, trains and now automobiles, to bridal companies and financial services. Sir Richard Branson realises the value in the Virgin name, in the fact that the consumer immediately recognises it and the familiar red and white colours. By putting that recognition together with a reputation for being slightly anti-establishment he can get consumers to buy into almost everything that the name is linked with. It also needs a healthy dose of self-publicity from Sir Richard himself in order to keep the name and the brand in the public eye.

Many bands are now recognising the value in the name, the brand, and are actively trying to put themselves into a position where they can make some money out of that brand.

BRANDING OF ARTISTS

To a greater or lesser extent, a successful artist or band is always going to be a brand in the sense of being a name that people recognise. The more successful you are, the more likely it is that your name, likeness and image will be recognised by members of the public. If they like or admire your reputation they will want to know more about you and will buy things that tell them more about you such as books, magazines and records. They will buy products that have your name or likeness on it such as calendars, posters, screensavers, T-shirts or other items of clothing. They will also buy products that you are associated with – food, sweets, drinks and so on. Part of this branding process is doing merchandising deals for these products. If you have taken steps as early as you could afford to protect your brand then you will have the means of stopping others from cashing in on your name without your approval.

If you have a name, likeness or logo that can be trade marked you can apply to register a trade mark. Not all names are registrable. If it's too common a name or it's descriptive of something then the Trade Mark Registry won't let you register it.

Even if you haven't got a trade mark registered, if someone tries to pass themselves off as you in order to cash in on your reputation and this results in loss or damage to you, you have the means to try to stop them. This is called an action for 'passing off' (see page 161).

If a company wants to use your name to promote their product, they will do a sponsorship deal with you. You lend them the use of your name and may agree to provide some other services, such as recording a single or performing in an advert, and they give you money in return (see Chapter 9).

If your fans are going to look for information on you or for copies of your records, they will look under your name or that of your band. They aren't going to start looking under your record company name. In fact many fans may not know or care what label your records come out on as long as they can find copies of them in their record shop under your name. When you look at the Internet you can see why the record companies are so concerned to own or at least control artists' websites and domain names. A fan is going to search for the artist's name. If you wanted to find information on Robbie Williams on the Internet you would search under 'Robbie' rather than under his record company, Chrysalis. There *are* record company websites but they tend to be corporate affairs where the services and information provided are intended for other companies or businesses. As we saw in Chapter 7, this opens up many new possibilities for marketing your brand name.

Is branding a good idea? To some artists it's anathema. Most artists know that they have to work on building up a name and a reputation in order to sell their records. Most also like the trappings of fame. Some, though, think that they are somehow selling out if they put their name to other products – selling their soul, as it were. It's obviously a personal thing.

Some artists, particularly those boy or girl bands with a relatively short shelf life before a new favourite comes along, do embrace branding in order to make as much money as they can as quickly as they can. Others are content to limit their branding activities to tour merchandise or sponsorship deals to help support a tour that would otherwise make a loss. It all comes back to the gameplan (see Chapter 2).

I've also come across artists who take the sponsor's or merchandiser's money and put it into charitable funds rather that spending it on themselves.

So is branding a sell out? I don't think it is. If it isn't right for you, don't do it. But before you come over all credible and refuse to entertain any form of merchandising or branding just remember that you're already doing it to some extent when you use your name to promote sales of your records or tickets to your gigs.

There are many artists and bands whose image doesn't easily lend itself to selling loads of posters, caps and so on. If that's you then fine, don't waste time or money on it. You don't have to have your name associated with every product that comes along. You can use it creatively and still leave yourself with some credibility. The products you choose to associate with should be selected with the overall gameplan in mind.

If you do decide to get into merchandising deals for your name, logo or likeness then you need to also decide how far you are prepared to go in protecting that merchandise from the pirates who will inevitably come along and try to steal your market, often with inferior products. Even if you don't do merchandising deals you may find that the pirates do. I know of artists that have decided, for example, not to do a merchandising deal for calendars only to find that unofficial versions appear in the shops anyway (see below).

MERCHANDISING DEALS

In its simplest form, a band is involved in merchandising when they sell tickets to their gigs. The band name attracts the fans who've bought the records and now want to see the band perform live. The ticket to the gig is bought on the back of the band name. If the band's core business is performing live then the band name is being used to sell records or other goods such as T-shirts and posters.

In the entertainment business, merchandising has been big business for years. People can buy the T-shirt, the football strip, the video game and the duvet cover bearing the name and image of their favourite cartoon character, football team or pop group. Disney and Manchester United Football Club are good examples. They know that there is a lot of money to be made from maximising the use of the name and likeness.

The Spice Girls have been one of the most successful UK acts in applying the concept of merchandising their brand name far beyond their core activities. Their manager, Simon Fuller, had the vision and the girls were willing to grasp the ideas and run with them. And now he intends to do a similar thing with S Club 7, using the medium of television and the tie-in with the successful TV programme *Miami 7*. He's not the first to use the television tie-in – you only have to remember The Monkees and The Partridge Family. He's just taking it to a different plane.

HOW DO YOU GO ABOUT GETTING A TRADE MARK?

Before you can begin to use your name to sell merchandise outside your core business of selling records, it's essential that you have a name or logo that is easily marketable and that you have or are starting to get a reputation that people can relate to. Most artists have a distinctive name and some form of logo. If your gameplan is to do a fair amount of merchandising, you should think of a distinctive name and logo from the beginning. We all know how difficult it is to find a name that no one else has thought of and we saw in Chapter 1 how to check this out. The same thought must go into making your logo as distinctive as possible.

If you're going to have any chance of holding off the pirates, you need to protect your rights in your name and logo as far as possible. If you want to prevent others jumping on the bandwagon and manufacturing unauthorised merchandise to satisfy market demand then you will need to have your own house in order. You'll be helpless to stop the pirates if you don't properly protect your name and logo. So it's important to get trade mark protection as early as possible.

• Elvis Presley's estate wasn't able to protect the use of the Elvis name for merchandising as a registered trade mark in the UK because it waited until ten years after his death.[1]

In 1989, Elvis Presley Enterprises Inc, the successors to the Estate of Elvis Presley, filed UK trade mark applications for Elvis, Elvis Presley and the signature 'Elvis A Presley'. The Estate had registered a number of trade marks around the world for a wide range of products.

The UK trade mark applications were accepted by the Trade Marks Registry but were then opposed by Sid Shaw, a trader who had been marketing Elvis memorabilia in the UK since the late 1970s under the name Elvisly Yours. He opposed the registration of the marks by the Elvis Estate on the ground, among other things, that they conflicted with Sid Shaw's own prior trade mark registrations for Elvisly Yours. The Registry upheld the Estate's applications; Mr Shaw appealed to the High Court, which allowed the appeal. In a judgement that was quite critical of character and personality merchandising in general, the court decided that the public didn't care whether Elvis Presley memorabilia were approved by the Estate of Elvis Presley or not. The Estate appealed to the Court of Appeal.

The Court of Appeal refused the Estate's appeal and refused registration of all three marks. The court concluded that the marks were not in themselves distinctive and, as there was no evidence produced by the Estate of any use of the marks in the UK which might have indicated that the marks had become distinctive of the Estate of Elvis Presley in the minds of the public, there was therefore no reason at all why the marks should be registered.

The courts are also showing that they are not prepared to interpret the Trade Marks Act too narrowly in favour of someone who has registered a trade mark in a band name.

• Another example is a case involving the band Wet Wet Wet: the Bravado and Mainstream case.[2]

Bravado owned a trade mark in the name Wet Wet Wet. Bravado asked for the Scottish equivalent of an injunction to be ordered against Mainstream from infringing that trade mark. Mainstream was publishing and marketing a book entitled *A Sweet Little Mystery – Wet Wet Wet – the Inside Story*. Mainstream argued that they weren't using Wet Wet Wet in a trade mark sense but rather that it was used to describe the subject matter of the book. They also said that they weren't suggesting in any way that it was published by Bravado and as such somehow 'official'. Bravado argued that if they couldn't prevent this use then it would be meaningless having the trade mark because they couldn't then stop it being used on other merchandise relating to the band.

1 Elvis Presley Trade Marks [1997] RPC 543.
2 *Bravado Merchandising Services Ltd* v. *Mainstream Publishing (Edinburgh) Ltd* [1996] F.S.R. 205.

The court decided that the words *were* being used in the course of trade but refused to grant the injunction because it said that would be interpreting the meaning of the Trade Mark Act far too narrowly. If it were so interpreted, any mention of the group name could be an infringement of the trade mark.

HOW TO APPLY FOR A TRADE MARK

You don't have to be already rich and famous to register a trade mark in your name or logo. In fact, as we saw in the Elvis case, there are dangers in waiting too long to apply for a trade mark. As soon as you can afford to, you should think about doing it. You can apply to protect your name or that of your brand worldwide, but this would be expensive. To start with I usually advise that you apply to register the name in your home market, for example the UK for a British-based band, and then in other places where you have or hope to gain a market for your records and other merchandise, for example the US, Europe or Japan.

Each country has its own special rules for registration of a trade mark and in many cases an application to register a trade mark in one country can help you with applications in other parts of the world. For example, the rules at present allow you to backdate an application for the US to the date of your UK application provided you apply within six months of the UK application. So if you apply for a UK trade mark registration on 1 July 1999, you have until 31 December 1999 to apply in the US and still backdate it to 1 July 1999. Just making the application itself can kick-start the trade mark protection. Even if it takes a year or more to get a registration, your trade mark, when and if you get it, will be backdated to the date you first applied. You also have priority over anyone else who applies to register a trade mark in the same or a similar name or logo after you. This is, however, a specialised area and you should take advice from a trade mark lawyer or a specialist trade mark agent. Your lawyer can put you in touch with a trade mark agent and a good music lawyer should have a working knowledge of trade mark law. While you may be happy to leave all this to your manager to sort out for you, do remember that the name should be registered in your name and not that of your manager or record company.

Once you've decided the countries where you'd like to apply for a trade mark – finances permitting – you have to decide what types of product or particular goods you want to sell under the trade mark. In most countries, goods and services are split for trade mark registration purposes into classes and so it's important to make sure that you cover all relevant classes of goods and as soon as possible. You can add other classes later but then you run the risk of someone selling goods with your name in a class that you haven't protected. For example, you may have applied to register a trade mark for the class that covers records, but not in the class that covers printed material such as posters. In theory someone else could apply for a trade mark in that area, but then you get into the whole area of passing off (see below). It's also not usually as cost-effective. You get a costs saving by applying for several classes at a time.[3]

3 In the UK there are 42 classes for goods and services. Some common ones used in the music business are Class 9 for records, Class 16 for printed material, such as programmes and posters, and Class 25 for clothing.

At the time of writing, the cost of applying to register a band name in the UK in one class, say Class 9 for records, is an initial fee of £395 plus VAT and, after that, costs to the final registration stage can be anything up to £600–800. However, a registered trade mark has distinct advantages over an unregistered mark. Actions to stop infringements of registered trade marks are generally quicker and more cost-effective than when you are relying on unregistered rights. A registered trade mark puts the world on notice of your rights. A registered trade mark is attractive to merchandising companies as it gives them a monopoly over the goods for which the mark is registered and gives the merchandising company more of an incentive to do a deal with you.

PASSING OFF

If you haven't registered a trade mark in the UK, you can try to rely on the common law right of passing off in order to protect your name and reputation. Before you can do this you'll have to prove there is goodwill in your name. This may not be the case if you're unknown and haven't yet got a reputation. You have to show that someone else is trading on your reputation by passing themselves off as you, using your reputation to confuse the public that they are you or are authorised by you. As well as having this goodwill or reputation you also have to show that this has actually caused confusion in the mind of the public resulting in damage/loss to you. For example, a band using the same name as yours or one confusingly similar might advertise tickets to a gig in the same town as your planned gigs. Fans might buy those tickets thinking they're coming to see you. This loses you ticket sales and might possibly damage your reputation if the other band aren't as good as you. You have to have established a reputation in the name in the particular area in question. If your name is associated with records and someone trades under the same or a very similar name in the area of clothing, where you don't have any reputation, there is less likely to be confusion in the mind of the public.

- One famous passing-off case involved the pop group Abba.[4]

A company called Annabas was selling a range of T-shirts, pillowcases, badges and other goods bearing the name and photographs of the band. The band didn't own the copyright in any of the photographs and Annabas had obtained permission from the copyright owners of the photographs to use them. Abba lost its application for an injunction preventing their sale because they were unable to show they had an existing trade in these goods or any immediate likelihood of one being started. The judge also went on to say that he thought that no one reading adverts for the goods or receiving those goods would reasonably imagine that the pop stars had given their approval to the goods offered. They felt Annabas was only catering for a popular demand among teenagers for effigies of their idols. These words have been often repeated in later cases.

4 *Lyngstad* v. *Annabas Productions Limited* [1997] FSR 62.

One importance of this case is that it is clear you have to establish that you already have a trade in that area which could be prejudiced or there was a reasonable likelihood of you starting such a trade. If you're seriously thinking about getting into merchandising then you should do so sooner rather than later. You should be setting yourself up ready for starting such a trade, for example by commissioning designs, talking to merchandise companies or manufacturers and applying to register your trade mark well in advance of when you want to start business in order to get around some of the pitfalls highlighted in the Abba case.

● In the same year as the Abba case, another one involving two members of The Beatles – George Harrison and Ringo Starr – came to court.[5]

It was a case against a record company that planned to release recordings of interviews given by The Beatles interspersed with Beatles songs. George and Ringo's copyright hadn't been infringed nor was there any breach of confidence, so they brought an action on the basis of passing off. They were arguing that anyone buying this record would think it was an official release endorsed by The Beatles. The court refused to grant them an injunction because it felt that anyone buying the record 'The Beatles Tapes' would know that there was no implication that The Beatles endorsed or authorised the release.

OTHER REMEDIES

If you can't rely on either a trade mark or the remedy of passing off then you'll have to see if there has been any infringement of copyright, for example in a design or possibly if there has been a false description of goods that might be unlawful under the Trade Descriptions Act 1968.

TRADE MARKS – CONCLUSIONS

Clearly getting registered trade mark protection is the best way to go about protecting your brand, but when you are just getting started you'll probably not have the money to spend on protecting the band name. A balance has to be struck. If you are ultimately successful and haven't applied for a trade mark, you may end up kicking yourself if others cash in on your name and market unauthorised products. If you apply late you may be too late, as in the case of Elvis (see above). On the other hand, it's often not at all certain whether a group is ultimately going to be successful enough to justify the expense. A sensible thing to do would be to register a trade mark in just one or two classes including, of course, records and perhaps only in one or two countries at first and then add more countries or classes as things develop.

It's also worth bearing in mind that a record company may advance you the money to make the trade mark applications. If you don't want your record company to own your trade mark then make sure the application for the registration is in your name, not theirs, even if they offer to register it on your behalf.

5 *Harrison and Starkey* v. *Polydor Limited* [1977] FSRI.

As we've already seen in the area of e-commerce, there is also a great deal of mileage to be had from registering your domain name. If I'm even partly correct in my predictions for the Internet, ownership of your domain name will give you control of the doorway to official information on you and what you have to offer (see Chapter 7).

UNAUTHORISED, UNOFFICIAL MERCHANDISE

● The line of arguments that we saw being developed in the Abba and Beatles cases was more recently expanded on in a case involving The Spice Girls.

In the case, The Spice Girls applied for an injunction against an Italian publisher of an unauthorised sticker book and stickers entitled The Fab Five. At this time the Spice Girls had no trade mark registrations and, in fact, it probably wouldn't have helped them if they had because Panini carefully hadn't used the Spice Girls' name anywhere in the book or on the stickers. So the Spice Girls were trying to use the law of passing off to protect the band's image. They argued that, even though the words Spice Girls weren't used, the book was clearly about them. The book didn't carry a sticker that it was unauthorised so they argued that this amounted to a misrepresentation that the Spice Girls had authorised or endorsed the book.

The judge wasn't swayed by any argument that it made a difference whether the book was marked 'authorised' or 'official'. He refused to give an injunction. As a consequence of this decision, if a company puts out an unauthorised calendar featuring pictures of The Spice Girls then, provided it made it clear that it wasn't a calendar that had the official blessing of the band and didn't reproduce copyright words/lyrics or photographs without permission, that would not be a passing off or a breach of copyright rights. The judge decided that even the use of the word 'official' wasn't a case of passing off provided the product clearly indicated it wasn't approved by the artist. In this particular case The Spice Girls had a trade mark application pending, but it hadn't been registered so they couldn't rely on arguing that there had been an infringement of their trade mark. This is a good example of why it's important to have a registered trade mark if you're going to try to put a stop to the sale of unauthorised goods.

You might be forgiven for thinking that all these cases involve millions of pounds and are only of interest to the megastars that can employ people to do all this for them. Well, it's true that it's usually only the big names that have the inclination or the money to bring cases to court. But protecting your name can start at a very low level – such as preventing the pirate merchandisers from selling dodgy T-shirts or posters outside your gigs or stopping another local band cashing in on the hard work you have put into starting to make a name for yourself.

HOW DO YOU GO ABOUT GETTING A MERCHANDISE DEAL?

You may start off by producing a small range of T-shirts that you sell at your gigs. You can get these printed up locally and you put up a temporary stall in the foyer of the venue and sell them from there. If it's clear that you can sell enough to make money then you might approach a merchandising company about doing it for you on a larger scale. The merchandising company could be a big multi-national company or a small independent company. You can get names of merchandising companies out of directories such as *Gavin* or *Music Week*. You can also get recommendations from your mates in other bands, your lawyer, accountant or manager.

If you are starting to sell out the larger venues and are a regular on the gig circuit, merchandising companies may approach you. If they do then you could try them out with your concert or tour merchandise before deciding if they are right to do your retail or mail order merchandising as well.

If it's part of your gameplan to market your brand as widely as possible then first you need to establish a name and reputation that has worldwide appeal and then you can start to put the plan into action and talk to merchandising companies.

THE MERCHANDISING DEAL

If you have a registered trade mark you will increase your appeal to a merchandiser. Without one, merchandise companies will still be interested in you if you are sufficiently well known for them to run the commercial risk of producing merchandise for sale. The merchandise company will take a view as to whether yours is the sort of image that will sell particular types of merchandise. They will know if your image will sells T-shirts or posters at gigs and if you will also sell merchandise through retail stores.

Even quite small acts can often shift reasonable numbers of T-shirts to fans at the gigs or through mail order. If there is a steady turnover, a merchandiser will be interested in doing a deal. Obviously, if you only sell two T-shirts a month, and then only to your close family, getting a merchandise deal is going to be a non-starter. In that case you should be looking to do it yourself. Why would you want to do this? Well, obviously, the more that you keep to yourself, the more of the profit you get to keep. There is, however, an awful lot of work involved in mailing out the merchandise to fulfil orders and in ensuring that you have enough products to sell at your gigs.

If things start to go only moderately well you'll probably need to employ someone to look after that side of things for you and you'll also need to do a deal with a company to make the clothing or other products for you to your design. You'll have to be responsible for selling it either by mail order, through selected retail outlets, such as your local record stores, and at your gigs. You will need to check on the quality of the product being produced, be a salesman and be able to market the goods and distribute them. You will need to make sure that the orders are fulfilled promptly and that the accounts are properly kept. This is quite a tall order, even if you do get to keep the lion's share of the profits. Not a wonder, then, that many bands find a specialist merchandising company to do this for them.

WHAT IS IN A TYPICAL MERCHANDISING DEAL?

Obviously, each merchandise deal will be different and once again it's important for you to use a lawyer who is used to doing these sorts of deals. There are, however, some points that are in issue in every merchandising deal.

Territory

You can do a one-stop, worldwide deal with one company for all your merchandise needs but this is still comparatively rare. It's more usual for you to do a series of deals with different companies for different types of goods. For example, you could do a deal with one company to sell T-shirts, sweatshirts, caps and so on at your gigs. This deal could be limited to the UK or Europe. You could then do another deal for the US, probably with a company that specialises in the US market place. If we are talking about merchandise in the wider sense of marketing your name or likeness on sweet packages or crisp packets then you will do your deal with the company that manufactures those goods. That deal could be a worldwide one or for specific countries. If you're going to do a worldwide or multi-territory deal make sure that your merchandise company has the resources to look after your interests properly in each country. Find out if they subcontract the work and if so to whom. Is the subcontractor reliable?

Term

If you're doing a series of concerts then you could do a merchandise deal that was just linked to those dates. If you were doing a world tour with various legs to it, you could do a deal with one merchandise company that covered the whole tour. Alternatively you could do a deal with one company to cover the period of the UK or European legs and with another company or companies in other parts of the world. The term of the contract would be the duration of the tour or of that particular leg of it.

If you're doing merchandise deals to sell goods in shops or by mail order then the term is more likely to be for a fixed period of time, probably a minimum of one year and up to three years or more.

The more money the merchandising company is investing in manufacturing costs and/or upfront advances, the longer term they are likely to want in return. The longer the term, the better their chances will be of recouping their investment.

Some merchandising deals are linked to recoupment of all or a proportion of the advance. The term of the deal runs until that happens. This can be dangerous if sales don't live up to expectations or if the merchandising company isn't as good as you'd like them to be. The best thing to do with these types of deals is to have the right to get out of the deal after, say, a year by paying back the amount of money that is unrecouped. This will give you the flexibility to get out of a deal that isn't working and into one that might.

Rights granted

The deal will usually be a licence of rights in your name and likeness for a particular period, not an assignment of rights. The rights granted will be the right to manufacture, reproduce and sell certain products featuring your name and/or logo. If you have a registered trade mark, you will be required to grant a trade mark licence to the merchandising company to use the trade mark on specific goods.

The rights granted could be for particular products or all types of merchandise. These days the trend is towards limiting the granting of rights to particular products. You could grant the right to use your name or likeness or your registered logo on T-shirts and keep back rights to all other products such as calendars, posters, sweets and so on.

You might grant the right to use your band name and/or logo for some types of a particular product and keep rights back to other forms of the same product. For example, you could grant a licence for ordinary toys and keep back the rights to use your name on musical toys. You could then do merchandising deals for all or any of those types of toys with one or more other companies. If your music is going to be used in the musical toys then you or your publisher will license the right to include the music for either a one-off buy-out fee or for a fee and an ongoing royalty (see Chapter 4).

Quality control

Once you've decided what goods are going to feature your name, likeness or logo, you have to make sure that the goods are of the highest possible quality. If you don't keep a tight hold on quality control you could do potentially serious and possibly irreversible damage to the reputation of your brand. If a T-shirt featuring your name and logo falls apart or the colours run on the first wash then that is going to reflect very badly on you. The fan that bought the T-shirt won't care that it was another company that made it – they'll blame you and give you a reputation for selling shoddy goods.

The contract will usually say that the merchandising company must submit samples of designs for you to approve. If they are making the goods to a design you've given them then they should make up samples to that design. Only once you are satisfied with the quality of the sample should you authorise full production to go ahead. Even then you should have the right to inspect the product at short notice and to insist upon improvements if the quality has dropped to an unacceptable level. The contract should contain a guarantee that the product would be of at least the same quality as the sample you have approved.

It's also important that the merchandising company make sure that what they manufacture complies with all local laws. Toys and other children's products in particular have very stringent safety standards. You may want to insist that the manufacturers take out product liability insurance. Be careful also if the company subcontracts any of the processes. The subcontractor must also stick to rigid quality controls and ensure product safety, carrying insurance against any damage caused by the product.

If the design is one created for you either by the merchandising company or a third party, make sure they assign the rights in that design to you. If you don't then you may find that the designer comes knocking on your door for more money.

Methods of distribution

The rights you grant may also be limited to certain methods of distribution.

You might grant mail order rights only or limit the rights to selling merchandise to retail shops or at your concerts. There are specialist companies that are good at doing tour merchandising but aren't as good at selling goods to retail shops and vice versa. It's important that you find the right company for the right method of distribution.

Depending on the means of distribution, the basis on which you are paid may also change.

Advances and Guaranteed Minimum payments

You can usually expect to get an advance against what you are going to earn from sales of the goods. This advance is recoupable from those earnings but, as we've already seen with other types of music business deals, the advance isn't usually returnable if you don't sell enough to recoup the advance. One exception is if you're doing a merchandising deal for a concert tour and you don't do some or all of the concerts. Then you can expect to be asked to repay some or all of the advance. Some tour agreements also say that advances are repayable in whole or in part if ticket sales at the concerts don't reach a particular level. For example, you may get a fixed sum, sometimes called the Guaranteed Minimum, which is not repayable unless you cancel the whole tour. Then there are other payments that are made which are dependent either on you doing a particular number of big, stadium-type concerts or on you selling a minimum number of tickets over the whole concert tour. If you don't do those gigs or don't sell enough tickets then you don't get those further payments.

There is also another catch with tour merchandise agreements, which is the one that I touched on above. The contract may say that the term continues until you have earned enough from sales of the tour merchandise to recoup either the whole advance or the Guaranteed Minimum. If you aren't certain that you'll be able to do this within a reasonable time then you'll want to have the option to get out of this by paying back the unrecouped amount. If you don't have this option, and say your 1999 tour isn't a big success, then you could be stuck with the same tour merchandising company for the 2000 tour without the prospect of any more advances. If you can get out of it you can try to find someone else to do a deal for the tour merchandise for the 2000 tour and may even get them to pay you another advance.

The advances could be payable in full when you sign the deal or may be payable in a number of instalments linked to concert appearances or sales of product with, say, 25% of that being payable on signature.

Royalties and licence fees

You will usually receive a percentage of the sale price of the goods as a royalty, which will go first to recoup the advances you've already had.

This percentage will either be calculated on the gross income or, more usually, on the net income after certain expenses are deducted. Deductions can include VAT or similar sale taxes, the cost of manufacture and printing of the goods and all or some costs of their distribution and sale.

When you are doing a tour merchandising deal, commissions or fees are often payable to the owners of the concert venues for the right to sell merchandise on their premises. It's usual for the merchandise company to deduct this payment from the gross income. Some companies will also try to deduct other expenses including travel and accommodation costs for their salesmen and other unspecified expenses. I'm not convinced that these should be deducted and it's a good rule with all these deductions to look at them very carefully.

Obviously, if you're being paid a percentage of the gross income it will be a much smaller percentage than if it were a percentage of the net. A fee of 20–30% of gross would be equal to about 60–70% of the net income depending on what is deducted from the gross. For example, if you had a gross income from sales of T-shirts featuring your name of £10 per T-shirt, a 20% royalty would be £2.00. If you had a net income of £2.00 then a 60% royalty based on the net income would be £1.20.

Accounting

Accounts are usually delivered for retail or mail order deals every three or six months. Obviously, from your point of view, you will want it sooner rather than later. You should have the right to go in and inspect their books regularly and at least once a year. You should also be able to go in and do a stock check from time to time.

Merchandising deals for tours are different. There is usually a tour accountant who will check the stock and the sales sheet on a daily basis. He'll expect to be paid within a very short period of time, preferably within 24 hours of each gig or at the very latest within seven days.

Trade mark and copyright notices

If you have a trade mark registered, the contract should confirm that they will include a trade mark notice on each product and a copyright notice for each design.

Termination rights

As with all contracts, the merchandising contract should say in what circumstances the deal could be brought to an end. These should include a persistent failure of quality standards, failure to put the product into the market place by the agreed date and other material breaches of contract, for example if they don't account to you when they should. If the company goes bust or just stops acting as a merchandise company then you should also have the right to end the deal.

Enforcement

This could be the subject of a chapter in its own right. The contract should say who is responsible for tracking infringements of your rights. There is usually a requirement that the merchandising company reports to you any infringements of your trade mark or copyright that it comes across on each product. It's as much in their interest as it is in yours to keep pirate activities to a minimum.

There are civil and criminal remedies to stopping infringements. You can also enlist the help of Trading Standards Authorities and Customs & Excise. Often, these authorities are prepared to seize unauthorised products bearing a name that is a registered trade mark. Even without a registered trade mark, Trading Standards Authorities are sometimes prepared to rely on the Trade Descriptions Act in order to make seizures and bring prosecutions. In my own experience, the Trading Standards Authorities are an invaluable help in clearing the streets of counterfeit products. It is possible to provide Customs & Excise with trade mark registration details to assist them in identifying and seizing unauthorised products entering the country at ports and airports.

CONCLUSIONS

- Merchandising is the use of your name and reputation to sell goods.
- Not everyone will want to do lots of merchandise deals and not everyone will be in a position to. You have to build up a name and reputation.
- Consider registering a trade mark in your name and logo.
- If you haven't got a registered trade mark but you do have a reputation, you may be able to stop people trading on your name through the laws against passing off.
- Make sure you own the copyright in any designs you commission.
- Make sure you have the right to get the design used in your album artwork from your record company.
- Think about limiting the territory and the rights you grant.

9: SPONSORSHIP

INTRODUCTION

This subject really fits into the whole area of branding. We saw in Chapter 8 how an artist or a band protects their name by registering trade marks, through taking advantage of the laws of passing off and of copyright.

Having protected your name, your brand, you can choose how far to exploit that brand. You can decide to only use it to sell your records and videos and to promote your live performances. Many artists choose to do just that and don't really expand outside their core area of activity at all. This is fine. No one is saying that you have to. But you may need to look at some kind of merchandising deal to bolster your income from live work. Many tours would make a loss if they weren't underwritten by merchandising deals and often by sponsorship.

Your merchandising activities could be limited to the sale of posters, caps and T-shirts featuring your name, logo or artwork from your album packaging. Or you can use your brand to sell a whole range of other merchandise, everything from sweets and soft drinks to bedding and wallpaper.

Sponsorship is a kind of extension of a merchandising deal. The sponsor uses the association between you and their product to increase awareness of their product and to encourage more people to buy that product. The sponsor gives you sponsorship money in return for the right to trade on your importance to a particular sector of the market. For example, a manufacturer of a soft drink might look for a sponsorship deal with a pop artist who would appeal to teenagers. An alcoholic drinks manufacturer, on the other hand, would want to sponsor an artist that had an appeal to over-eighteens and, in particular, those in their early twenties.

Pepsi have been a keen sponsor of artists in recent years. The Spice Girls released a track as a Pepsi single and featured that track in a Pepsi ad on television.

Sponsorship deals are often done for tours. You'll often see the name of a sponsor on the ticket. For example, 'Band X sponsored by Guinness'. When you arrive at the gig you'll find that there are banners and posters from the sponsors. There may be more than one sponsor. You could have a sponsor for the programme and the tickets, another one for the soft drink on sale at the venue and yet another for the alcoholic drinks. But watch out – venues often restrict the extent to which they will allow outside sponsors to plaster their brands all over the venue (see Chapter 10).

HOW DO YOU FIND A SPONSOR?

There are a number of ways to get a sponsor. You might be surprised to know that it's possible for a band to approach a designer or company to ask for sponsorship. The shoe company Doc Marten has, on at least one occasion that I know of, sponsored the cost of making a whole album following a direct approach from the band's manager. Doc Marten wanted to promote itself as a brand supporting and encouraging youth culture of which, of course, music plays a huge part. Such sponsorships by clothing companies are not common.

AN ENDORSEMENT DEAL

What is much more common, though, is for clothing companies such as Doc Marten to loan clothes for photo shoots or live appearances in return for a suitably prominent name-check. If you are lucky you can sometimes get to keep the clothes. Diesel and other similar 'youth' brands have looked at sponsorship in the past and up-and-coming new designers or those trying to break in to the UK market may be keen to do a deal. A number of designers have really made their name by having a 'star' seen out and about in their clothes. Even Shaun Ryder has a sponsor – Admiral. If the star mentions the designer's name in press or TV interviews then so much the better. These kinds of deals are closer to what I would call endorsements than pure sponsorship. You let it be known that you support or endorse a particular product. For example, you might mention in an interview that you do all your shopping at a particular shop in fashionable Notting Hill. Suddenly all the wannabes are queuing at the door of that shop, partly on the off chance that you'll be in there but also to copy your look.

SPONSORSHIP AGENTS

Apart from the direct approach, another means of getting a sponsorship deal is to approach a specialist agent who either represents one or two big companies looking for suitable projects to sponsor or who will act for you and go to potential sponsors on your behalf. There are lists of these agencies in the *Music Week Directory* and magazines such as *Audience*. There is also the tried and trusted word of mouth recommendation from friends or other contacts in the business. If you are sufficiently successful to have a brand that a sponsor might be interested in, they or their agents are likely to approach you or your manager direct. As with all these things, don't feel you have to grab the first thing that comes along. If you are desperate for some funding to underwrite a shortfall on a tour then by all means do a deal, but keep it short and see how things work out before you get in too deep.

What do they charge?

If you employ an agent to find a sponsorship deal for you then they will usually take a percentage of the deal they get for you. This percentage can vary between 5% and 15% of the gross sponsorship income. For example, if the agent brokers a deal for Heineken to sponsor your next UK tour and Heineken are prepared to offer £100,000 for the privilege, the agent would take between £5,000 and £15,000 of that as their fee. If the sponsorship is made up partly or wholly of goods rather than cash then the agent will expect to get their percentage in the cash equivalent to the value of those goods. So if Heineken were to give you £80,000 in cash and £20,000 worth of free lager to give away to your fans then your agent on 15% would still want their £15,000 in cash.

The money is usually paid to the agent at the same time as you are paid. If you are paid in two instalments, half at the beginning of the deal and the rest when you finish the tour, then your agent would get 50% of their fee upfront and 50% when you get the balance of the money. They have a vested interest in you completing the tour and, if the amount of money is large enough, they may decide to insure you against your failing to complete the tour.

They might want to be exclusively employed as your agent for a period of time. This is usually about a year but could be longer. During that time you wouldn't be able to use any other brokering agents so you'd have to make sure that they were good enough first. The advantage you get from an exclusive arrangement is the incentive that the agent has to bring deals to you as opposed to anyone else. The disadvantage is that you can't go to anyone else if they don't get you particularly good deals. If you can get an agent on a non-exclusive basis then that would give you more flexibility.

If the agent gets you a deal for some tour sponsorship and that sponsor comes back to you to sponsor your next deal then some agents insist that they should also get commission on that repeat work, even if they are no longer your exclusive agent by the time of the second deal. The logic is that they made the initial introduction and so should benefit from any follow-up. I can see this logic but obviously other factors also play a part in your getting the follow-up deal such as the professional way you dealt with the first deal, the benefits that the sponsor saw that came from your efforts and your increased fame in the meantime. So while it might be acceptable to agree to pay the agent for a short while after the end of your relationship with them, I would try to draw the line at somewhere between six and twelve months. This is all subject to negotiation when you take them on.

The agent could be your only agent worldwide and be solely responsible for getting you sponsorship deals around the world. As many sponsors are multi-national companies this may not be such a bad thing but if you think your agent doesn't have the necessary overseas connections then you might just agree that they can act for you in the UK and decide to use other agencies overseas.

If the agent were representing a company that comes to you with an offer of sponsorship, you wouldn't expect to have to pay them a fee for brokering the deal. In those circumstances the company concerned should pay them. If he also looks to you for payment then you would be right to be suspicious.

INTEGRITY

No, don't worry, I'm not going to go all serious on you and talk about your moral values – well actually, I am a bit. What I want you to think about is whether you will accept sponsorship from *any* company that offers it and the more the merrier, or are you going to select who sponsors you on moral or ethical grounds.

When you decide on your gameplan to look for sponsorship deals, you have to think about what effect that will have on your brand and your reputation. There is a narrow line to be drawn between using sponsorship by selected companies to enhance the brand and of being accused by fans of 'selling out'. The products you choose to be associated with must complement the image you have established for yourself. For example, if you are aiming at the teenage market then you might alienate them (or perhaps the parents who supply the pocket money) by being associated with alcohol or tobacco. On the other hand, if you cultivate a bad boy image then you won't want to be associated with cuddly toys. The exception to this would be if your plan were to reposition yourself in the market place. For example, if you wanted to move out of the teen or pre-teen market then you might choose sponsors associated with adult products to show you're growing up. You should also consider the moral sensibilities of your fans. You could alienate a large proportion of them if you chose manufacturers of GM foods or a fur company as your sponsor.

Don't forget that the companies that you are being sponsored by will also expect things from you. They won't want you to do anything that will bring their brand into disrepute or show them up in a bad way. Bear this in mind when negotiating your sponsorship deal. You need to be careful that you keep an even balance between your and their expectations. If you feel at all uncomfortable about what you're being asked to do then that should give you a signal to either try to change it a little or to pull out of the deal.

Your public is a very fickle thing. It is very difficult to know whether they will accept what you're doing as par for the course and what they expect from you. If your fans think you're selling out then your press people are going to have quite a bit to do to redress the balance.

The other issues you need to think about are whether you want to be associated with companies that are involved either directly or indirectly in activities or causes that you disagree with. For example, if you are a committed vegetarian you might not want to be involved with a company that has a subsidiary that is in the business of raising battery hens. If you have a strong aversion to anything to do with cruelty to animals or animal testing then you wouldn't want to do a sponsorship deal with a company whose French sister company ran laboratories that used animals to test their products. If these things matter to you then you need to have an ethical check on the company to make sure that they are not in any way involved with things that would be unacceptable to you. Remember, although they are using their association with you to benefit their business, you are being associated with them too – and with the sorts of things that they stand for.

SCOPE OF THE SPONSORSHIP DEAL

The sponsorship deal could be for a particular tour or for a series of tours. For example, it could be just for the UK or European leg of your tour or could be for the whole world tour. It could also just be for a particular project. A company could sponsor you for a particular event, for example a one-off concert, or they could expect some personal endorsements of their product. They might want you to do personal appearances, to give private performances at their company sales conferences to rally the troops. They might want you to write and record a song especially for them, which they might want to release as a promotion or as a proper commercial release. I'm sure you will have seen special offers where you get a single or album by your favourite artist if you collect a given number of ring-pulls, packet tops or special coupons. The problem here is that if you have an exclusive record deal you can't do these deals unless you first get their agreement to waive their exclusivity. They may agree to this if they think that the publicity will help sell lots more records or if the sponsoring company has access to markets in parts of the world that your record company can't break into without spending a lot of money. For example, some of the soft drinks companies have a huge market in parts of South East Asia or in South America. By being associated with them in those countries you are getting a huge amount of exposure that should help to sell lots of your records. This exposure could be much more valuable than any amount of marketing money that your record company may be prepared to put into launching you in those areas. Obviously it makes sense in these cases for there to be a considerable degree of co-operation between what your record company is planning, what you are doing in terms of live appearances and what the sponsor intends to do. If you can dovetail these plans then your chances of world domination come a lot closer.

Whether it's a tour sponsorship or an individual event sponsorship it's a reasonable rule of thumb that the more a sponsor expects from you, the more you can expect to be paid.

EXCLUSIVITY

You could only have one sponsor at any given time or you could have a series of sponsors for different products, as The Spice Girls did. If you're only going to have one sponsor then, in return for that exclusivity, you should get a lot more money.

If you're going to look for a number of different sponsors for different products then take care that you don't narrow down your options too much. If you're going to have a drinks sponsor then limit the extent of their sponsorship to either alcoholic or non-alcoholic drink, which leaves you room to look for another sponsor. For example, if Pepsi or Coca-Cola were looking to sponsor you, you might agree to that if their sponsorship was limited to soft drinks. You couldn't have another soft drinks sponsor but you could have a sponsor for alcoholic drinks. If you have a food sponsor then try to limit the deal to their particular product, for example biscuits or crisps or whatever. This would leave you with a lot of opportunities to find sponsorship deals among the many remaining food products.

• Hot off the press is the decision in a case brought by The Spice Girls against Italian scooter company Aprila.[1]

The Spice Girls were suing the company for payment of the balance of the monies they said they were due under a sponsorship deal that they'd done with the scooter manufacturer. Aprila had produced a series of scooters each in the trade mark colours that were associated with each member of The Spice Girls. For example, they had produced a bright orange version as the Geri Spice Scooter, Geri Halliwell being otherwise known as Ginger Spice. The scooter company refused to pay and counter-claimed that The Spice Girls had misled them because at the time they did the deal they knew that Geri Halliwell intended to leave the group. She did in fact leave shortly after the deal was done. In February 2000 the court decided against The Spice Girls and found that they had misled the scooter company who did not have to pay them the balance of

1 *The Spice Girls Limited* v. *Aprila World Service BV* Ch.Div.24/2/2000.

their sponsorship money. Furthermore, The Spice Girls were ordered to pay damages to the scooter company for the losses they had suffered.

WHAT'S IN A TYPICAL SPONSORSHIP DEAL?

THE SERVICES

The first thing you have to establish is what they want you to do or what event they expect to be sponsoring. Remember to keep the scope of their sponsorship as narrow as you can to allow you the possibility of getting other sponsors.

If the sponsor expects you to do a series of things, for example writing a new song, doing a live concert tour and making a television ad or a TV special, then make sure that you aren't over-committing yourself and taking too much on to be able to do it all properly and professionally. If you agree to do too much you'll end up either not doing it or doing it badly. This will reflect back on you and could do you more harm than good.

EXCLUSIVITY

Once you've agreed what they are going to sponsor and what the product is that will be associated with you, you have to decide whether you are only going to have one exclusive sponsor or whether you are going to give them exclusive rights for a particular product or type of product and still have the option to take on other sponsors for other products.

TERRITORY

Then you have to decide whether the deal is a worldwide one or whether it's to be limited to particular countries. You could do a deal for just the US or the Far East depending on the type of sponsorship. For example, the Far Eastern section of your tour could be sponsored by one company that is 'big' in that area of the world but not so well known in other parts of the world. You could then switch to another sponsor for the US or Europe.

CREATIVE CONTROL

If the sponsor intends to feature your name and likeness in any way in the campaign, whether on packaging, ads or otherwise, you might want to have approval of those uses. You might want to insist or ask for a special photo shoot with a photographer of your choosing. You could then submit to them a number of examples of photos that you like and agree that they can have the final choice. If you are writing a special song then you ought to have some say in what it sounds like, even if the sponsor does give you a brief to work to. If you are recording a song for them that has been specifically written, you will want to know whether they require any particular lyric or theme to be featured. You need to be comfortable with that.

If you're being asked to record a new or special version of an existing song, or to allow a particular track to be used in the campaign, you will need to know whether they intend to change the lyrics or music. If they do then you will probably want some control over that and to have final approval. Bear in mind that that approval should extend to any co-writers or composers of the original work and that your publishers and record company may have to give their permission to you making the recording of the new version. You may also want to check the context in which the song is being used.

The American singer-songwriter Tom Waits has a consistent policy not to endorse products or do adverts. He has taken at least two legal cases against companies that used soundalikes to imitate his distinctive gargling-with-razor-blades voice. One case involved a US advert for Doritos snack chips that used a singer to imitate Waits's voice and the way he sang a particular song used in the advert, 'Step Right Up'. Waits sued and received $2.6 million in compensation for appropriation of his voice.[2]

TERM

You have to agree how long the deal is to last. If it's for a specific event or a tour then the sponsorship deal will run from the days leading up to the event or the tour and end shortly after the event or tour has been completed. The sponsor may have the right to use up printed materials or products they have already manufactured. This would not normally be for more than three to six months and you'd want to know that they hadn't manufactured too many products in anticipation that the deal was about to come to an end. Obviously during the time that they are allowed to sell off the product any exclusivity they had would end so that you could go off and look for a new sponsor. If it's a general sponsorship deal for a particular product then you might agree that it runs for a year, perhaps with an option to extend it by mutual agreement. You would normally only agree to an extension if you got paid a further sum of money. With a general sponsorship deal there would usually be a right to sell off the product for a limited time after the end of the deal. You will want to make sure that any remaining stocks are sold off as soon as possible. You don't want this hanging around for too long as it could interfere with either the sponsorship deal for the next part of the tour or a new sponsorship deal for the same type of product.

You should also bear in mind that the longer your name becomes associated with one company for a particular product, the more difficult it will be to get a deal with another company. For example, if the public has come to associate your name with Pepsi then Coca-Cola are less likely to want to sponsor you. Now wouldn't that be a nice problem to have?

BANNER ADVERTISING AT VENUES

If the sponsorship is for a tour, or part of a tour, the sponsors will usually want to have their name on banners in each concert arena. They may agree that these only go up in the foyer or they may want them in the concert hall itself. Some artists insist on no banners over the stage and if the sponsor's name is being projected on to the stage backdrop that this stops several minutes before they go on stage. Whether you want to insist on these kinds of restrictions will depend on your own views as to how closely you want to be associated with the sponsor as well as your bargaining power. I don't think it unreasonable, though, to ask that the banners are not so intrusive that they detract from your own performance.

2 Entertainment Law Review 1992 (3(6) 208).

If your sponsorship deal involves publicity for the sponsor at the concert venue then you have to be careful that you don't run foul of any restrictions within the venue itself. The venue owner may already have given the drinks concession to another company. For example, Coca-Cola may already have the right to have their soft drinks on sale at the venue to the exclusion of all other competing brands. If that's the case, they won't take it too well if your sponsor Pepsi then drape their banners and logos about the place. That doesn't mean that you will definitely not be able to do the sponsorship deal – just that you must be aware of any restrictions and make sure you don't agree to do anything in the contract that you can't put into effect on the ground.

MEET AND GREETS

Whatever type of sponsorship deal you do, it is likely that the sponsor will require you to be involved in some kind of 'meet and greet' sessions. These are where the sponsors and their key customers get to meet you. This may be before or after a concert or at specially organised events. Bear in mind that a live performance can be very draining. You may not want to meet a lot of people beforehand and afterwards you may need time to come down from the adrenaline rush of performing. Don't over-commit yourself. I know of some bands that share out the meet and greet sessions between them. It is the job of your manager to make sure that your sponsors don't get over-eager and expect or even demand too much of you.

FREEBIES AND PROMOTIONAL ACTIVITIES

No, this isn't free goods – it's stuff that the sponsor will expect to get for nothing as part of the sponsorship fee. They'll usually want a guaranteed number of free tickets to your concerts. They will always want more than you will want to give. There will need to be a compromise. You could offer more tickets at bigger venues and less or none at all at smaller ones.

The sponsors may want you to attend press conferences for product launches or to make personal appearances. These should always be subject to your availability and any other professional commitments that you have. If you're on a concert tour in Europe you don't want to find yourself committed to having to return to London for a press conference. You should also try to limit these appearances to a maximum number of days over the term of the deal.

Take care before you guarantee that you will do a concert tour in a particular region. You may not be able to deliver this or, if you do, you may lose a lot of money. However, the sponsor may agree to underwrite all or part of such a tour if it's important to them that you perform in those parts of the world.

If the sponsor wants to feature you in adverts, they need to specify how many ads, whether TV or radio and the extent to which you have to be involved. You should have some rights of approval. It's unlikely that you'll be able to limit the number of times they can repeat the ads unless you have considerable bargaining power. If you do then you should aim to allow them a reasonable amount of repeats without it getting to the stage that every time you turn on the television there you are. There's nothing more off-putting than that. The sponsor shouldn't want that either but sometimes they need to have the brakes applied for them.

TRADE MARK LICENCES AND GOODWILL

I discussed in the last chapter the advantages of registering a trade mark. If you have a trade mark either pending or registered in your name or logo then, in your sponsorship deal, you'll be expected to grant a licence to your sponsor to use that trade mark. You should limit the licence to the uses covered by the sponsorship deal and the licence should end when the sponsorship deal does.

PAYMENT

I bet you were wondering when I was going to get to this. What are you going to get paid for all of this work? The amounts can vary widely depending on what you're expected to do, the size of the company, your fame and the length of the deal and how exclusive it is. Each will have to be negotiated on a case-by-case basis. The sponsor or the agent will usually come to you with a figure for what the sponsor thinks it's worth and after due consideration you may want to accept that or try to push it higher.

The sponsorship contract will not only spell out how much you will get paid; it will also say when you get the money. The sponsorship fee could be money alone, or cash and goods or, occasionally, just goods – although, in that case, that's more of an endorsement deal. It isn't usually recoupable or returnable. There are exceptions though. If you break your side of the bargain, for example by not doing the tour, or if it is a case of misrepresentation, as in The Spice Girls case (see above), then the contract might say that you are required to repay some or all of the money. Or you may get sued for its return. You may also be required to return some of the money or to pay compensation if you bring the sponsor's brand into disrepute.

When you'll be paid will usually be some kind of compromise. The sponsor will want to hold back as much of the fee as they can until they're sure you are delivering your side of the bargain. On the other hand, you will be actively promoting the sponsor's product (well, you will, won't you?) and you will want to get some, if not all, of the sponsorship fee in the bank. At the very least you will want to be paid as soon as specific things have been achieved; for example, some of the money should be paid when you sign the deal, some when you start the concert tour and the balance at the end of the tour.

You should also be clear what is included in the fee. If you're doing a recording of a song, remember that there will be mechanical royalties to be paid to your publisher and that of any co-writer (see Chapter 4). If you have an exclusive recording deal then your record company may want payment in return for releasing you from that exclusivity. If the advert is going to be put together with, for example, visual images for television, a synchronisation fee will be payable to your publisher and to the publisher of any co-writer. These can be significant amounts of money. Who is going to be responsible for these fees? Are they included in the sponsorship fee so that you have to sort it out with the publishers? Or is it the sponsor's responsibility? The answer can make a considerable difference to what you end up with in payment.

You should have the right to end the deal if the sponsor breaches the payment terms or otherwise doesn't fulfil their side of the bargain.

CONCLUSIONS

- Decide on the types of product you want to be associated with.
- Either target those companies that produce those products yourself, or through an agent, or decide that you'll wait until they come to you.
- Decide if you're looking for one exclusive sponsor or a series of deals for particular products.
- Decide if you want to do a worldwide or limited country deal.
- Make sure that the services you have to provide are manageable and that you have any necessary permissions from your record and publishing companies.
- When setting the level of the fees agree what is to be included.
- Try to get as much of the fee paid upfront as possible.

10: **TOURING**

GETTING STARTED

When you're starting out you'll probably get gigs in a very hand-to-mouth way. You or your manager will hustle for them, probably starting in your hometown with local pub dates. If you live in a town with a large student population you might get on to the university/college circuit. Local bands are often very popular for 'rag' or Summer balls, possibly as support to other better-known acts. Getting to know the local social secretary at the university/college can help but remember that all local bands with a bit of ambition will be doing the same thing.

If you can get the local media behind you this can open up more local gigs. Don't forget college radio. If you make a fan of the station manager or a particular DJ they'll plug not only your local dates but also if you're venturing further afield. Take copies of your tape or CD to the station and use your best selling skills to convince them they could be in at the start of a future Oasis, Radiohead or whatever.

Once you have a local following you can look to venture outside the area to bigger and hopefully better-paid gigs. A word of warning: don't even think of inviting A&R people to your gigs unless you're well rehearsed and 'tight' in your playing and command an enthusiastic local following. I've been to many showcases where the band makes the fatal error of treating it as just another session in front of their mates. They act far too casually and are under-rehearsed. If the local record company scout happens to be at that gig they could be put off you for life, or it could set back your campaign for a record deal by several months while the damage is repaired. The same disastrous situation could happen if there is a reporter for the local newspaper at the gig who gives you a bad write-up. Don't get me wrong. I know that every act has its off day when, for whatever reason, it just doesn't come off. Scouts and newspaper reviewers will take an off day into account. What they won't forgive is if you aren't acting in a professional way. You should treat every gig as the one when you will be discovered.

Try to find out who are the local scouts for the major record companies – it may be someone at the local college or radio station. Local bands that have been around for longer may be able to tell you, otherwise ask the reporter on music events at the local newspaper. It may even be them. Whoever the scout is, they may be looking to move into the business themselves using the discovery of a great local band as a stepping-stone.

Doing all this is very hard work and mostly unrewarding. Some bands get to play in venues in larger towns by doing a deal with the venue owner or promoter; for example, in return for the booking, the band guarantee there will be a minimum number of tickets sold. If you don't sell enough tickets you have to make up the shortfall. It pays to drum up 'rent-a-crowd' from among your local fans, friends and family. I know of bands that sell package tours – they sell tickets to the gig and hire a coach to get you there and back. This proves especially popular where the band manages to get a gig in a larger town or city. Then the trip to the gig is combined with the chance of a day out in the city at a reasonable price.

As I mentioned in Chapter 1, you might also consider entering one of the many competitions around the country. These might be billed as 'Battle of the Bands' or similar. Look out for adverts in the local press or the music papers such as *NME* or *Melody Maker*. These contests are often viewed as slightly cheesy, not quite a credible way to break into the business. But if it gets you noticed, what's the problem? If nothing happens then quietly stop mentioning you were ever involved in it.

There are also some venues that have special showcase evenings for unsigned artists or writers. The ones I know about are in London but there may well be others in a town near you – ask around.

The Kashmir Club holds regular nights for unsigned acts. The Barfly Club, which has recently moved to the Monarch pub in Camden, also has similar events. The PRS occasionally supports events for artists who are either completely unsigned or only signed for records or publishing. At the time of writing, these were being held at the Kashmir Club but venues do change. The American collection societies ASCAP and BMI also hold unsigned artist events from time to time (see Appendix 2).

You can try to get in on the unsigned acts part of the annual UK music festival called In The City. It is run by Tony Wilson (ex-Factory label boss). The event is usually held in mid-September. As well as being a place for UK music business people to gather and have a drink or five, it is also the venue for a whole series of music events – mostly for unsigned acts. The unsigned gigs are held in local music venues and pubs and are a magnet for A&R scouts and record label honchos. This is because in the past this event has been a fruitful source of new talent including, 'allegedly', Suede, Oasis, Kula Shaker and Younger Younger 28s. To be part of the unsigned section you have to submit your demo and a brief biography to the unsigned organisers who then have the unenviable task of wading through a vast pile of material to come up with a shortlist of about 30–40 bands over the 4–5 nights of the event.

Even for some signed acts, doing live concerts is an essential marketing tool. People that haven't yet bought one of your records may go to one of your gigs and love what you do so much that the next day they go and buy up your entire recording output. A good review of a live gig can give your latest release very valuable publicity. Also, the current emphasis being placed on radio-friendly artists means that if your records aren't the sort that Radio 1 or other powerful radio stations are going to play, you've got little alternative than to build a fan base through live concerts (see Chapter 6).

GETTING A BOOKING AGENT

The next stage on from you or your manager doing all the legwork yourselves is to get a booking agent. This will probably happen after you sign a record deal (see Chapter 3). It may, however, happen before that if you've established a reputation as a good live act and have attracted the attention of local agents because they can see you're a safe bet for venues they regularly book acts for.

Do you need a booking agent? Possibly not. If your horizons are set at only playing local pub venues and you don't mind doing the work yourself you probably won't need one. You certainly wouldn't expect to have one at the beginning of your career. It's another person that you're going to have to pay commission to so you want to make sure it's going to be worthwhile before you get one. Also they are not likely to be interested in you unless you've already established a reputation for live work.

What you may find is that certain venues are closed to you because the venue owner only books acts brought to him by selected booking agents.

Having a booking agent can also give you credibility to get into more prestigious or bigger venues and open up the possibility of supporting bigger name acts. As the booking agent is on a percentage of what you get it's in their interests to drive a hard bargain. If the agent is any good you should end up with a better deal than if you'd argued for it yourself.

You might think that your manager could do the job of a booking agent. Yes, they could and in the early days they probably will. But these specialised booking agents are the experts in putting together larger events such as a UK or European tour of the medium to large venues and stadiums. They know all the promoters; they can get the best deals and have a better chance of getting the prime dates than you or your manager, who won't be doing this on a day-by-day basis. The agents also know details about all the main venues you are likely to want to play and one or two that you won't have thought of. If the venue is outside the main concert circuit they have the specialised expertise to negotiate a good deal for you. With everything else that is going on around a tour, you or your manager are not going to have the time to do this properly. It pays to find someone who can.

HOW DO YOU FIND A BOOKING AGENT?

You can ask your mates in the music business. Which agent do they use, which ones do they rate and which have they have found to be trustworthy? Word of mouth is often a very reliable method of finding a good booking agent. But be sure that the booking agent works in the same area of music as you, otherwise he won't have the contacts in the right places to be of use to you.

Booking agents are also listed in directories such as the *Music Week Directory*. You could call local ones and try to find out which sort of acts they regularly work with and what venues they book. Another good source of information on which agents do what is the monthly magazine *Audience*. It also gives you music business news including details of up-coming festivals and other music industry events.

If you have a record deal then it's likely that your A&R contact will direct you or your manager to a good booking agent. While obviously you should take on board their suggestions, you shouldn't blindly follow their advice. As with finding a manager (see Chapter 2), you should also ask around and arrange to meet more than one agent. You should get them to come and see you perform live. This should show which one seems most enthusiastic. You should also ask around as to which booking agents are seen as having the most 'clout'. Your record company, accountant and lawyer should all have had experience of dealing with booking agents and can give you some guidance. It's also important that your agent has a reputation as being honest. You don't want a booking agent that's going to run off with the ticket takings. If the agent who is interested in you works for a big organisation find out if you'll be dealing with them in person or if they'll be passing you on to someone else in the organisation.

If there's a good buzz or hype about you, and you are signed to a record deal, booking agents will probably approach you or your manager either direct or via the record company. If this happens, the same tips apply. Ask who else is on their books. Ask around about their reputation, honesty and reliability. Get them to meet the band and see you perform live. Make sure the agent 'gets the picture' as to what you're trying to achieve.

One thing that you should also be aware of is that some booking agents may also be getting a financial kick-back from the record label to come on board as your agent. I know of record labels that are keen to see their artists perform live and encourage agents to get involved by paying them either a retainer or a small percentage of record sales (usually 0.5–1%). This should be at the record company's expense and not recoupable against you or deducted from your royalty or other record income. It isn't necessarily a bad thing but there could be a conflict of interest between what you want and what your record company thinks is best for you. Also, when you work out your deal with the agent you need to bear in mind what they're also getting from the record company.

WHAT'S IN A BOOKING AGENCY CONTRACT?

It is often the case that agents do not have written contracts with the artists they represent. They prefer to work on trust. They tell the artists what commission rate they take, they leave it to the artist's tour manager to sort out things such as the riders (see page 195), security requirements and so on. The risk for an agent in not having a written contract is not as great as for a manager. A manager who has no written contract may find it difficult to claim that they should be entitled to commission on records sold after the end of the deal. An agent is less concerned about this because they are probably only booking one tour at a time and will have sorted out in advance their commission on that tour. Agents have no interest in ongoing record or publishing royalties or in merchandising or sponsorship income. That said, even though some agents don't bother with written contracts, most booking agents like to have them to keep things clear and to give them some certainty so that they can plan what is to happen in the future. In many ways the booking agency contract is very similar to a management contract (see Chapter 2).

There are several parts of the contract that are common to all booking agency contracts.

Exclusivity

Your booking agent will be looking for an exclusive arrangement. They won't want to be competing for your work with other agents. Your arrangement with your booking agent sits alongside your management agreement. Indeed your manager may be very involved in the appointment of the booking agent. Your management contract will usually give you the right to approve the identity of any booking agent that your manager appoints on your behalf. Your manager looks after all other aspects of touring other than the actual booking of the concerts. There is a danger of an overlap in the commission arrangements. You don't want to be paying a booking agent and your manager out of the gross income. The management contract will usually say that the manager takes his commission after any commission to a booking agent has been deducted. The management contract will usually give you approval over the terms on which your agent is appointed if they want to charge more than the industry norm of 15–20%. Your booking agent's fee should be deducted from the gross income first and the manager's commission should be calculated on the net amount that is left after the agency commission and any other deductions agreed in the management contract.

Territory

The contract could be a worldwide one or it could be for a specific territory, for example North America. If it's a worldwide deal then it's possible that the booking agent will want to use local sub-agents in some territories. For example, your booking agent may have their own offices in the UK and Europe but be linked in with another company or individual in the US. You may want to have the right to approve the identity of any sub-agents. You will also want to say that any sub-agent's fees come out of the booking agent's fee and aren't payable by you on top.

If you're doing a worldwide deal then you will want to be satisfied that the booking agent has the necessary contacts to do a good job in all countries where you are likely to want to perform live. It's no good you appointing a UK booking agent worldwide when they can do a great job in the UK but haven't a clue how do deal with promoters or venues in other parts of the world.

Term

The length of the term can vary considerably. It could be for a particular tour, for example your 2000 UK Arena Tour. In that case the contract will end after the last date of the tour. You would probably be free to do a deal for the next tour or for the US leg of the same tour with another agent immediately, so long as you didn't run across the UK booking agent's rights. On the other hand, the term could be open-ended; you continue with the booking agent until one of you gives the other notice that you want to end the arrangement. The usual notice period is a minimum of three months. There may also be an agreement that notice can't take effect during a tour or that the agent gets commission on the whole of a tour they have set up even if you terminate the arrangements with them before the tour is finished. This is only fair because tour arrangements often have to be set up many months in advance.

Many booking agents are looking for the certainty of a fixed-term contract. This could be as short as a year but terms of three to five years aren't unusual. Obviously, from your viewpoint, the longer time you are committed to one booking agent, the more you need to have a contract that puts definite obligations on the booking agent to get you work. The contract should also give you a get-out if it isn't working, for example the booking agent can't get you any work or is otherwise falling down on the job.

The booking agent's duties

As we saw with management contracts, the agency contract doesn't often set out in any great detail what the agent will do for you. Their duties are usually expressed in very general terms. There should at least be some kind of obligation on your booking agent to try to get work for you. After all, that is their job. If you've got a fixed-term contract you may also want to make sure that, if you are ready to do gigs and your agent can't or won't get you any, you have an option to go to another agent.

If the booking agent does get you live touring work you should have the right to decide whether you actually want to do the work. The contract will probably give you the right to turn down offers of work if you do so on reasonable grounds. For example, if the booking agent gets you three dates in the north of England and a fourth a day later in Torquay, it might be reasonable to say that you can't get yourself from one end of the country to the other in that time. Or, if you did, it would not be cost-effective once you take into account the travel costs in getting you from A to B. If, however, your booking agent has got you work which you turn down for no good reason, you can't then turn around and say that he hasn't done his job.

Your duties

You will usually have to agree to refer all offers for live work that come to you to your booking agent. Because of the exclusive arrangements you mustn't act as your own booking agent. You will also usually agree to keep your booking agent aware of your plans, for example, if the plan is to release your new album in September. You will be expecting to do live dates to help promote that release. You'll need to tell your agent at the beginning of the year so that they can begin to outline a tour in consultation with you and your manager. Many of the bigger venues are booked up months if not a year in advance for key dates and the earlier you can tell your agent of your plans, the sooner they can start to take options on the key venues and dates. These provisional bookings are confirmed when the details of the tour are firmed up. If you're tying a tour in with the release of your album then it's probable that the dates won't be confirmed until the album release date is confirmed. That said, it doesn't always work to plan. In 1999 Gary Barlow postponed his concert tour at least once because he said he had so many ideas for his new album that he kept reworking it. Therefore, it wasn't ready for release when it was supposed to be.

You will also usually agree to use your best efforts to do the dates that your booking agent has got for you and which you have agreed to do. Obviously illnesses do occur and sometimes tours or particular concert dates are cancelled at short notice due to illness. It is usual to take out insurance against having to cancel a tour or one or more dates on grounds of illness or accident affecting one or more band members. These insurance policies are not cheap but, if you get laryngitis halfway through a world tour, it's comforting to know that insurance will cover any losses. Insurance policies can also be taken out to cover dates that have to be cancelled because not enough tickets have been sold to make it worthwhile. These are of course very expensive and are probably only worth it for big stadium dates. If you've got yourself a decent manager you shouldn't have to worry about whether the necessary insurance is in place as they, or the tour manager, will do this for you.

Insurance policies can also be taken out to cover such things as bad weather on open-air gigs. I remember the owner of the site that hosts the Glastonbury Festival describing in the press how he'd been offered insurance cover against bad weather but hadn't taken it up because the premium was too high. I wonder if he was kicking himself because that particular year the weather was so atrocious that the site turned into a giant mudbath. You can get insurance cover for most things at a price. I remember one of my colleagues dealing with a situation some years ago, when a member of a band was doing a tax year out of the country to save tax. The rules at the time allowed you to return to the UK for a given number of days in that year. The band was doing a world tour that included some dates in the UK. The last of these dates fell on the last day that he would have been entitled to be in the UK and still gain the tax advantages. The concert was due to finish at 11 p.m., which meant that, with a helicopter standing by, he should be out of the country in time. If he wasn't, he would lose significant amounts of tax savings. So an insurance policy was taken out to cover him against that happening. Everything was going very well until the band got a little too enthusiastic in the number of encores and it was getting to nearer 11.30 when the band finally left the stage. A very swift dash to the helicopter followed and, luckily, our man was away just in time. This left a very relieved insurance man who would have had to pay out a lot of money.

Your booking agent may want to have a free hand in deciding which promoter to use for particular tours. So long as you aren't being asked to take less money as a result, you may well be happy to leave this decision to your booking agent. After all, it's also in their interests to get you a good deal.

The fee

What is the agent paid? His fee is usually a percentage of the gross income from your live appearances. It will include the appearance fee but also any benefits that you receive in kind as opposed to cash. For example, the payment you get for a particular contract could be made up of a £10,000 appearance fee plus a car provided by the tour or venue promoter or free travel or hotel accommodation. The agent will usually want to add the value of the car, the travel, the accommodation and so on to the gross income in working out their fee. It's here, of course, that you can see the value of a tour accountant. One of their many jobs will be to see if a proper value has been placed on these non-monetary items.

The fee is usually between 10 and 15% of the gross income. If you are paid £10,000 in appearance fees and a car worth £10,000 then your booking agent will receive 10–15% of £20,000 (i.e. £2–3,000). The agent will negotiate with the promoter or with the venue direct and will usually agree that the promoter or venue pays them their fee direct, with the balance being paid through to you. There may be a deposit paid, which the agent may well hold as security for their fee. Once it is clear that there are sufficient ticket sales to mean that date will not make a loss, the booking agent may well agree to release that money to you less their agency fee. Or the agent may negotiate Guaranteed Minimum payments from the venue or promoter, which are not returnable even if not enough tickets are sold to make the date viable. The booking agent will usually insist on being paid for any work that has been contracted for or substantially negotiated during the term of the agency contract. For example, you may contract to a 40-date tour through a particular agent and then move on to another agent for the rest of the dates or for the next tour. You may well be free to do that but you will still have to pay the first booking agent for the work they did in putting the original 40-day tour together. Sometimes the agent will limit their commission to concert dates that you do within six months of the end of the term of their contract in the UK. This could be a little hard on the agent. If you are doing a world tour then it's likely that it could run well beyond six months. If the agent has done the work in setting up the tour, there are strong arguments for saying that they should be paid for it. As it's unlikely that you'll have to pay any other booking agent for that same tour you aren't going to get a double-hit for fees. If the booking agent has done an all-right job and the contract isn't being disputed or hasn't been brought to an end because the booking agent is in breach of contract, this position is a reasonable one to take.

Accounting

The booking agent will usually want to collect the money and deduct their commission before paying the balance through to you.

You'll want to make sure that the money is paid into a separate bank account, preferably one where the money is held in trust for you. You'll need to see detailed statements of what's been received, from where and how the commission is calculated. You will want to be paid through the balance quickly and you'll need to have the right to carry out an audit of the booking agent's books and records to make sure you've received your proper due.

This is particularly important where some payments may be received upfront in the form of deposits from the venues or as guaranteed sums regardless of the number of tickets sold. The deposit may be returnable in some circumstances. One of the jobs of the tour accountant is to keep track of all these arrangements as well as keeping a close eye on any sums paid in cash on the night.

You should be paid the balance due to you at the end of each gig but that may not be possible, in which case, if you're doing a number of dates, it should be at least weekly. Sometimes payment may come at monthly intervals if the arrangements are particularly complex or involve overseas tax issues (see page 201). If you aren't going to be paid on the night, or payment is delayed, then a rough outline, called a settlement sheet, should be prepared at the end of each concert and given to you or the tour accountant within three days to check.

Assignment and key-man provisions

You need to establish who is going to be your agent – your key contact at the booking agency. The larger the booking agency, the more important it is to get this sorted out. There's nothing worse than signing up to an agency thinking that you are going to be dealt with by one of the hot-shots only to discover that they've passed it to a junior nobody with no experience or clout.

If you can, you should get a right in the contract to terminate it if your key-man isn't available to you as your agent when you need them. Obviously a good agent is going to be working for more than one artist and is going to be in great demand. You can't therefore expect them to be there for you every minute of the day. But when it comes to putting together a big tour, whether you are headlining or as a support act, you need to know that the agent is there for you to lend their experience and bargaining skills to sorting out the details. The agency isn't going to be very happy about agreeing to key-man clauses in the contract. If a particularly good agent wants to go off to another agency, or wants to set up on their own account, that puts you and them in a very good bargaining position. You can terminate the contract if they go and then move to their new agency if you want to. They can use the fact that you could terminate to negotiate better terms for them to stay with the agency or a better settlement term if they still want to leave. If the agency does agree to it then they will probably say that the right to terminate only arises when the agent is consistently not around for 30 days or more. They will also usually exclude periods when the agent is genuinely ill or on holiday. This is fine as long as the agent doesn't take three-month holidays.

If your agent wants to bring in someone to work on your account then you should have approval over who that is.

Also, if the agency plans to sell up or sell on your contract to another company, or it wants to buy into a bigger company, you need to have the right to refuse to be tied to these arrangements unless they first get your approval.

Finally, the contract should give you the right to terminate the contract if the agent is insolvent or they breach their obligations to you, for example if they don't pay the balance of the ticket money through to you when they should and they fail to put this right within a reasonable time of you putting them on notice that they should.

PROMOTERS

As the name suggests, a promoter is responsible for booking artists to perform live at particular venues.

Promoters can be one-man bands promoting single venues or be multi-million-pound multinational corporations owning a whole raft of large and small venues. At the time of writing, a company owned by one of the best-known UK promoters, Harvey Goldsmith, has gone into receivership leaving a large gap in the market place. Harvey is expected to reappear in some form in the near future. No one wants to accept that such a character could just disappear from the scene. His companies were responsible for promoting many large-scale events at Wembley and Earls Court, among others.

Another development that is causing some concern among UK promoters is the aggressive expansion by the US company SFX Entertainments into the UK media and leisure industry. SFX Entertainments owns a large number of the New York Broadway theatres and is the largest concert promoter in the US.[1] In 1999, SFX embarked on a series of acquisitions

1 Source: Jamie Doward's article in the *Observer*, 10 October 1999.

of UK promoters. In mid-1999, SFX bought up the Midland Concert Promotions Group and the Marquee Group. In September 1999 they bought Britain's biggest theatre operator, Apollo Leisure Group, and at the end of 1999 they bought out Barry Clayman Concerts. SFX was also said to be interested in bidding for Stoll Moss, which owns a number of London theatres including the Lyric and the Garrick, but was beaten to it by Andrew Lloyd Webber's Really Useful Group, which apparently paid £87.5 million for the theatres. In less than three years SFX has become the world's largest and most diversified promoter of live events. It has recently announced a deal with the Internet company World Online International apparently with the view to setting up a pan-European live entertainment portal on the Internet. The idea, it seems, is to give World Online International access to SFX's worldwide venues and for SFX to have access to the million-plus users of World Online International's services. Just as I was putting this book to bed, news broke that SFX itself had been sold to a company whose stable of assets include radio stations.

Some promoters and booking agents are concerned that a reduction in the number of promoters will mean less competition and fewer opportunities for artists. The opposite view is that a small number of big and powerful promoters may unlock a greater potential for corporate sponsorship and advertisers. The bigger name stars are most likely to benefit from the concentration in the number of promoters. We may see a split into small venues with no overall promoter and the small number of bigger venues dominated by one or two promoters. The smaller promoters may even be moved to form an alliance to stand up to SFX and their like, as has happened in the States.[2]

WHAT DO PROMOTERS DO?

Promoters are responsible for securing the venue and for selling the tickets. The promoter may be the venue owner or it may be a separate company that has an arrangement with a particular venue. This arrangement may be exclusive or non-exclusive.

The promoter may deal direct with the artist or his manager or they may negotiate through a booking agent.

Promoters make their money on their margins. If they own the venue then they want to cover their costs and make a profit. Promoters dealing with venues make their money on the difference between what they have to pay through to the venue and what they have to pay to the artist/booking agent after allowing for their own expenses.

A promoter may be promoting just one venue or perhaps a festival or a series of venues. There are promoters who operate nationwide but also those who operate only in particular parts of the UK.[3] A promoter may be trying to put together a tour linking a number of venues. If it's just one venue then the contract is likely to be for only one or two concerts. If they're stringing together a tour then, obviously, they're hoping to be the promoter of your whole tour. It will be their responsibility to make the necessary arrangements with all the venues.

2 Eleven major US promoters joined forces in August 1999 and formed the Independent Promoters Organisation (IPO). This was intended as a national tour alternative to SFX.
3 The Regional Promoters' Association is an informal grouping of promoters in the north of England.

Once the dates are pencilled in, the promoter will want an agreement committing the artist to do these dates and the terms on which the artist will perform.

Naturally, these sorts of arrangements are only likely to affect the main artists on the bill – the top billing or headline acts. If you're a supporting artist you have little or no say on the terms of the deal with the promoter. The promoter will usually agree a fee with the headline act and it is up to that act to agree a deal with the supporting act as to the terms on which they appear on the bill.

WHAT'S IN A PROMOTER'S CONTRACT?

Artist's obligations

The contract will set out what concerts the artist will do, when and where. The contract could spell out the length of time the artist is required to perform. For example, it may say that the artist is expected to do one set (performance) of at least 40 minutes' duration. For smaller venues it may say that the artist is expected to do two 40-minute sets with a break in between.

Promoter's obligations

The promoter will agree to provide at least the venue, ticket sales facilities and basic door, stage and backstage security arrangements. Thereafter it's down to the individual arrangements agreed in each contract. The promoter may agree to supply certain equipment and personnel, for example a particular sound desk or sound engineer. If the concert dates include any overseas then any personnel should come equipped with all necessary permits, including work permits for overseas dates or for overseas personnel working in the UK.

The promoter will also usually be required to provide an agreed level of backstage amenities for the artists in the form of dressing rooms, toilets and meet and greet or VIP areas.

It's also usually the responsibility of the promoter to provide insurance cover against injury or death caused to members of the public. This is called public liability insurance. It is vital to ensure that this cover is in place. Obviously this will be your manager's job, not yours. However, in the early days, when perhaps you don't have a manager on board, it's worth remembering that you can get injured too – so do think about this. Unfortunately accidents do happen at live concerts; people fall or get caught up in the crush at the front of the stage. If there isn't insurance in place, the person injured could look to you for compensation. In the same way, if you employ anyone else to do any construction work for you for the stage or lighting rig then make sure those subcontractors are also carrying insurance or, once again, responsibility could fall back on you.

The promoter may also insure against cancellation by the artist or bad weather for open-air festivals. However, they won't necessarily add you to the people covered by the policy. They may only be concerned that their losses are covered and not be concerned about whether you can recover any of the sums you have paid out to musicians, stage crew, on equipment hire and transport and so on. It is usually your or your manager's responsibility to get all insurance necessary to cover against cancellation on grounds of accident or illness; possibly against poor ticket sales and the equipment provided by you against loss or damage.

Riders

Anyone who has seen *Spinal Tap*, the spoof film about the music business, will know about the occasionally ridiculous artist riders. These are the lists of specific requirements that the artists have for their comfort and entertainment backstage. Only black jellybeans and sandwiches cut in circles will do! I have seen some very strange riders in my time – ranging from twelve pages of very detailed menu requirements including very specific types of cereal and drinks that can only be bought in the US. On a European tour, that was pretty unreasonable and changes had to be negotiated and substitutes found. Other riders specify only that they want a crate of good whiskey and five crates of beer. Well, this *is* rock'n'roll!

Some artists take their own caterers with them or will only use a caterer that they know is familiar with their particular requirements. Some riders are there for a very good reason. For example, an artist may be a vegan or vegetarian or allergic to particular food. I've also seen riders that insist that all hotel rooms have hypo-allergenic bedding and pillows.

It is usual to leave the negotiation of the details between the manager or the tour manager and the promoter. It is not usually cost-effective to get your lawyer involved in this. The riders do form part of the contract so the promoter has to make sure that the requirements are reasonable, affordable and obtainable. If they don't, and the omissions are sufficiently serious, this could be a breach of contract. Even if the omissions are more minor in nature it can cause major grief with the artist, which is the last thing a promoter wants just before the artist goes out on stage.

Fees

You and your booking agent are dependent upon the promoter for ticket sales and income. You'll want to be sure that you are guaranteed a certain level of income. If you are an already established artist you may be able to get a Guaranteed Minimum included in the contract. If it is, you will be paid this regardless of whether the promoter sells enough tickets. This is where the promoter runs a risk. He has to get the level of the Guaranteed Minimum right because he'll have to pay it even if he doesn't sell a single ticket.

Over and above any Guaranteed Minimum sum you might receive a fixed percentage of the promoter's net receipts less what you've already received. For example, if the Guaranteed Minimum is £10,000 and after the promoter has paid out certain agreed expenses you are entitled to 10% of the net receipts then, if the net ticket sales are £100,000, you will only get your Guaranteed Minimum. If the net receipts are £250,000 then your 10% is worth £25,000. After deducting your Guaranteed Minimum of £10,000 you are then due another £15,000. If you are using this method then you have to check very carefully that the expenses that the promoter can deduct are reasonable and that the percentage you receive of the net represents a reasonable return. The alternative is that you receive a further fixed payment dependent on levels of ticket sales. For example, it could be agreed that you get a Guaranteed Minimum of £10,000 and if ticket sales exceed £250,000 then you receive another £15,000. With this type of payment arrangement you need to assess how realistic it is that ticket sales will be high enough for you have a reasonable chance of receiving further payments.

Payment

The contract should set out when the Guaranteed Minimum is to be paid. Usually at least half of it should be paid upfront and the rest on the night of the first of the concerts.

The balance of any payments should be made on the night of the concert or possibly at the end of a particular leg of a tour or end of each week of a tour.

It's important that your tour accountant has access to the box office tills and receipts on the night of the concert and that all ticket stubs should be kept for at least three months after the concert in case they need to be checked by the accountant. Further payments under your merchandising deal may be dependent on you having a given number of people at your concerts (see Chapter 8). The ticket stubs and any on-the-spot head count on the night will prove the number of people at a particular deal, so you *must* have access to that information and proof. Receipts for any expense that the promoter is allowed to deduct should also be scrutinised and kept for later checking. Only those expenses allowed by the tour accountant should be deducted.

Other income

The promoter or the venue owner may have done deals with catering companies or drink suppliers. The contract should set out whether or not you should get any share of the profits from such sources. For example, the venue may have a deal with Coca-Cola that they are the official suppliers of soft drinks to the venue. If you are an artist that commands a very loyal following of fans who will ensure that your concerts are a sell-out then this can only benefit Coca-Cola in the number of soft drinks they will sell. If you have sufficient bargaining power you can insist on sharing some of the money that Coca-Cola pays to the promoter or venue for the right to be the exclusive supplier.

The sale of merchandise can be an important source of income for an artist. The promoter/venue may make a charge for the right to set up merchandising stalls at the venue. In your merchandising deal you will have covered whether the merchandising company is allowed to deduct some or all of this charge from the gross income before you receive your percentage.

If you have sufficient bargaining power you could insist that you alone have the right to sell food or drink and that the promoter gets no income from these or from merchandise sales. You can then do suitable sponsorship deals with food and drink companies as well as your merchandising deals.

Restrictions

You should insist that the promoter stops anyone from recording your performances unless you intend to make a live recording or film of the concert. Your record contract will probably say something about you not allowing anyone to make a recording of your performance. While it is very difficult for you to prevent a bootlegger unofficially and unlawfully recording your performance, you can show the right spirit by putting it in your contract with your promoter that you do not condone this sort of activity. If you do intend to make a film of your performance, perhaps to make a video or for a live webcast or television broadcast, you should make sure that the promoter will allow you to get access to the venue for the recording at no charge.

Each venue has its own restrictions on parking and when your crew can gain access to load equipment in or out. Any particular stipulations or restrictions should be set out in a rider or schedule to the main agreement. In residential areas you may have severe restrictions on how late you can play and there may be an early curfew on when your crew can load the equipment back out. You may have to come back the next morning. If so you need to ensure the equipment is kept securely and that you are insured against loss or damage. If you are doing a nationwide tour then you or your tour manager need to know these restrictions well in advance. It wouldn't be funny if you had a date in Scarborough on the Friday night and your equipment was still in Torquay because your crew couldn't get in to load out the equipment after Thursday's Torquay gig until seven o'clock the next morning.

An important part of protecting your brand is to ensure that there are no sales of unauthorised merchandise inside or outside the venue. It's easier for a promoter to control illegal merchandise inside the venue but they may say they have no control over what happens outside. In that case you should try to make sure that the venue and the promoter co-operate with Trading Standards Officers or other personnel who are trying to stop unauthorised or pirate merchandise.

GETTING FUNDING

Funding for a tour can come from a number of different places. At the lowest level, where you are just starting out and doing local gigs, you will expect to be paid little or nothing over and above some petrol money and a few free pints of beer. As you progress you may get a small percentage of the ticket sales and may make some money from sales of T-shirts or recordings of your performances that you sell at the gigs. There probably won't be much in the way of profits after you hire a PA, pay for transport and maybe an agent or manager.

It is possible for an unsigned act to get sponsorship for live work. As mentioned in Chapter 9, companies such as Doc Marten have sponsored live tours by unsigned acts. Pub chains such as The Firkin pubs also sponsor live music at their pubs around the country. As I said at the beginning of this chapter, some artists can make a decent living from live gigs if they can keep their costs down, can play decent-sized venues and have a loyal following of fans. But it is very hard work.

It isn't usually until you get signed to a record company that proper funding is available for touring. Sometimes you can make specific provisions for the availability of tour support money in the record contract at the time you negotiate your deal. If you and your manager have worked out a gameplan that requires you to do a lot of live gigs in order to promote your records then you may want to make it a condition of the record contract that the record company gives you support funding to do that, particularly in the early stages.

Once you are signed to a record deal, bigger venues may open up to you. A booking agent may come on the scene and get you slots as support bands or lower-down-the-order gigs at summer open-air festivals. You may also make money from merchandise sales or from tour sponsorship.

However, it's likely that you won't make a profit on your live work until you've achieved quite a degree of success and fame as a recording artist. Even then you may barely break even if you have an expensive live set with lots of special effects and a cast of thousands. If you keep your live set very simple and don't have loads of backing singers, or a live orchestra, then you can stand a better chance of making money. But you have to balance cutting back your expenses to a minimum against the risk that your show is a disappointment to your fans, which would be counter-productive.

Most artists need the financial support of their record company to get them out on the road. The record company will rarely agree to put this in the record contract unless you have a lot of bargaining power or if you are prepared to hold out for this support at the expense of perhaps a lower advance or royalty. Even if it isn't specifically in the contract it is usually in the record company's interests for you to be out touring and promoting your new album. If you can only do this by making a loss (the shortfall) then the record company has to come to your rescue and underwrite this shortfall. This is usually called tour support.

Tour support is usually 100% recoupable from all your record sales. This is, however, negotiable and could be reduced to 50% recoupable with the remainder being treated as a non-recoupable marketing expense of the record company. Sometimes, if the tour support is for a tour in a particular part of the world, you could agree that the tour support is only recouped from record sales within that particular area.

In addition to making up any shortfall, the record company may pay a 'buy-on' fee. This is the fee payable to the headline artist on a tour or to his record company for the privilege of being allowed to support them. For some new artists the association with a more established name gives them an opening to a much wider potential audience as well as the chance to perform in bigger venues. For the headline act this is an additional source of income, reducing the amount of tour support they'll need from their record company. Buy-on fees for large venues and for concerts by big name artists can run to tens of thousands of pounds. It's one of the reasons why you will often see a big name artist being supported by another smaller act on the same label. That way the costs are kept in the family.

HOW MUCH TOUR SUPPORT WILL YOU NEED?

Before you can go to your record company to ask for tour support, you need to have an idea how much you'll need.

First, you'll need to get someone to prepare a tour budget. This could be your manager or your regular accountant or bookkeeper. However, when you're doing a bigger tour, either as headline or support, you should consider getting a specialist tour accountant on board. The tour accountant could be someone at your regular accountancy firm or one recommended by them. You could find one by asking round your friends. Your A&R contact or manager can suggest people, as can your lawyer. Most importantly, the tour accountant must be honest, must understand how tour promoting works and be brave enough to tackle unscrupulous promoters about to run off with the cash midway through the gig.

The tour accountant, or any other person doing that job, will put together an outline budget that will make guestimates of income and expenditure. As details such as any Guaranteed Minimum, buy-on fees, merchandise advances and so on become known, they are factored in. The accountant works very closely with you or your manager to work out what type of shows you intend to put on. The number of musicians and how elaborate the stage set and lighting effects are to be will all affect the tour budget.

Once the tour accountant has a good idea of the likely profit or loss, they prepare an outline draft budget that the manager then takes to the record company in order to negotiate the level of tour support. It's important, therefore, that they try not to make wild guesses and are as accurate as they can be as to what you are likely to need.

The record company will usually set a maximum amount that they'll pay to underwrite the shortfall. For example, your tour accountant may have estimated a tour loss of £18,000. The record company checks the figures and make their own assessment of how valuable it will be to them in record sales if the tour goes ahead. They may decide that one or two dates should be dropped or that some of the costs could be saved. They will set a limit on how much they will pay. In this case, and after some adjustments, they might say that it will pay up to £16,000 in tour support. You and your manager have to then sit down with the tour accountant and any production manager working on the tour to see if savings can be made. The tour then goes ahead and the record company pays the shortfall up to the maximum of £16,000. If you do better than expected and only lose £15,000 then the record company underwrites a £15,000 shortfall, not £16,000. The actual amount they will pay up to that maximum is determined by the actual costs supplied by the tour accountant after the end of the tour with supporting invoices. If you do worse than you thought you were going to do and make a £17,000 loss then the record company is only obliged to pay £16,000 and may insist that you sort out the rest yourself.

The record company will usually agree to pay part of the tour support upfront. This means that your essential personnel can get paid some of what is due to them and essential equipment can be hired. The tour accountant then has to juggle who gets paid along the way and who waits until the final instalment comes in from the record company. Needless to say, the tour accountant is rarely the most popular man on the tour.

Even if you do have something in your record contract about tour support it is unlikely that all the details will be in there and so it is usual to set out the arrangements reached with the record company on tour support in a side letter to the main record contract. Copies of all side letters should be kept together with the record contract. If you are reviewing the accounting statements, or are considering doing an audit, you need to have details of all the arrangements you have reached about what amounts are or are not recoupable and from what sales. Unless the side letter is very simple, your lawyer should review it before you sign it.

This is an example of the sorts of things you'd expect to see in a tour budget for a band doing a number of overseas concerts or a tour involving overnight hotel stays and transportation.

Rough budget for overseas tour

DESCRIPTION	COMMENTS	RATE		PERIOD	TOTAL
		£/Day:		Days req'd:	
Equipment					
Tour Rentals:	*(Add details below of all items*				
Fixed Lights	*& costs)*				
Moving Lights					
Risers					
Sound					
Security		per day			
Band Tour Bus					
Crew Tour Bus					
Trucking					
Flight Case Rental					
Equipment Rental	*(Any extra equipment required)*				
Wages (Band & Crew Party)		Rate:		Period:	
Band members	*(Names of any band members*				
Crew members	*on wages and any crew)*		pw		
Daily Expenses	*No. of people on expenses*	Rate per day		Days:	
Band Party	*How many in band*		pd		
Crew Party	*How many in crew*		pd		
Crew Driver	*Usually 1 per transport*		pd		
Truck Drivers	*1*		pd		
Band Driver	*1*		pd		
Accommodation	*How many needing beds*	£/Night:		No. of nights:	
Band Party					
Crew Party					
Transport	*To and from hotel/venue*				
Taxis	*Taxis & Cars*				
Travel to and from	*Band & Crew Party*				
London					
Flights	*Internal – to national gigs*				
Flights	*International – to overseas gigs*				
Freight	*To and from gigs for equipment*				
Local transport	*From airport/station to gig*				

DESCRIPTION	COMMENTS	RATE		PERIOD	TOTAL
		£/Day:		Days req'd:	
Administration & Commissions/fees **UK & Europe** (or wherever tour is)					
Tour Insurance	*Cancellation of tour*				
Tour Insurance	*Equipment loss/damage*				
Insurance	*Public Liability for concertgoers*				
Tour Accounting	*Fees for tour accountants*				
Itineraries	*Printing/binding of gig details*				
Passes	*Printing/laminating of security*				
	passes				
Tips	*Hotel/porters/taxis etc*				
Design Fee	*Stage set design*				
Design Fee	*Lighting design*				
Commission	*Booking Agent's percentage*	%			
Commission	*Management*	%			
Miscellaneous	*Any special items*				
Phone & Fax	*Long-distance costs*				
Laundry					
Pre-production	*Rehearsals*				
Subsistence	*Food/living expenses*				
		Sub-Total:			
	(In case anything goes wrong:)	5% Contingency:			
		Total:			
	(Amount you are guaranteed	Guarantee:			
	to receive:)			USD	
	(Ticket and merchandise sales)	Income:			
	Profit after costs:	Approx. UKL			

OTHER PLANNING ISSUES

There are other things that have to be taken into account when planning a tour.

TAX PLANNING

Your accountant should advise whether there are any tax advantages to you in putting your touring services through a limited company and, if so, should that be a UK-based or offshore company (see Chapter 11).

If your accountant does decide that you should have a limited company, a service agreement should be put in place between you and the company (see Chapter 11). The contract with any promoter will then be with the limited company.

If some or all of the dates are in another EU country then the band (or company) may need to register for VAT in each country you are going to visit. This can be avoided if the promoter agrees to account for the VAT on the performance fees using what is known as the 'reverse charge' method. And no, it doesn't have anything to do with telephone calls. Essentially, what it means is that the promoter takes responsibility for accounting for all the VAT in his own country so the band need not get involved. You need to set this out clearly in the contract with the promoter to avoid a situation where the VAT authorities in the country concerned demand that the band (or the company) pays VAT.

In some countries there is an obligation to pay tax in the country on your earnings from the live work. The promoter may have to deduct the tax before they hand the money over to you. In that case your contract with the promoter must make sure that they have to hand over the sums they have withheld to the relevant tax authorities. In countries where there are reciprocal tax treaties in place, it is possible to claim exemption from some of these taxes or, if they have a tax treaty in place, you might be able to reclaim some or all of the amounts withheld. The promoter should be obliged to do all the necessary paperwork and the local tax authorities should either confirm you are exempt from tax on the income or give you a certificate of how much tax has been withheld so that you can offset some or all of it against your UK income for tax purposes.

Until recently, when a band was embarking on a long tour, when a large proportion of a tax year was to be spent outside the UK, the band might have decided to take a tax year out. This meant that the band members would remain out of the country for long enough not to pay tax in the UK for that particular tax year. At the time it didn't mean that you had to be out a full year – you could spend some days in the UK during that tax year. If this was carefully planned, the artist could also avoid paying any income tax at all on his earnings during that tax year. These arrangements were altered in 1998. You will no doubt have seen the press stories about The Rolling Stones cancelling their UK dates in 1998. This was on tax grounds. They and several members of the crew were apparently taking tax years out from the UK. The tightening up of the rules meant that, in order to get the maximum tax benefit, they couldn't set foot into the UK the whole of that tax year. The UK dates were cancelled because otherwise the Stones and their crew would lose all of the benefit of their tax year out.

Obviously everybody's tax circumstances are different and these are only very general comments. Nothing will substitute for proper, professional tax planning and advice. Such planning should be done as far ahead as possible.

PUBLICISING THE TOUR

This is the joint responsibility of you and the promoter. Your record company also has a vested interest and will want to co-ordinate their own marketing efforts with the tour dates. For example, if they had planned a poster campaign in particular towns in the UK then they may decide to target those towns where you are doing live dates. The tour posters may also give information on when the latest record is to be released. The promoter or the venue will publish adverts in the music and local press listing forthcoming tours. The band's press officer and the internal press office at the record company will get to work placing the information in the press, getting interviews and personal appearances for the band to promote the tour. The band will be expected to mention it in interviews with the press or on radio or TV.

Increasingly the Internet is being used to advertise tours. This could be on the record company's website but more usually it will be on the artist's website, possibly with a link to the promoter's site, or that of the venue, and the possibility of ordering tickets online.

Your fan club can be invaluable in publicising your tour. The regular newsletter sent out to your fans can give details of forthcoming live events and where tickets can be bought. Sometimes the fan club does a deal with the promoter and/or a travel company to offer special travel, accommodation and ticket packages at a reduced rate to fan club members. What your fan club has to be careful of is offering things that it can't then deliver. For example, members of the Boyzone fan club were apparently offered special top-of-the-range seats at Boyzone concerts as part of a special package. It seems that the promoters did not deliver the expected good seats, leading to a demand for the return of monies. Such bad experiences can have a very negative effect on the fan base and their support for the artist.

OTHER PERSONNEL

TOUR MANAGER

Depending on the size of the tour, and your degree of success, you may appoint a tour manager to work alongside your manager in organising the day-to-day details of the tour. Tour managers go out on the tour and handle all crises as they come up. They are generally paid a weekly fixed fee and receive free travel and accommodation and probably a fixed daily sum for expenses.

SOUND AND LIGHTING ENGINEERS

How your music sounds and how you look on stage are crucial to the success of your live performances. Most bands learn at an early date the importance of having their own sound engineer and not relying on some stranger in a strange venue. As soon as they can afford it, most bands also like to bring along their own lighting engineer. Both of these will be on a daily or weekly rate with free accommodation and travel and daily expenses.

BACKING BAND AND SESSION MUSICIANS

If you're a solo artist or only one of you is signed to the record label then any backing musicians and singers have to be engaged for the tour. There are many different types of arrangements that can be reached with regular band members. They can be on a year-round retainer or on a small, daily-based retainer for when they aren't needed and a higher fee when they have work to do, such as at rehearsals, personal appearances, interviews and during the tour. When they aren't needed they could be on a first-call basis, which means they have to drop everything to make themselves available for you. They may be completely free to do other work but on the understanding that if you call for them and they aren't available then you will get someone else. You can only afford to do that if they are replaceable. If they are crucial to your sound then you would be better advised to put them on a retainer on a first-call basis.

Other non-regular members of the band will generally be engaged on a daily or weekly rate plus accommodation, travel and daily expenses. Additional fees may be payable to regular or non-regular members for other promotional work such as appearing in a video, a live TV or radio performance or a webcast to promote the tour. Or the fee that they are paid could include any of these extra activities and fees. It is important that you agree a 'buy-out' of all rights on the musicians' or vocalists' performances whether they are your regular band members or not. If they are Musicians Union or Equity members there will be minimum rates for the work you want them to do and rules on what can be bought out in the way of rights and what will be the subject of further repeat fees. If you don't buy out the rights, you may get into difficulties if you then go ahead and do a TV or video deal for performances including those of the session musicians or singers. You may believe you have cleared all rights and say as much in the contract. If you haven't then the musician or vocalist, or their union, can come out of the woodwork at the most unhelpful moment.

All these personnel should be given written agreements specifying their fee, when it will be paid and what you expect to get by way of services and rights in return.

For personnel who are not regular members of the team it may be wise to look at getting them to enter into confidentiality agreements. These are agreements that make it clear that they have to keep confidential anything that they find out about you from being on the road with you. They are intended to stop people selling salacious stories and, even worse, pictures of you misbehaving on tour. If you don't know the person very well then it might be an idea to go for these. If, however, they are regular band members then it could be counter-productive because they could get upset at what they might see as you not trusting them.

● The importance of getting things clear in contracts with musicians is borne out by a case involving Elvis Costello.[4]

Elvis Costello employed Thomas as a musician to perform on the European tour with him as part of his band. He was also going to do the US tour but as a part of a separate contract. He employed Thomas through his service company, Elvis Costello Limited. The tour had breaks in it between countries in Europe, when Thomas's services were not required. Thomas took a seven-day break between the UK and USA tours and put in a claim for payment. When he didn't get paid he applied to the court to wind up/liquidate Costello's company for insolvency. The court declined to do that but did order that Thomas be paid on the basis that the court did think it was part of the European tour. The lesson for lawyers is to make absolutely sure that your tour agreements are clear as to when someone is working and when it is unpaid leave.

4 *Elvis Costello Limited* v. *Thomas*, Chancery Division June 1997.

THE FUTURE

What we've talked about so far are largely traditional methods of touring and promoting yourself through live work. We're already seeing glimpses of what might happen in the near future. What I'm talking about is virtual touring – or webcasts. As the name suggests, these are broadcasts of your live performances (or interviews) over the Internet.

Webcasts can be an additional means of promoting yourself alongside the actual tour. By this I mean that you could be doing a normal tour and agree to have your performance filmed and the sound 'streamed' (i.e. digitally presented in a way that means it can be listened to on a computer but not downloaded). The webcast could be available on one or more sites, either at the same time as the concert is taking place – called a simulcast – or at a later date.

Alternatively, what is now increasingly happening is that the artist doesn't go out on the road at all but just goes into a studio. His performance is then streamed and filmed and broadcast, either on the artist's own website or in conjunction with another site or portal.

In fact, in the near future, artists may not need to rely on record company support and will be able to fund their own records and concerts via the Internet and partnerships with IT or telecom companies.

As I said in Chapter 8, imaginative use of your brand name and the Internet can make it possible for you to target your marketing at your potential or actual fans. For example, if you had access to a database of the people who visit your site, or who listened to your last webcast, then you could email them all and tell them when you're going to be performing live and let them buy tickets to the gigs online. Or you could dispense with touring altogether and just do webcasts. There are already a couple of UK venues that are either converting themselves into specialist webcast venues or are setting themselves up from scratch as Internet venues.[5]

You may ask how you make money from webcasts. Well, you could have an arrangement where your fans have to pay a small fee to have access to your webcast. This would be similar to the pay-per-view system offered by some satellite and cable TV companies for special concerts or sporting events. Alternatively, you could decide to broadcast the webcast for free and get your money from other sources. For example, you could do a deal with a sponsor so that, in return for being associated with the webcast, you get a fee (see Chapter 9). Or you could do a deal with one or more advertising companies who might want to put what are called 'banner adverts' on the home page of the site offering the webcast. These companies are prepared to pay for the right to advertise on that site. Or you could turn yourself into an entertainment channel and members will then subscribe on a weekly or monthly basis to listen to whatever is on your site during that time.

The possibilities are endless, and the future is as wide as your imagination will allow.

5 One London venue, the Mean Fiddler, has now closed its doors to regular gigs and has set up four permanent cameras to facilitate webcasts.

CONCLUSIONS

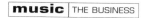

- Get yourself a good agent.
- Tie your touring in with your record company's marketing plans.
- Use the Internet to advertise forthcoming tours.
- Look at doing webcasts as the only or an additional way to make money from touring.

11: **BAND ISSUES**

INTRODUCTION

The solo artists and songwriters among you may want to skip this chapter but if you co-write or plan any kind of recording collaboration it would be worth you reading it to see some of the potential pitfalls.

It may seem very negative to talk about problems and issues before you've released a record or even got a deal. But that's exactly when you should be looking at the things that can cause friction within bands. If you sort some of these things out at the beginning when everything's going well you'll do so much more easily and with less tension. If you wait until you've been on the road non-stop for six months and can't stand the sight of each other then, believe me, it'll seriously strain, if not destroy, the relationship.

WHO OWNS THE BAND NAME?

As we saw in Chapter 1, choosing the right name is vital, but once you've decided on a band name, and have done what you can to check that no one else has it, you have to decide who owns that name.

Your record company won't normally expect to own your band name and you should be very wary of any company that says they want to. It does sometimes happen in the dance world where a record company thinks up the name and concept and hires in people to perform. In these cases they might have a very good reason to say that they should own the name, but these are relatively rare exceptions. What the record company *will* expect you to do is to confirm (to warrant) that you have the right to use the name and that they have the exclusive right to use it in connection with the recordings you make during the term of the record contract and a non-exclusive right after the contract ends if they go on selling your records. The same goes for the music publishers. They will want the exclusive right to use the name in connection with exploitation of your songs during the term of the publishing contract and a non-exclusive right after the end of the term for any ongoing uses of the songs that they still control. You don't want to give exclusive rights for all uses of the name to any one company, for example your record company, as that would mean that you couldn't then use your name to sell merchandise or do a sponsorship deal.

WHO *WITHIN A BAND* OWNS THE NAME?

It's essential that you sort this out at the beginning. I also firmly believe that you should put that down in writing. But I realise that I am probably whistling in the wind. I tell every band about to sign a deal that they should have a band agreement. They usually nod and say that they understand why they should have one but most of them never do anything about it. It doesn't have to be a terribly formal document – although as a lawyer I would have to advise that a proper agreement drawn up by a lawyer would be best. Even if you don't go for that it would be better than nothing to write down what you've all agreed and sign it and then keep it in a safe place. You may think that this is over the top and a bit unnecessary but if you can't prove who owns the band name you can get the very unedifying spectacle of two or more band members arguing over who has the right to use the name.

Although it can happen, it would be quite unusual for the band name to be owned by just one member of the band. An exception would be where one or more members form the core of the band and the others are not permanent members. For example, a band may be made up of a core of the vocalist and the lead guitarist, who do most of the writing, and a rhythm section of bassist and drummer on a wage and not signed to the record contract. The core members may not want to share ownership of the band name with the other two unless and until they become full time permanent band members.

It's most common to agree that all members of the band own the band name. More sophisticated band agreements could set out who gets to use the name if the band splits up. You may decide that in that case none of you could carry on using the name or that those who carry on performing together as a band can continue to use the band name and that the one who leaves can't. Then you get problems if two or more members leave and set up another band. There's no simple solution and it's something that you should talk over with your lawyers as they will have some suggestions that you may want to adopt.

That said, you may not in fact get any say in what happens to the band name if the band splits up, because the record contract may well decide the issue for you. The contract might say that the record company has final say over who can continue to use the band name. This may seem unfair but if you think about it the record company has invested a lot of time and money in building up your name, and the reputation in your name, through their marketing efforts. They won't want to risk losing control of that if one or more members of the band were to leave and, as a result, no one could continue to use the name. You may get a chance to say no to this if you already have a band agreement in place or, as usual, if you have a lot of bargaining power. If the record company does decide who gets to use the band name then you have to think about whether the other band members should be paid some kind of compensation for the loss of the right to use the name. It's possible that, either under the terms of the partnership/band agreement or by the operation of the Partnership Act 1890, the band name will be treated as an asset of the partnership that forms part of its 'goodwill'. There are formulas that accountants can use to work out how much that goodwill is worth. If the partnership is dissolved because the band splits up and, for example, the vocalist continues as a solo artist then the others could have the value of their share of the goodwill in the name calculated and paid to them as part of the settlement between the band members. It's quite a difficult and delicate question and needs to be treated carefully. This is another good reason why you should sort it out at the beginning – before any tensions or pretensions get in the way.

STRUCTURE OF BAND ARRANGEMENTS

You can decide on things such as the ownership of the name and how the income is to be divided between you. Before your lawyer can put what you've agreed into a legal document you need to also decide what legal form the arrangements between you are going to take. There is no simple answer as to which is best. Each has their good and bad points. Each band's needs are going to be different and you have to look at each on its own facts. It's important that you involve both your lawyer and your accountant on this question as your lawyer will be looking to protect you from a legal viewpoint and your accountant will be looking at the financial and tax implications for you of the different types of agreement. Your accountant will know your personal circumstances and will be able to advise whether one type of structure works better than another.

The two main types of arrangement are a partnership and a limited company.

If you decide that the band should be a partnership then the band agreement will usually take the form of a partnership deed. This is like a legal contract that sets out how the partnership is going to operate on a day-by-day basis and puts in writing what you've agreed about the band name, the split of earnings and so on. If you decide to become a limited company then you will probably be advised to have a shareholders' agreement, which does the same thing essentially as a partnership deed but also deals with what happens to your shares in the company if the band splits up or one or more members leave. At the risk of confusing things even more, it is also possible for the band to take the form of a partnership or a limited company and for the individual members to decide to set up their own company to provide their services to the band through the company. I'll go into this in more detail below.

LIMITED COMPANY

A few years ago accountants regularly advised bands to set up a limited company for some or all of the band's services in the entertainment business. There were good tax reasons for doing so; especially the tax year out that was only available to employees and not to self-employed individuals or partners. This particular tax loophole has now been closed and so the tax advantages have been considerably reduced. The reasons for setting up a limited company are now more complex and, if you are considering this option, I strongly suggest you have specialist advice from your accountant.

The main advantages are:

- You can spread your income (for example a large advance) over a number of years and therefore not have it all taxed in the year in which you get it.

- It may be a more tax efficient way of distributing income to band members.

- Increased flexibility for pension contributions.

- Increased flexibility for capital gains tax planning.

- It might protect you from legal actions because anyone bringing such an action would have to sue the company in the first instance.

Also, if a lot of the band's income is going to be earned overseas you can use an offshore company to avoid paying UK tax until you decide you need to have access to the money in the UK.

One of the main downsides is that there are more rules governing what companies can and cannot do and they have to publish accounts, so members of the public could find out how much you earn. There are also higher administration charges with a limited company.

Obviously, the sooner you get advice and decide on the band structure the better. If you leave it too late, and try to put the structure in place after you've already signed contracts, things get much more complicated. If you've already done a record deal as individuals and you then decide you're going to have a limited company then the record deals would have to be 'novated' (renewed) in the name of the company. Also, if you have already received some money as an individual this might jeopardise a scheme to take money out of the country or may result in the Inland Revenue deciding you are not a limited company and should be taxed as individuals.

On a more basic level, if you decide halfway through the negotiation of a record or publishing deal to change the structure then the business affairs person at the record or publishing company isn't going to find this very funny as they will have to redraft the contract to deal with the new structure.

If you do decide on a limited company then bear in mind that you'll have to pay to get the company, to have it set up with the name that you want (assuming that name is available) and you will have to pay the annual running costs. These have been reduced for smaller companies because they do not now have to file full accounts and the administrative burdens have been reduced. This was in order to encourage small entrepreneurial businesses. However, there are still formalities that you have to deal with, and do remember that your accounts are open to the public.

The band members will be the shareholders and you will have to agree how many shares each member is going to have. This will probably be equal but need not be. Day-to-day decisions on the running of a limited company generally require a 50%-plus majority. If it's a two-member band and each has 50% of the shares then each can block a decision by the other. Major decisions of the company require a 75%-plus majority. If you have a four-member band with equal shareholdings then one member could block major changes but three could gang up on the fourth to push through day-to-day decisions requiring a 50%-plus majority. To get around such problems you are usually advised to put a shareholders' agreement in place. This agreement decides how day-to-day matters are to be dealt with and couldn't state that major decisions require unanimous agreement (for example, three out of four couldn't vote through a major change against the wishes of the fourth). The shareholders' agreement will also deal with what is to happen if a member wants to leave. It will usually require that they resign as an officer of the company and that they first offer their shares to the other band members. If a value for the shares can't be agreed then an accountant is usually brought in as an arbitrator to decide the matter.

PARTNERSHIP

This is the main alternative structure for bands. The band members are in partnership together for the particular venture of being a band. All partners are treated equally and earnings and losses are shared by all. You will usually be advised to put a partnership agreement in writing. That agreement will decide how the venture is going to be run on a day-to-day basis, whether all partners are equal (or whether some are more equal than others) and what is to happen to the band name if the partnership is dissolved. It will record whether anyone has put any money (or goods such as equipment) into the partnership and, if so, whether the money is intended to be working capital of the business or a loan and whether the equipment has been gifted to the partnership or is still owned by one member and is on loan. Does each band member own the equipment they use, for example a drum kit or a guitar? What if it was bought with band advances – does that make it joint property? What about the vocalist who has no equipment other than a microphone or two? The partnership deed should also deal with these things. The other main thing that the partnership agreement can deal with is the question of who is entitled to what shares of the songs and the publishing advances and income. This is a very tricky subject and a very emotive one, which is why I say that you should sort it out at the beginning of the relationship, before money starts to come through from the songs (see Chapter 4).

Even if you don't have a written agreement there can still be a partnership. The taxman will look at the reality of how you work together and how things such as the band income are dealt with.

SERVICE AGREEMENTS

Whether or not you have a partnership or a limited company, it is possible for an individual band member to have their own company, which we call a service company. This service company is exclusively entitled to some or all of the individual's services in the entertainment business. The service company then enters into the record or publishing deal and holds shares in the band's company or an interest in the partnership. Record and publishing companies are used to these arrangements and are usually happy to incorporate them into their contractual arrangements, especially if they're told at an early stage. They will usually want the individual to sign a supporting letter, called an inducement letter, to confirm that the service company is entitled to the band member's services and agreeing that if the service company drops out of the picture for any reason then the individual will sign the contract personally.

Someone will usually have a service company for tax reasons. Recently the Inland Revenue announced that it was looking closely at service companies as they are often used as a device to add weight to someone's claim that they are self-employed and not an employee. For example, an individual record producer with a service company can claim to be self-employed when engaged as in-house producer/engineer at a recording studio. However, the Inland Revenue would now look behind the service company in order to establish the real relationship between the producer and the studio and if the indications are that this relationship is actually one of employee and employer then the producer will be taxed accordingly.[1]

This issue often comes up when an artist engages musicians for a particular tour or to record an album or both. The musicians may want to be treated as self-employed. The musicians' contracts have to be very carefully drawn up to establish the existence of a self-employed relationship. However, whatever you call it and whatever the intentions of the parties, the Inland Revenue will make up its own mind.

BAND INCOME

Whatever the structure you put in place, you have to decide what is to happen to the income.

Record, video, touring, merchandise and sponsorship income is usually shared between all band members. As we have seen, there are exceptions where a band consists of one or two core members who are signed up to the record or publishing deal and the other members are employed to work alongside these. In such cases these 'employed' members are usually either put on a retainer or a weekly wage or they are employed as session musicians. Session musicians are only paid when they work but as they are not usually signed up exclusively they are free to work for others (see Chapter 5).

While most disputes usually arise in the area of songwriting income, this doesn't mean that arguments never arise in relation to recording income, as the following case shows.

● The Cure's drummer and co-founder, Laurence Tolhurst, was asked to leave the band in 1989 and subsequently sued the lead singer and the record company for damages arising out of deals done in 1986.[2] He argued that the record deal with Fiction Records Limited gave Robert Smith the lion's share of the recording income and left him with 'the crumbs'. He asked the court to agree that there was a partnership in place and to order Smith to account to him for 50% of all profits receivable under the 1986 agreement. He also argued that he had been forced to enter into the 1986 agreement by undue influence exerted by the record company and its owner Chris Parry. He said that Mr Parry and Fiction Records should account to him for all their profit under the 1986 deal after an allowance for their skill and labour.

The case turned into a bit of a character attack on Tolhurst as allegations were made that his contribution to the band's success had declined as a result of his drinking problems. Tolhurst claimed that he hadn't been given enough information about the deal before he signed it and that he hadn't had independent legal advice. Once again we see that familiar theme emerging – Tolhurst argued that the deal should be set aside and that the court should order an account of all record income to determine how much he was actually entitled to.

The court dismissed his claim and said that no presumption of undue influence arose because, although the record company would have been in a position to use it, the terms offered were not obviously bad. In fact the judge thought that Tolhurst was lucky to have been offered

1 The Inland Revenue has issued a pamphlet containing guidelines and some quite useful examples of what are the main indicators to someone being either employed or self-employed. It can be obtained from your local Inland Revenue office.

2 *Tolhurst* v. *Smith and Others* [1994] EMLR 508.

these arrangements at all in the circumstances. The court found that he hadn't signed the 1986 agreement under undue influence. The fact that he hadn't had independent legal advice didn't affect the court's decision. The judge also decided that there was no partnership in place in respect of the 1986 agreement as Smith and Tolhurst had in fact come to a different arrangement on what was to happen to the income.

With regard to the area of songwriting income, there's no problem if all members of the band contribute equally to the songwriting process. Then the income from songwriting should be split equally. This is, however, rare. Much more common is the situation where only one or two members of the band write all the songs. This can give rise to two possible sources of resentment. Firstly, those who write the songs could come to resent sharing advances or royalties with the non-writing members of the band. Secondly, if the writers don't share the income this then gives rise to resentment from the non-writers who miss out on a potentially lucrative form of income. As we saw in Chapter 4, songwriting deals often recoup faster than record deals because lesser amounts of money are usually advanced on a recoupable basis. Also the writer's share of performing income is paid through to the writers four times a year regardless of whether the publishing account is recouped. This can be a very welcome boost of income at a time when the band is broke.

Of course, leaving aside these tensions, there may also be arguments about who actually wrote what, as we saw in the Kemp case. The other members of Spandau Ballet brought a case against Gary Kemp, arguing that they were entitled to a share in the publishing income as co-writers of the music on the songs they recorded. They were unsuccessful but there will be other arguments as to the extent that all band members actually contribute to the creative process by the way in which they interpret or perform the song. If the contribution is a genuine one then they should be credited as a co-writer. But is their contribution the same as that of the main writers? If not, what is the value of their contribution?

What do you do if not all members of the band write and a publishing advance comes in when the band is broke? Just imagine the tensions that could then occur if the main songwriter or writers take the publishing advance and don't share it with the others. The main songwriters might agree to share the advance equally with the others. You then have to decide what will happen when the advances are recouped and publishing royalties start to come through. Should the royalties then go to the main songwriters or continue to be divided equally? There's no simple answer to this because it's so personal to the individuals concerned. You only have to look at the above cases to realise how important it is to try to sort this out properly, and preferably in advance.

Here are three examples of ways in which I have seen bands deal with this issue. There are many more possibilities.

One band I know has an arrangement where one member controlled all the songwriting and took all the publishing income. When this began to cause tensions he volunteered to share percentages of his publishing income from some songs with the other band members.

I've also heard the story, which may be urban myth, that the members of mega rock band Queen had an agreement where they got to write the songs on the singles in turn. If true, this is very democratic but doesn't really deal with the problem if some of the band members are weaker songwriters than other band members.

A third way of dealing with it would be to share the advances and royalties equally until the advances have been recouped. After that, each band member would have his own account with the publisher and the income from each writer's contribution to the songs would then be paid into his own account.

Three very different solutions to a very ticklish issue. Whatever works for you should be written down as soon as possible. If circumstances change then review the arrangements and see if it would be fair to change them.

ACCOUNTING AND TAX

One of the main things that cause problems with a band is tax. This is often closely followed by VAT. In both cases bands don't keep enough money back to pay the bills. The Inland Revenue and Customs & Excise (the VAT man) have very heavy powers to impose penalties on you. They are often among the main creditors forcing a winding up of a limited company and they can and will make you bankrupt. Even if they give you time to pay, there will be financial penalties and interest to pay. Believe me, you won't get away with it.

Your accountant will advise you how much should be kept to one side for tax and if he is doing your books for you he will be able to tell you what to expect to have to pay the VAT man. He will also probably advise you to keep all your receipts. You can then sort out which ones you can legitimately recharge as business expenses against tax. If you haven't kept them, there's no proof. So do yourself a favour and get a big cardboard box and get into the habit of throwing all your receipts into it. If you were more organised you could have a file divided into the months of the year and could put the receipts in the relevant month. This makes life a lot easier for you or your bookkeeper/accountant when it comes to doing the books.

You will need a band account and, unless your accountant is doing all the books for you, you will need a basic accounting system. This could be a simple computer spreadsheet. In it you'd keep a diary for the income you received, what it was from and what your outgoings were in doing that work. So if you did a gig in March you'd record how much you got and how much it cost you to do the gig.

LEAVING MEMBER PROVISIONS

These are the clauses in recording or publishing agreements that deal with what happens if one or more members of a band leave or the band disbands totally before the contract is over. The record or publishing company naturally wants to try to prevent this happening. They've invested a lot of money in supporting the band, making records or videos and in promoting them around the world. The last thing they want is a band falling apart on them. But of course no words in a contract are going to keep a band together if one or more of them have decided to call it a day. Band members develop personally and creatively and not necessarily in the same direction as other band members. One member of the band may get married and have children and not want to spend as much time on the road. Or they may change their artistic style, which might be more suited to a solo career than as a member of a band. Of course there are also the possibilities that the band members will grow to hate the sight of each other after years on the road or that the band just comes to the end of what it can do together creatively. It used to be the case that when this happened the deal ended and the companies moved on to the next potential big thing. Nowadays, when so much money is resting on building a reputation, when the inevitable happens the record and publishing companies want to be able to salvage what they can of their investments. They will want to have the option to pick up the rights in any new projects that the writers or artists get into without having to compete in the open market.

The record company will also want to try to get the right to continue to use the name of the band in which they have invested a lot of money in building as a brand.

Record and publishing companies will also want to have the option to pick and choose whom they continue the deal with (sometimes called the Remaining Members) and whom they drop. For example, if the drummer leaves the band, the record company will want the right to continue with the remaining members of the band on the basis that they continue to perform and record as a band and with any replacement drummer who they'll also put under the same contract.

If the whole band splits up then the company will want the option to do new contracts with each individual member or not. A publisher might only pick those writers who will probably go on to do other things. A record company might decide only to continue their deal with the lead vocalist or other main focus of the band, guessing that they will team up with other artists to form another band or will have a solo career.

So how does the record or publishing company decide? There is usually a system built into the contract that gives the record or publishing company a breathing space while it tries to work out what they're going to do. The record contract will usually give the company the option to call for a leaving member to deliver to them demo tapes of what he would do as a solo drummer or with his new band. It will usually provide studio time for him to make those demos. It may also require the remaining members of the band to demo new tracks with or without a replacement member to see if they think there is a future for the band or if they should drop them now. Alternatively, the record or publishing company may know whether they want to continue with a leaving member or any or all of the remaining members and may come to a quick decision. But don't hold your breath. They will probably take the maximum time they have under the contract in order to continue to look at their options.

Once demo tapes have been delivered to the record company they usually have a month or two in which to decide what they want to do. In that time both the leaving member and the remaining members of the band are in limbo. The term of the contract is usually suspended while they make up their mind what they want to do.

The record company may decide to take up an option on the leaving member's new project but not that of the remaining members or vice versa. They may also decide to take up their option on the remaining members. They may decide to abandon all members to their fates.

For the leaving member or remaining members who are dropped from the contract, that is the end of their obligations to the record or publishing company. They don't have to repay to the company their share of any unrecouped balance on the account. However, their share of royalties from recordings made or songs written by them up to the time of the decision to drop them will go to recoup the unrecouped balance. The dropped artist or songwriter won't see royalties from those recordings or songs until that advance has been fully paid back.

For example, let's assume that there was an unrecouped balance on the record account of £100,000 and that the record company continues with the three remaining members and drops the fourth, leaving member. Let's also assume that the band shared their advances and royalties equally. The leaving member's share of the debt and of the income will be 25%. So the leaving member's 25% share of the royalties from the recordings made while he was a member of the band will go to recoup £25,000 of the unrecouped £100,000 debt.

If the record company continues with the remaining members and pays them further advances then the leaving member doesn't have to also use his share of royalties to recoup those additional advances as he won't have received any share of those. His debt is fixed at the time he is dropped. Or at least it should be. This is something your lawyer has to look out for when he negotiates the contract. Once the leaving member's 25% share of the royalties has gone to recoup the £25,000 he is then entitled to his 25% share of on-going royalties.

The situation with the remaining members, whose contracts carry on, is slightly more complicated. Their 75% of the old recordings goes to recoup their 75% share of the unrecouped balance (£75,000 in our example). Then, anything else that is earned from the old recordings first goes to recoup any new advances they've received and only when both the old account and the new account are recouped will they see any royalties. It also works the other way around. The royalties from their new recordings go first to recoup the new advances and then any surplus goes to recoup their share of the old debt. Only when both are recouped will they see royalties from the new recordings.

If the contract continues with any remaining members, or if a new contract is issued to the leaving member, the record or publishing company will want to continue to have the same rights to the leaving member and/or remaining members as it had under the original recording or publishing contracts. There are, however, one or two parts of the contract that they like to try to change. The record company will often try to change the minimum recording commitment from an album to singles. The rationale being that until they know how the new line-up will perform in the market place they don't want to risk committing to make an album. With singles being seen as largely a promotional tool for album-based artists, if your music is not directed to the singles market you should hold out for an album commitment.

The record label will also usually want options to future albums. This could either be for the number of albums left under the original deal or that number plus one or two more. This should be agreed at the time the record deal is originally negotiated, when you will have more bargaining power. There is no guarantee that the record company will want to negotiate this with you in the middle of a leaving member/band split situation.

The record royalties are usually the same as under the old agreement but may go back to the rate that applied in the first contract period, so if you've received an increase in your royalty based either on record sales or because it's later in the contract, it will go back to the rate before the increase took effect.

The advances are usually a fraction of the advance that you would have got for that period. For example, if a four-piece band can expect an advance of £100,000 for their next album it doesn't necessarily follow that, after one member leaves, the remaining three are entitled to £75,000. Your lawyer will have to fight for it on your behalf.

Because an artist can walk away from an unrecouped debt and have a chance to start again, many are actually in the position where they are crossing their fingers and hoping they'll be dropped. This is a fairly short-term response, though, because it will all depend on whether you can get into a new deal. It's certainly no reason to split up a band in the hope you'll get dropped.

There are leaving member clauses that have special arrangements. There may be different rules on recoupment, or different levels of new advances, depending on which member of the band leaves and how 'key' he is seen to the proceedings. For example, they may feel that the lead vocalist/front man should command a larger advance and more preferential terms than, say, the bassist. They may even say that they are only interested in leaving member rights for the key people.

As you can imagine, these sorts of provisions can be very disruptive and indeed if it's the band's first deal then such arrangements ought really to be avoided as much from the record company's viewpoint as the band's. At this early stage no one knows who is going to turn out to be the 'star'.

Different arrangements can also occur with publishing deals. For example, one of the four writer-performers in the band may be a prolific writer for adverts or jingles in addition to his work for the band. In these circumstances it is possible for all four members to have separate accounts and to initially receive an equal share of the advances. It only really works if each writer also earns an equal share of the income, which first goes to recoup the band's advances. If after that one writer earns significantly more from his earnings as a jingles writer he will have his income from that source credited only to his account. At the next accounting date he will then receive the correspondingly larger royalty cheque.

One area that will probably have to change in publishing deals is the Minimum Commitment. If one songwriter previously wrote 25% of an album and the others 75% and after a split both are expected to deliver 100% of an album each then there's going to be a problem. So with leaving member clauses in publishing deals you usually try to reduce the commitment pro-rata.

WHAT HAPPENS TO A BAND'S ASSETS ON A SPLIT?

If there's a partnership or band agreement then that will say what happens if a band splits up or one or more members leave (see above).

If there's no provable written or verbal agreement between the band members, and if they are treated as being in a partnership, then the rather antiquated Partnership Act 1896 will govern what happens. Essentially the partnership is dissolved unless all partners elect that it can continue. If agreement can't be reached on a fair way of dealing with the assets then, again, the partnership is dissolved and the assets have to be realised (i.e. sold) and the proceeds divided equally between the partners. If agreement can't be reached on whether something such as the goodwill and reputation in the band name should be given a value and if so what value, the matter is usually referred to an accountant acting as an arbitrator. The way, if at all, that the record company deals with the name in its recording agreement may help determine if it has a value (see above).

If the band were not a partnership but had shares in a limited company then the shareholders' agreement and/or the Memorandum and Articles of Association will say what is to happen. Usually the remaining members would want to have the right to require the leaving member to resign from any office as director or company secretary and also to sell their shares. Normally the arrangements would give the remaining members the right to buy those shares back at a certain price or in accordance with a fixed formula. Or they may require the shares to be valued by an independent accountant. Tax questions could arise here so, in the event of a split, everyone should take advice from an accountant or a tax lawyer. In the absence of written arrangements there is a danger that the company could become unworkable. If the leaving member is a director or a company secretary, and if not guilty of any wrongdoing, it will not be easy to remove them from office. If they have service contracts, employment advice should be sought before terminating those arrangements. As shareholders without a shareholders' agreement, you can't easily get them to sell their shares and, depending on the size of their shareholding, they could 'block' votes requiring 75% or more majority. Indeed, they could also block those votes requiring a simple majority if it's a two-man band or two or more members out of a four-piece band have left.

Once again, this argues in favour of a written shareholders' agreement.

Once agreement has been reached as to what to do with the band's assets this should be recorded in a settlement agreement, which should be drawn up by your lawyer. This is particularly important for matters such as rights to band names or copyrights.

If no agreement can be reached then the parties head, almost inevitably, towards litigation and the courts. Even though the reform of the legal system in England and Wales now places considerable emphasis on conciliation and alternative dispute resolution (ADR) we still witness the largely unedifying spectacle of bands fighting it out in court.

In my view, the partnership or band agreement should be very clear as to who owns what and who has brought what into the deal. For example, if one of the band members had a transit van that he allowed the band to use then that should be noted. It could also be money that one band member has that he puts into the band to keep it going. Either these are loans to the band with or without interest or, more practically, they are gifts for the use of the partnership but which they should be allowed to get back if they leave. It's also usual for the band members to take with them any band equipment that they particularly use. This is fair unless one person has the use of a lot of expensive equipment paid for out of band advances. In that case you'd expect the equipment to be valued and for each band member to either get the equipment or be paid his share of its value by the one who is going to get to take it away.

If a band name is genuinely closely associated with one individual then it is fair to say that that individual should be allowed to continue to use the name after the band splits. But as it will have been all the band members that will have helped to make the name successful the person using the name after a split should compensate the others. If a figure can't be agreed it can be referred to an accountant to value it. In many cases, however, the name dies with the end of the band. Each band member should continue to be responsible for his share of the record or publishing company's unrecouped balance. This will usually be covered by the record or publishing deal. Once the old accounts are recouped the individual band members should be entitled to their agreed share of any royalties.

It is also wise to decide whether all the band members have to agree before something can happen with the material that they created together or if it is going to be a majority decision. For example, a few years after a band splits, the record company wants to put out a Greatest Hits album. The record contract may give the band approval over whether the record company can do this. The band agreement should say whether all the band members have to agree or not. The democratic thing would be to say yes, they should. The practical thing would be to say that it was a majority decision so that the minority couldn't hold a gun to the head of the others or their record company. The same situation arises with approvals of the use of material in adverts or films. My own view is that it should be a decision of all band members.

CONCLUSIONS

- Decide on a good name and protect it as far as you can.
- Decide on a band structure and put a partnership or shareholders' agreement in place.
- Decide who is going to be allowed to use the name if you split up.
- Make sure any leaving member clauses in your contracts are fair.
- Decide these things while you are still friends.

12: **MORAL RIGHTS**

INTRODUCTION

When you're looking at ways in which to protect your work, and to make sure that where it is used you are properly credited, you shouldn't neglect the area of moral rights. Sounds like something they taught you at Sunday School? Well in fact moral rights have their origins in well-established European principles of law aimed at protecting you and ensuring your works are treated with respect. These are also called droit moral. This chapter gives only an overview of these rights and where they can be used. There are many books on the subject if you want to read into this further.[1]

Moral rights are separate from your rights in copyright. In some circumstances you can hang on to your moral rights even when you have to assign copyright.

In Europe it has long been felt that an artist's rights to receive economic (i.e. financial) reward for the use of his work could be adequately protected by the copyright laws. However, the integrity of the work itself deserved separate protection. Hence the development of separate droit moral. In the UK legal tradition, economic rights have been more important than those of artistic integrity. Why doesn't the UK value the integrity of creative works, you may well ask. It's not that we don't give them a value. It's a question of emphasis and the answer lies in the cultural differences between the UK and the rest of Europe and in their different legal histories.

These European principles of moral rights were included in the major international convention on intellectual property, the Berne Convention,[2] and in particular the 1948 Brussels Revision of the Berne Convention.[3] The UK lagged a long way behind and, indeed, the fact that we didn't incorporate the two basic moral rights into our laws meant that for many years we were unable to fully comply with the Berne Convention.

As the UK gradually integrated with Europe it became clear that we were out of step not only with the Berne Convention but also in not giving sufficient weight to these rights. The general principles of harmonisation, which govern the operation of the European Union, meant that the UK had to come in line on these moral rights. As we shall see, it did so, but in a peculiarly British way.

The 1988 Copyright Designs & Patents Act was the first UK statute that effectively incorporated all the principal moral rights. There had been limited moral rights in the 1956 Copyright Act but the 1988 Act was the one that brought the UK in line with Europe and enabled us to comply with the provisions of Article 6 of the Berne Convention.[4]

The moral rights are not necessarily linked to who owns the copyright in the work in

1 See Chapter 11 of *Copinger & Skone-James on Copyright* for a more detailed legal description of UK moral rights.

2 It first appeared in the 1925 Rome Act.

3 Article 6 bis of the 1948 Brussels Revision to the Berne Convention contains two basic moral rights: the right to be identified as an author of a work and the right not to have that work distorted, mutilated or otherwise altered in a manner which would be prejudicial to the author's honour or reputation.

4 The moral rights are found in Chapter 4 of the Act in sections 77–89. The remedies are found in section 103ff.

question. For example, you could have assigned your rights to the copyright to a publisher but, as the author of the musical work in question, you retain the moral rights. In fact you can't assign these moral rights – they remain with you, or your beneficiaries on your death. This restriction on assignment is intended to protect you from unscrupulous people who may want you to assign your rights alongside your copyright. However, there is more than one means to an end.

If you and your fellow band members write the work together then you each have these moral rights independent of each other. Just because one of you has decided to abandon his moral rights doesn't mean that the rest of you have.

In reality, the 1988 Act merely put into law that which had previously been dealt with in contracts. The crucial difference being that in a contract you can only bind your contracting partner whereas with moral rights you can enforce them against third parties that were not party to the contract. For example, you may have a clause in your record contract that says you have to be credited as the composer of the music. If your record company forgets, it's a breach of contract and you can sue them. If, however, the record company licenses your tracks to go on a compilation album and the compilation company doesn't credit you then, unless you have your moral rights, you can't take action because the contract is between the compilation company and your record company, not with you. However, if you have your moral rights then you could take action against the compilation company for breach of your moral right to be identified as the author – whether or not your record company wants to take any action.

WHAT ARE THESE RIGHTS?

There are four moral rights but only three of them are likely to affect you. These three rights only exist in respect of copyright works.[5] If a work is out of copyright then you don't have moral rights in relation to it.

THE RIGHT OF PATERNITY

The first moral right is the right to be properly identified as the author of the work. This is also known as the paternity right. No, I'm afraid there isn't an equivalent maternity right for female authors.

The author of a copyright literary, dramatic, musical or artistic work owns the right. So, as a lyricist or composer of original songs, you would have the right to be identified as having written the words or composed the music. It's also possible that you will have moral rights in the artwork used for the packaging of your records (if you created that work). You will notice, though, that the owners of the sound recording copyright don't have moral rights in that sound recording.

The right exists in relation to a musical work and lyrics when that work is exploited in one of five ways:

5 Sections 178 and 1(2) CDPA.

1. When the work is commercially published; this includes not only sheet music but also in sound recordings or as soundtracks to films.

2. The issue to the public of copies of the work in the form of sound recordings.

3. The showing in public of a film, the soundtrack of which includes the work.

4. The issue to the public of copies of a film, the soundtrack of which includes the work. Remember that the definition of 'film' will include videos.

5. If a work has been adapted and the adaptation is exploited in one of the above ways then you have the right to be identified as the author of the work that has been adapted. If the arrangement itself is capable of copyright protection then the author of the adaptation may also have a right to be identified as its author.

You'll notice that there's no moral right to be identified as the author of a musical work when that work is broadcast, performed in public or included in a cable broadcast service. Just think of all those poor DJs who would be in danger of breaching your moral rights every time they irritatingly didn't give you a name check after playing your record on the radio. It seems it was thought to be unrealistic to put this burden on the broadcasters.

If you have moral rights in the artistic work (the artwork) then that right comes into effect when that work is exploited in one of the following ways:

1. If the work is published commercially.

2. If it is exhibited in public.

3. If a visual image of it is broadcast or included in a cable broadcast service.

4. If a film including a visual image of the work is shown in public or copies of the film (which will include videograms) are issued to the public.

Section 77(7) of the Act sets out details of how the author is to be identified. One example is that the author of the musical or artistic work must be identified on each copy. This is logical: you wouldn't want a record company to be able to get around the right by identifying you on the first, say, one hundred copies issued and not on any of the rest.

Assertion of the right

There is, however, one very big 'but' here. In order to be able to rely on the paternity right, you have to first have asserted that right. You may have noticed on the inside cover of books published since 1988 that there is a statement along the lines of 'the right of [author's name] to be identified as the author of this work has been asserted in accordance with sections 77 and 78 of the Copyright, Designs and Patents Act 1988'. This is the book publishing world's way of asserting the author's right of paternity. If you write a song and don't want to have the right to be identified as the author then you just don't assert your moral right of paternity and you don't insist on having a credit clause in your contracts. But why wouldn't you want to be identified?

Your right of paternity can be asserted generally – as in the statement above – or in respect of any particular act. For example, you could assert your right to be identified as the author of the musical work in the sound recording but not if that sound recording is then included in a film. Again I wonder why one would make the distinction. Whichever you choose, you can assert your moral right in the document in which you assign any copyright in the work, for example in an exclusive music publishing deal where you have to assign your rights for a period of time (see Chapter 4). Alternatively, you can do it by some other written means that bring your assertion to the attention of someone. They are then responsible if they breach your right. The problem with this is that it is only binding on those people to whose attention the assertion of rights is brought. You cannot rely on your moral right if someone who is unaware of your assertion fails to identify you as the author of the work. Putting it in the assignment document is the best way of ensuring that anyone who later takes any interest in the work will have notice of your paternity rights.

If the musical work has been jointly written, for example by all members of a band, then each is responsible for asserting their own right of paternity. One band member can't take it upon himself to assert it on behalf of the others.

There are a number of exceptions. The most important one for you is likely to be the fact that, if the copyright work was done as an employee, your employer – and anyone acquiring rights from him – doesn't have to identify you as the author of that work. For example, if you wrote a jingle as part of your job as an employee of a jingle company then your employer wouldn't have to give you a credit and you wouldn't be able to rely on any right of paternity (unless there was anything in your contract that stated otherwise).

THE INTEGRITY RIGHT

The second moral right is the right of an author of a work not to have that work subjected to derogatory treatment (i.e. to have someone treat your work in a way that reflects badly on the work and indirectly on you). This is sometimes called the integrity right. The right is owned by the author of a copyright literary, dramatic, musical or artistic work and by the director of a copyright film (which includes a videogram). Once again the right only applies in relation to a work that is in copyright and it doesn't apply to sound recordings.

The right has several hurdles to it. To begin with, you have to establish that the work has been subjected to some form of treatment, i.e. that it has been added to, or parts have been deleted, or the work has been altered or adapted in some way. Something has to have been done to it. This can be as little as changing one note or one word of the lyrics. It *isn't* a treatment of a work if all you do is put it in an unchanged form in a context that reflects badly on its author. For example, if someone uses your song as part of a soundtrack for a porn video then that of itself is not a treatment of the work for the purpose of your moral rights. Nor is it a treatment if someone just changes the key or the register of the music.

During a case involving George Michael, the court was asked to consider the question of what was a treatment.[6]

Someone had put together a megamix of George Michael's tracks using 'snatches' from five songs. They had also slightly altered the lyrics. The court decided that this was definitely a treatment.

One you have established that there has been some form of treatment you then have to show that that treatment was derogatory. For these purposes that means a distortion or mutilation or something that is prejudicial to your honour or reputation.

When you have established both these points you then have to look at whether the treatment has then been subjected to a particular type of use.

In the case of a literary or musical work the integrity right is infringed by: publishing it commercially; performing it in public, broadcasting it or including it in a cable broadcast service; issuing copies to the public of a film or sound recording of, or including, a derogatory treatment of the work.

In the case of an artistic work the treatment has to have been used in one of the following ways: publishing it commercially; exhibiting it publicly; broadcasting or including in a cable programme service a visual image of a derogatory treatment of the work; showing in public a film that includes a visual image of a derogatory treatment of the work or issues to the public copies of such a film.

In the case of a film (which includes a videogram) the integrity right is infringed by a person who shows in public, or includes in a cable programme service, a derogatory treatment of a film or who issues to the public copies of a derogatory treatment of the film.[7]

FALSE ATTRIBUTION

The third right is an extension of a right that existed under the previous Copyright Act of 1956. It is the right not to have a work falsely attributed to you. This would happen if someone says that a piece of music is written by you or that you directed a particular film and that is not in fact the case. This false attribution need not be in writing – it can be verbal. It also need not be express – it can be implied. So someone could say on a television programme that you were the author of a particular piece of music, when you weren't, or could imply that you were. In many ways it is the mirror image of the right of paternity.

If there has been a false attribution then it has to be applied to a work that has been used in one of the following ways before it can be said to be an infringement of this moral right:

1. If a person issues to the public copies of a literary, dramatic or artistic work or a film in which there is a false attribution. So, for example, if the film credits wrongly identify you as the author of the music, this could be an infringement of you moral right.

6 *Morrison Leahy Music* v. *Lightbond*, 1993 EMLR 144.
7 See section 83 CDPA for details of other persons who could be liable for infringement of this right and section 81 CDPA for exceptions.

2. If a person exhibits in public an artistic work, or a copy of an artistic work, in or on which there is a false attribution.

3. If, in the case of a literary, dramatic or musical work, a person performs the work in public, broadcasts it or includes it in a cable programme service, saying wrongly that it is the work of a particular person. If, in the case of a film, a person shows it in public, broadcasts it or includes it in a cable programme service as being directed by someone who hadn't in fact directed it.

4. Material issued to the public, or displayed in public, which contains a false attribution in relation to any of the above acts is also an infringement. This could catch publicity posters for films or adverts in magazines for a book or the false credit on the packaging for a recording of a piece of music.

There are also rights against those who indirectly infringe this right.[8]

PRIVACY OF PHOTOGRAPHS

The final moral right is the right to privacy in any photographs that you commission. This is intended to protect against unauthorised use by newspapers and suchlike of private photographs that you have commissioned. When you're starting out in the business this right may not be of immediate practical interest to you. There's always the motto that there's no such thing as bad publicity. However, later in life, when you're a megastar seeking to protect your privacy at all costs, you may remember this right and use it against unscrupulous photographers keen to sell their soul and your life to the tabloids.

OWNERSHIP OF RIGHTS

As we've already seen, the moral rights belong to authors – to composers of musical works and writers of lyrics intended to be spoken or sung with music. Performers on sound recordings don't have these rights unless they are also the writer or composer of the musical works. So, for example, if you have a band member performing on a record who has not contributed to the writing of the words or the lyrics then they cannot expect to be credited as an author. The same applies to record producers. If the record producer contributed to the writing of the words or music then they may have moral rights but they don't have them if they acted purely as a record producer (see Chapter 5).

The real beauty of these rights is that they are rights of the author, who can't be made to assign them. So, for example, a songwriter may have been required to assign the copyright in his words and music to a publisher as part of a publishing deal (see Chapter 4), but he can't be made to assign his moral rights. If he retains his moral rights then he is in a

8 Section 84(3) CDPA.

position to take legal action against someone infringing those rights, even if the publishing company wants to take no action.

There are, of course, difficulties with the moral right of paternity: you would have to show that you had the right, that it had been infringed and that you had asserted the right in such a way that the person infringing it had notice of the assertion. If your assertion was in an assignment document and was general in nature then you could take action against the assignee of the rights and against anyone else taking an interest in the rights subsequently. This could help you take action for infringement of your paternity right against your publisher or one of their sub-publishers but not so easily against someone who was acting unlawfully.

The other moral rights do not have to first be asserted.

DURATION OF RIGHTS

The paternity and integrity rights last for as long as copyright exists in the work in question. The same applies to the right of privacy in commissioned photographs and films. After a person's death the right to take action for infringement passes to whomever he specifically directs. This can be more than one person. The right against false attribution lasts for twenty years after the person's death. If there is an infringement after his death then his personal representatives can take action.

THE CATCH

There is, however, one other big problem with these rights and it is a peculiarly British way of dealing with a problem. You will recall that the two main moral rights were introduced into UK law in 1988 in order to enable us to fully comply with the requirements of the Berne Convention. The Convention said that the laws of signatory countries ought to contain the author's moral rights. There was, however, nothing in the Convention that prevented a country incorporating the rights into its laws but then making concessions to other economic interests. This is exactly what then happened. It arose largely as a result of intensive lobbying by the powerful record and publishing interests in this country. It is also a result of the long-standing laissez-faire tradition that we spoke of earlier. In the UK we still favour economic interests over author's rights. So what happened was that, after including the rights in the 1988 Copyright Act, the law went on to say that the author could then elect to waive his rights, to agree not to assert the right of paternity or to enforce any of the other rights. The waiver must be in writing and signed by the person giving up the right. The waiver can be for a specific work, for works within a specific description or works generally. It can apply to existing and future works and can be conditional or unconditional and can be revocable.

What was the consequence of this waiver provision? I'm sure you can guess. As soon as the industry realised these rights could be waived, all contracts were changed to include, as standard, a waiver of these rights in the widest possible terms. Clauses were included which provided for an absolute, unconditional and irrevocable waiver of any and all moral rights of whatever kind in relation to all existing or future works. They even put them in record contracts where there was little or no chance of the right existing in the first place.

So why bother discussing these rights if you're going to have to waive them anyway? Once again it comes down to bargaining power. If creative controls are important to you then you could try to insist on not having to waive them. If you are forced to waive your moral rights then try to only waive them against uses of your works by properly authorised people. Try to retain the right to enforce your moral rights against unlawful users of your works and infringers of your rights.

Also, if you are made to waive your rights then your lawyer will usually use that as a lever to try to get some of the benefits of the rights through the back door. It helps us to negotiate more favourable credit clauses for you and what happens if you aren't properly credited. We rely on the integrity right to get you contractual consents as to what can or can't be done with your work. For example, that you words and music can't be changed without your consent.

It's not a criminal offence to infringe your moral rights but, if proven, you have the right to seek injunctions and/or damages. Most importantly, you can exercise a degree of control over what is being done with your work.

CONCLUSIONS

- Try to retain your moral rights if you can.
- Assert your right to be identified as an author of a work as early and as widely as you can.
- If you have to waive your moral rights, use this to get improved creative controls in the contract.

13: **SAMPLING AND PLAGIARISM**

INTRODUCTION

Sampling and plagiarism are two sides of the same problem. Plagiarism is the taking of someone else's ideas and passing them off as your own. Sampling is more or less the same thing. The subtle difference between them, as we'll see in the cases below, is that with plagiarism you need to show that they had access to your material and hadn't just come to it by some coincidence. Sampling, of course, is always only a deliberate act. The person doing the sampling deliberately takes parts of someone's work and then, possibly after manipulating it, includes it in their own work. Both sampling and plagiarism are infringements of an individual's copyrights.[1] You can sample the actual sound itself by copying the digital recording. This is an infringement of the sound recording copyright.[2] If you don't actually make a copy of the sound recording copyright you could take the piece of music that you are interested in using and get someone to replay it, to re-perform it in an identical way. This is still sampling but it would then only be an infringement of the musical copyright in the music and the literary copyright in the words.[3]

Is sampling theft? Many people argue that all cultural evolution is based on taking bits of existing popular culture and adapting and changing them. They argue that all new musical genres 'borrow' or are influenced by earlier ones: R&B from gospel, and rock'n'roll from R&B and so on. Those that believe this think that clamping down on sampling stifles this growth. They would be behind the removal of all restrictions on using parts of someone else's copyright.

This is all very well but if you were to take that to its logical conclusion then no one would be able to protect their work, music would be devalued and people wouldn't be able to make a living from their work. Surely that is likely to lead to less creativity rather than more. I believe that it is wrong to deliberately take someone else's work without their permission, without paying them anything for it and without giving them proper credit.

HOW MUCH IS A SAMPLE?

Although sampling has been around since the 1960s, it only became more widely used when affordable digital sampling machines arrived in the 1980s. When they first became available they were expensive (around £20,000). Now they are available for less than £1,000.

Sampling now forms the core of the dance music scene. But there is still an awful lot of confusion about what is a sample. A lot of people think that, just because they've only sampled a couple of notes or a few seconds of someone else's work, they haven't sampled

1 Sections 16–21 CDPA.
2 Section 5A CDPA.
3 Sections 3 and 4 CDPA.

at all. That simply isn't true. The Copyright Act says that there has to have been copying of a 'substantial part'.[4] It is a question of the quality of the part sampled and not the quantity. There are a whole series of cases that have considered what is a 'substantial part'.

- In the case of Hawkes & Son, Paramount had included the sound of the 'Colonel Bogey' military march in a newsreel.[5] They used 28 bars of music lasting about 20 seconds. The question was whether 20 seconds out of a 4-minute piece was a substantial part. The bars performed by the band made up the main theme of the march. The court clearly looked at the quality of what had been copied as well as the quantity and found that an infringement of copyright had taken place. Judge Slesser said, 'Though it may be that it was not very prolonged in its reproduction, it is clearly, in my view, a substantial, a vital, and an essential part which is there reproduced.'
- So, could something shorter than twenty seconds constitute a sample? Well, this question was considered in the Hyperion Records case.[6] The band The Beloved sampled eight seconds of a recording of a piece called 'O Euchari'. The sample was repeated several times in The Beloved's track 'The Sun Rising'. Hyperion, which owned the rights in the sound recording of the performance by Emily Van Evera, from which the work was sampled, sued. At a preliminary hearing the judge gave his opinion that he didn't think that an eight-second sample was too brief to constitute a substantial part. He wanted the matter to go to a full hearing. However, as happens with so many sampling cases, Hyperion settled out of court and permission to use the sound recording sample was given retrospectively.
- In a case my firm was involved in last year, a claim was brought by my clients Produce Records Limited that the dance hit 'Macarena', which had been released by BMG, infringed the copyright in a sound recording by The Farm called 'Higher and Higher'. The sample consisted of a short sound made by the vocalist Paula David that had been used or 'looped' throughout 'Macarena'.

Because so few sampling cases get to court, a lot rested on this case. If it went to a full court hearing and the court confirmed that such a short sample could constitute a substantial part then this would be a firm ruling that could be relied on in later disputes. After such a judgement it would be very difficult to rely on the fact that three seconds is the minimum amount necessary to constitute a substantial part. It was more important as a potential guideline for the samplers than it was for BMG to win this particular case. A decision that the part sampled didn't constitute a substantial part wouldn't necessarily have given any guidance on what is a 'substantial part' and so each subsequent sampling case would continue to be decided on a case-by-case basis. On the other hand, if the case had gone against BMG and such a short sample was said to be a substantial part, BMG would have lost this particular case but it and all other record companies would also have lost the argument in subsequent cases that such a small sample couldn't constitute an infringement of copyright. BMG later settled out of court on terms that I am not allowed to reveal. Possibly the potential downside was too great.

4 Section 16(3) (a) CDPA.
5 *Hawkes & Son Ltd* v. *Paramount Film Service Limited* [1934] 1 Ch 593.
6 *Hyperion Records Limited* v. *Warner Music (UK) Limited*, 1991.

The question also comes up from time to time as to whether you can sample a rhythm or a drum beat. I would argue that you can if it can be shown to be original and distinctive and if a substantial part has been copied. There are of course only so many rhythms in popular music and many drum and bass lines used in current works are in fact the same as earlier works. This is particularly true in the area of reggae music. So inevitably there is going to be duplication. I tend, however, to agree with Aaron Fuchs. He is the man behind an eight-beat drumbeat used in the classic hip hop track by The Honeytrippers, 'Impeach The President'. In 1992 he brought legal actions against Sony and Def Jam alleging that this particular drum sound is one of the more distinctive in the hip hop genre and worthy of the protection of copyright. I can find no report of that case coming to court so I presume it was settled out of court like so many of these cases.

In the US the courts are handing down decisions that suggest they are leaning towards giving protection to a distinctive or unique 'sound'. One example of where the US courts have tended towards this view is one involving the actress and singer Bette Midler.[7] Ms Midler successfully stopped Ford Motor Cars using an imitation of her very distinctive voice in a television advert. There are no signs that the UK courts are moving in this direction and, as we saw in Chapter 8, the UK courts are much less likely to accept that someone has personality rights that should be protected.

HOW DO YOU CLEAR A SAMPLE?

So, what if it's clear that you've sampled someone else's work? This is an infringement of their copyright and unless you get their permission to copy and reproduce their work they could sue you for damages for the copyright infringement and also for an injunction stopping you from continuing to use that sample in your track. As you can imagine, record companies are not very happy about having an artist who samples material from others and doesn't get their permission. It's very expensive for the record company if there is an injunction and they have to recall all the copies of the single or album and remove the offending sample before recutting, remastering and reissuing the record. In fact, if it's too expensive, they may not bother redoing it and just kill the single or album. That isn't a very good solution for you so you need to get permission to use any samples. This is called 'clearing' samples.

Most record contracts, whether they are exclusive recording agreements or licences, will have a clause in them that says you are guaranteeing that all samples are cleared before the recording is delivered to them. This makes it clear that it's your responsibility. This is only fair if you are the one who has put the sample in there in the first place. But bear in mind that producers and remixers can also have the opportunity to introduce samples into the recording at various stages in the process. You will want to make sure that the contract with them makes them responsible for clearing any samples that they introduce. Sometimes it is the record company that has the idea that including a particular sample will turn a good song into a monster hit. In those cases, if they are encouraging you to put the sample in, they can't

7 *Midler* v. *Ford Motor Company*, 9th circuit 1988 decision.

expect you to take sole responsibility for clearing it. They will have to share that load with you and probably pick up some if not all of the cost of clearing it, possibly as an additional recording cost. Those costs may or may not be recoupable depending on your deal.

With some types of music, particularly in the dance area, the record company is fully aware that there will be loads of samples. In such cases it will often help you to clear the samples. This can be an advantage if they can use their greater resources and clout to pull favours and get things cleared quickly – things that you wouldn't be able to do so easily. It can have its downsides. If you're a small struggling dance label that is asked to clear a sample then the person whose work is sampled is less likely to ask for stupid amounts of money than if you were EMI or Sony, for example.

WHEN SHOULD YOU SEEK PERMISSION?

Ideally, you should try to get clearance before you've recorded the sample. Then if you don't get permission you haven't wasted recording costs and time. In reality this won't usually be possible. It can take time to track down the owners of the work sampled, to find out whom you have to ask for permission. Even once you find them they may take a time getting back to you. You may then have to negotiate terms for the clearance. In the meantime you can't get on with finishing recording that track. This could hold up delivery of the record and its eventual release. Also, you are going to need a recording of what the sampled work is going to sound like in your version of it even if it's only a demo. In practice the clearance process usually takes place after the recording has been made or during the recording process. Sometimes it's left until the record has been delivered. I think this is too late to start the whole clearance process. Some 'feelers' should have been put out beforehand, at least to find out who owns what and to get an idea of whether they are likely to give you a problem.

Most record contracts and licences will say that delivery of a recording hasn't taken place until evidence has been produced (usually in the form of clearance letters or agreements) that all samples have been cleared. If you haven't used any samples, they'll want you to give a warranty (a sort of guarantee) to that effect. Until delivery has taken place it is unlikely that you will get any advances due to be paid to you on delivery (see Chapter 3). Nor will time start to run for your record to be released and the marketing plan will not be put into action. So the sooner samples are cleared and deals done, the better.

Some people say that they'll take the risk that the use of the sample will be spotted. They think that if it's sufficiently obscure or hidden in the track it won't be discovered. Well, it is just possible that you'd get away with this if your release were a limited edition low-key release. For example, if you were only going to press up 5,000–10,000 copies of the record for release on your own small dance label then you might get away with it. Even if it were spotted, the copyright owner of the sample may not bother to take any legal action because of the amounts involved and the legal costs and hassle of suing you. However, A&R people at the bigger record companies look to these dance labels as the source of new material. They might license your track in and give it a big marketing push. Or you might make it a big success in your own right and find you are licensing it to loads of different compilations. If you haven't cleared it, and you are found out, you'll end up with a big problem on your hands because now the copyright owner of the sampled work has an incentive for taking you to court. The copyright owner may sue the bigger record company that has licensed the track from you and then released it but, in turn, the record company will usually have an indemnity from you. This means that if they are sued then they in turn can make you responsible for the damages and costs involved because you have breached your warranty that there were no uncleared samples in the recording. By lying to them you may also have irretrievably damaged your relationship with that label for the future. Is it worth it? That's for you to judge.

TO WHOM DO YOU GO TO CLEAR SAMPLES?

If you've sampled the actual sound recording you need to seek permission from the owner of the original sound recording copyright, although they may have passed it on to someone else by licence or assignment of rights (see Chapter 3). You can start by looking at the recording that you sampled it from. It should have a copyright notice on it that will say who was the copyright owner at that time, for example '© Sony Music 1999'. So your first point of call would be Sony. If they don't still own the rights, or they own them for only part of the world, they should be able to tell you that. If you don't want to show your hand too soon you might want to do this on a 'no names' basis. You must allow yourself plenty of time.

At this stage you are looking for their agreement, in principle, to the use of the sample. Some artists will not allow their works to be sampled under any circumstances so it's best to know this as early as possible.

Once you've got the agreement in principle then you can negotiate the terms. This can also take time but you should know fairly early on whether they are going to ask for a ludicrous amount for the clearance, which will make it uneconomical for the sample to be used.

Remember that, as well as clearing the use of the sound recording sample, you have to clear the use of the underlying music and, if appropriate, words. In 1991 a US court granted a preliminary injunction against a rap artist called Biz Markie to stop him from exploiting a sample of three words and the accompanying music for Gilbert O'Sullivan's hit song 'Alone Again, Naturally'.[8]

The owner of the copyright in the words and music may be the writers credited on the sampled recording.[9] It's quite possible, though, that the writers may have assigned or licensed their rights to a music publisher (see Chapter 4). So you'll have to look at whether a publisher is credited and go to them to see if they still own or control the rights. They may only do so for part of the world or they may have passed the rights on or back to the original writers. The MCPS/PRS database should contain details of who claims to own or control the publishing rights (see Chapter 15). They would be a good starting point. If the title or the writer's name is a common one, for example John Smith, then the database is going to throw up a lot of names. Try to narrow down the search by giving them as much detail as you can.

8 *Grand Upright Music Limited* v. *Warner Brothers Records Inc.* No. 91 Civ. 9648 1991.
9 See Section 9 (1) CDPA for a description of who is the first owner of copyright in a musical or literary work.

Again, once you've found the copyright owner or administrator you should try to get an agreement from them (in principle) to the use of the sampled music and/or words. Then you can start negotiating the terms.

What sometimes happens is that it is possible to clear the underlying words and music but not the sound recording. If you are adamant that you have to use that sample then you can try to get it reproduced almost identically. It's replayed or recreated. Then you haven't used their sound recording so you only have to clear the underlying music/words. Of course if you do a very good job of it and it sounds identical to the original then they may not believe you've replayed it and may still sue you. Then you may need independent evidence from, for example, the studio engineer that you didn't use the sample sound recording.

I'm currently involved in a case where this happened. My client sampled part of a sound recording, asked for permission, which was denied, and then set about replaying the sample to recreate the sound. He even went to the trouble of getting a specialist report from a musicologist to confirm that he hadn't used the original sound recording but had replayed it. Nevertheless, the owner of the original sound recording was not convinced and threatened to sue my client's record company, which had released the track. Using a right they had under their record contract with my client, they 'froze' the royalties that would otherwise have been payable to my client on the track in question until there was an outcome to the dispute. The money has now been 'frozen' for over a year and, as it's a substantial amount, my client is understandably very frustrated. Ah but, I hear you say, it serves him right for copying someone else's work. Well, before you get all high and mighty just make sure that no one can ever accuse *you* of sampling or plagiarism.

HOW MUCH DOES IT COST?

This is always a question of negotiation. It will depend on how important the track is that you've sampled and how crucial it is to you that you use it.

Record companies will usually clear sound recording copyrights for an upfront fee and then a further fee when you sell a certain number of records. For example, £1,500 upfront and another £1,500 when you've sold 10,000 copies of the record that includes the sample. They may want a royalty, which usually comes out of the artist's royalty but may be shared with the record company if it really wants you to keep the sample in. The owner of the rights in the sampled track will usually also want an advance against the royalty, which should be kept in proportion to the advance that you are getting as an artist.

Publishers of sampled works may clear rights for a one-off fee or a fee and a further sum based on numbers of records sold. However, it is more likely that they will want a percentage of the publishing income on the track. In effect the publisher of the sampled work is saying that its writer should be treated as a co-writer on the work and receive a co-writer's share of the income. That share could be as much as 100% if a substantial use has been made of their work. For example, in the track by All Seeing I called 'The Beat Goes On', substantial use was made of the Sonny and Cher song of the same name, although the band had altered the track and given it a 1990s feel. Warner Chappell, who publish the Sonny and Cher song, insisted that the All Seeing I version be treated as a cover version and retained 100% of the publishing. If the use is less substantial then a lower percentage may be agreed.

If you are going to do a lot of sampling in your work and are going to end up having to give away some or all of your publishing on certain tracks then do bear in mind that this may make it very difficult to fulfil your Minimum Commitment to your publisher, unless you take this into account when setting the original level of that commitment.

WHAT HAPPENS IF YOU DON'T CLEAR SOMETHING?

If a sample isn't cleared and a dispute arises, your record company may suspend payment to you until the dispute is resolved. There may be a limit on how long it can suspend payment but this could be a year or more. MCPS also has the right to suspend any payments of publishing income and has a disputes procedure that has to be followed but they will not directly intervene to resolve a dispute.

- In 1992 the MCPS brought an action against dance label Shut Up and Dance (SUAD) on behalf of ten of their publisher members claiming twelve separate infringements of copyright of works by writers such as Prince and Suzanne Vega. Action was taken after the owners of SUAD, PJ and Smiley, told the music press that they would never clear samples legally. At the time a very macho culture prevailed over the use of samples with some one-upmanship going on over who could get away with the most in terms of uncleared samples. It's thought their comment was a throwaway one which reflected this cultural approach to sampling. In the end, SUAD did not defend the case and damages were awarded against them.

Failure to clear samples in good time could result in an injunction preventing distribution of copies of your record or an order that they be recovered from the distributors and destroyed. You could also be sued for damages for the copyright infringement.[10]

However, it's not all bad. Not all copyright owners sue or want payment when their work is sampled. The track 'Ride On Time' by Black Box may have attracted a fair amount of litigation in its time but there was no claim from Don Hartman whose work 'Love Sensation' was sampled. Apparently Mr Hartman loved the new work so much that he wanted neither payment nor a writer credit.

PLAGIARISM

For the purposes of this chapter, when I am talking about plagiarism as opposed to sampling I am talking about a situation where someone takes another's work and copies it, passing it off as his own work. There are, of course, overlaps with the situation where you replay a sound sampled from another's work. But what I'm describing here are cases where a writer has claimed that another writer has stolen or copied his work, where the similarities between two pieces of work are so striking that you'd have to believe the one was copied from the

10 As to remedies for infringement of copyright see Sections 96–100 CDPA for civil remedies and Sections 107–110 CDPA for criminal sanctions.

other. As we'll see from the cases below, once you've established similarities between two pieces of work, the crucial test is whether the person being accused of plagiarising the work has had access to the other work. It is possible to unconsciously copy something or indeed to arrive at a very similar-sounding piece of work purely by chance.

- The composer Lord Andrew Lloyd Webber is no stranger to claims of plagiarism being brought against him. In the late 1980s John Brett, a songwriter, accused him of copying two songs written by him. These songs now featured in Lord Lloyd Webber's musical *Phantom Of The Opera.* In this particular case, although there were similarities between the pieces, Lord Lloyd Webber was able to show that he had written the song first. He produced evidence that it had been performed in mid-1985 whereas Mr Brett's evidence suggested that he hadn't sent demo recordings of his songs to his solicitor until a month later.
- In another case involving Lloyd Webber, a songwriter called Ray Repp brought a legal action against him in New York, accusing him of plagiarism. Mr Repp claimed that Lord Lloyd Webber had stolen a passage from his song 'Till You' and had used it, again, in *Phantom Of The Opera.* Once again Lord Lloyd Webber was cleared of plagiarism and afterwards made a passionate statement condemning the increase in cases alleging plagiarism. He blamed the lawyers and people with an eye to the main chance. He said there were too many people around who thought it was worth a chance because record companies would rather settle than fight potentially damaging court cases. I understand that he now returns, unopened, all unsolicited demo tapes sent to him or his office.
- An early case in this area that set out a number of guidelines for what constitutes plagiarism is the case of Francis Day & Hunter.[11] Here it was argued that eight bars of the chorus of a song entitled 'In a Little Spanish Town' had been copied in the song 'Why'. The judge found a number of similarities between the two works but decided that copying hadn't been proved. It went to the Court of Appeal. That court also agreed that copying hadn't been proved but took the opportunity to consider the subject of copying generally. The Appeal Court judges said that you had to establish that there was a definite connection between the two works or, at the very least, you had to show that the writer accused of copying had had access to the work of the other.
- In another case, the writer Logarides, who had written a piece for television called 'City Of Violets', claimed that the writer Vangelis had copied four crucial notes from this composition when writing his theme tune for the film *Chariots Of Fire.*[12] Logarides said that consciously or unconsciously Vangelis had infringed his copyright. The court decided that there was insufficient objective similarity between the works for there to have been an infringement. This ruled out the argument that he had unconsciously copied it because it was not similar enough. The evidence that was produced to show that Vangelis had had access to the work was also not very strong, although the court thought that it was possible that Vangelis had heard the song 'City Of Angels'. Logarides was not able to prove that Vangelis had actually had access to the work.

11 *Francis Day & Hunter v. Bron* [1963] Ch 587.
12 [1993] EMLR 306.

- Other cases involving plagiarism include a claim by the Italian writer Al Bano, who has been described as a middle-of-the-road crooner, that Michael Jackson plagiarised his song 'I Cigni di Balaka', which then appeared as 'Will You Be There' on Jackson's *Dangerous* album. That wrangle ran on in the Italian courts for over two years.
- Tynesiders Lindisfarne took on pop star Whigfield in 1996, claiming that her hit 'Saturday Night' sounded like a copy of their 1969 hit record 'Fog On The Tyne', and Polygram Music Publishing sued Oasis, alleging that their song 'Shakermaker' sounded too much like 'I'd Like To Teach The World To Sing' written by Roger Cook and Roger Greenaway.

MORAL RIGHTS

If you sample or copy the work of another and you do not credit the original author, or if you do something to the work you've copied or sampled that distorts it, you may well also be infringing the author's moral rights of paternity and integrity of their work (see Chapter 12).

SOUNDALIKES

This is where someone deliberately sets out to imitate a successful piece of music. It is often used by advertising agencies when they don't want to pay the price for the right to use the original of a piece of work so, instead, they commission songwriters to write a piece that's a close imitation of the original. This is an art form in itself.

- In the second *Chariots Of Fire* case, Clarks Shoes deliberately set out to gain a financial advantage from using a piece of music that had a very close similarity with the film's theme music.[13] This was found to be blatant plagiarism but, because it was so obvious, the case didn't really set any guidelines.
- Another case involved the advertising company Pearson, which used a parody of the song 'There Is Nothing Like A Dame' in an advert for a coach service.[14] The lyrics were changed but the layout of the verse and chorus was similar. The manager of the licensing division of the MCPS heard the advert and thought it sounded like 'There Is Nothing Like A Dame'. He told the publishers of the song in the UK, Chappell Music Library. Williamson Music Limited were the exclusive licensees of the song in the UK. They and the other plaintiffs complained of infringement of copyright. Williamson Music Limited retained the right of approval to all requests for a synchronisation licence in relation to that song. No such consent had been given. The judge applied the test of whether an ordinary, reasonably experienced listener would think on hearing the track that it had been copied from the other work. He granted an interim injunction on the basis that the plaintiffs had established that there was a case to answer but it seems he was of the opinion that there had been infringement of the music but not of the words. It seems that the test for whether something is a parody that is allowable and one that infringes

13 *Warner Brothers Music Limited and Others* v. *De Wilde* [1987].
14 *Williamson Music Limited* v. *The Pearson Partnership and Another* [1987] F.S.R. 97.

copyright is that, in the case of the former, the parody has to conjure up the idea of the original and, in the latter case, it is an infringement if it uses a substantial part of the original.

CONCLUSIONS

- If you sample someone's work you will have to get permission to use both the sound recording copyright and the copyright in the underlying music and/or lyrics.
- Put the process of clearing samples in hand as early as possible.
- If there's any chance of an uncleared sample being found and legal action taken, don't take the risk – clear it or remove it.
- If you can't clear the sound recording copyright then see if you can replay the sounds to sound like them and clear the rights in the underlying music/lyrics instead.
- If you copy another's work and pass it off as your own you are guilty of plagiarism unless you can show that the similarity was completely coincidental and that there was no way that you could have heard of the work you are accused of plagiarising.
- There is a very fine line to be drawn between soundalikes and parody and plagiarism.

14: **PIRACY**

INTRODUCTION

Piracy is a huge, worldwide problem. The worst offenders are Eastern European and Far Eastern countries with weak copyright laws and little or no enforcement. In Eastern Europe, pirate recordings account for 80–90% of the market place. Of course, these illegal records are also exported to the UK. Even though the UK has strong copyright laws and a vigorous enforcement policy, pirate records account for about 3% of the total retail market for records. This is before you even begin to think about what is happening on the Internet. Even the most cursory search of the Internet will show up thousands of sites offering MP3 or similar music files for free download. Some of these are put up there legitimately by artists or record companies that want to promote their music. There are companies such as poplesound.com whose purpose it is to make music by unsigned artists available as downloads as a means of getting the artists noticed. However, for every site with legitimate MP3 files there are many more that feature illegal, pirated works (see Chapter 7).

WHAT IS PIRACY?

Piracy is theft. It is the reproduction of someone's copyright without their approval and generally on a commercial scale.

There are three different types of pirate records.

COUNTERFEIT RECORDINGS

These are copies of CDs, cassettes or vinyl records that also copy the packaging, artwork and graphics. For example, someone gets hold of a master recording; they make copies of it, which they then pass off as the original – they don't care what the sound quality is like. They don't really care if the tape or CD will play at all. They just want to make them look as much like the original as possible so that they take your money and you don't find out until you get home that they are not the originals. The trade marks and logos of the original copyright owners are also copied to make them look as much as possible like the originals. This is of course an infringement of the trade mark, which could give rise to a legal action in its own right (see below and Chapter 8). Of course if you're buying these CDs or tapes off a market stall at half the usual retail price you have only yourself to blame if they turn out to be dodgy copies. You don't get something for nothing, as the saying goes.

PIRATE RECORDINGS

This is the unauthorised duplication of an original sound recording. The pirate takes a master recording and copies it without the permission of the original copyright owner. The sound quality is usually as good as the original. This process has obviously been made much simpler with the introduction of digital recording processes. Pirate recordings are usually put out on a different label from the original and in different packaging. The trade marks and logos of the original copyright owners aren't usually on the record or packaging. The aim is to undermine your market by putting out a pirate copy first or in a different form from the way you were going to present it. For example, you release so-called white label copies of your next single to the press and to DJs for review in advance of the commercial release. They are called white labels because in their vinyl form they have a white label that says they are not for commercial use. Unscrupulous characters then copy that recording and put it on their own compilation without getting permission and without paying anything for it. Confusingly, the music industry has now taken to calling these releases 'bootlegs'. They aren't, as we'll see below, but this is a term that is being used more and more to mean all illegal copying of records.

Pirate recordings are generally made in countries with little or no copyright protection and then exported to other countries. However, the practice is spreading to other countries where the agencies in charge of anti-piracy are less effective. Sometimes publishing rights have been cleared and authorisation obtained from a collective body such as the MCPS but no permission has been obtained to reproduce the master sound recording. For example, if you were putting a pirate copy of a master recording on you own dance compilation you might apply for a mechanical licence from someone such as MCPS to get the right to reproduce the song on that master. This lends you an air of respectability and means you have one less collective body to worry about. You don't bother to get permission from the owner of the sound recording. You hope that they either don't get to hear about your release, or they haven't the money or the inclination to sue you for copyright infringement. You could also, in some cases, take advantage of different laws on copyright. For example, you might get permission to use the song and the original sound recording might now be out of copyright in your country. You make copies of it without going back to the original copyright owner and you can export it to other countries where the recording is still in copyright and undercut the legitimate market in that country.

This was more of a problem when the sound recording copyright in the EU was different in different countries. For example, the sound recording copyright in Denmark was 20 years after the end of the year in which it was first released while in the UK it was 50 years. This meant that after 20 years Danish companies could legitimately say that the sound recording was out of copyright so no permission was required to reproduce it in Denmark. They then used the principles of freedom of movement of goods within the EU to export these recordings to other EU countries. This began to be a real issue when early Beatles and Stones albums started to come out of copyright in Denmark. This has become less of a problem since the Directive on the Harmonisation of Copyright and Related Rights made the duration of the sound recording copyright 50 years throughout the EU.[1]

Sometimes pirates argue that they are entitled to a valid licence to release a sound

1 This was implemented into UK law as Section 13A CDPA. The term is 50 years from the end of the year in which the sound recording was first made or, if it is released in that time, 50 years from the end of the year in which it was first released.

recording because of a chain of contracts going back many years. Often, in the 1960s and 70s, ownership of copyright was not properly recorded and there are many changes of ownership down the years. It was not unusual for deals to be one-page sketchy outlines that didn't make it that clear who owned what and who could do what with the recordings. This confusion has been successfully exploited by later record companies claiming to have the right to put out recordings under some dodgy deal struck 20 years earlier. It's sometimes very difficult to prove them wrong.

BOOTLEGS

A bootleg is a recording of a live performance, whether it's at an actual gig or off a television, radio or online broadcast, which is made without permission of the performers.

You used to see shifty-looking people at gigs with tape recorders under their macs making terribly bad recordings of the concert. Now, with the improvements in technology and the miniaturisation of the devices, it is easier than ever to make reasonable digital recordings.

- In the early 1990s, Phil Collins, ex-Genesis drummer turned successful solo artist, brought an action against Imrat, a record distributor, in respect of royalties for sales in Germany of a CD recording of a concert in the US, which was made without his consent. Under German law, German nationals are entitled to stop distribution of performances made without their consent regardless of where the performance takes place. Foreign nationals couldn't rely on this law where the performance had taken place outside Germany.[2]

  The court decided that all European Union countries should provide nationals of other European Union countries with the same degree of protection as they would have had in their own country.

HOW DO YOU SPOT A COUNTERFEIT, PIRATE OR BOOTLEG RECORD?[3]

COUNTERFEITS

These are often on sale in markets and at car boot sales and are often obtainable from street traders selling goods out of suitcases on street corners. The prices are usually 50% or less of a full-price record in the shops.

The packaging will often be of poor quality, possibly blurred print, especially when it gets to the small print. Sometimes there is a white border on the edges of the inlay card for the cassette or CDs. These inlay cards may look genuine on the outside; it's only when you open it that you see it's a poor representation on the inside. The trade marks may be removed, smudged or partly obscured as the pirates try to get around an allegation of infringement of trade mark. The name and logo of the original record company may also be missing, blurred or obscured. There may not be a Source Identification Code. This was something introduced

2 *Collins* v. *Imrat Handelsgesellschaft mbH* [1994] W.M.L.R 108.
3 Source: *Protecting the Value of British Music*, published by the BPI Anti-Piracy Unit.

a few years ago to show the place of manufacture. The sound quality will often be very poor, particularly on cassettes.

BOOTLEGS

These are often found on sale at music festivals, second-hand and 'underground' record stores and collectors' fairs. They are aiming at the die-hard fans who want to own every available recording by their favourite artist. The price is often the same or higher than the legitimate product to reflect their desirability to collectors and fans.

The packaging may leave off company information and there could be no catalogue numbers or proper credits. Bootleg CDs can be very good sound quality, particularly when compared to the very bad quality of bootleg cassettes. The inlay cards will often be simple colour photocopies.

HOW CAN YOU STOP PIRACY?

There is a view that it will not be possible to prevent pirate, illegal music uses on the Internet and that rights owners should accept this and concentrate on putting systems in place to make sure the copyright owners and creators are paid whenever their music is used. There is certainly a view that not much can be done to prevent pirate recordings of sound recordings that are already in the market place. The music industry is concentrating its efforts into putting security systems in place within the digital computer files of the music (see Chapter 7).

When it comes to physical copies of records, such as cassettes and CDs, the problem is a different one as to how to control the illegal manufacturing plants and in seizing illegal copies.

In both cases the underlying rights being infringed are the same.

COPYRIGHT

The sound recording copyright and the rights in the music and lyrics as well as the artwork may be infringed by pirate recordings. It is an infringement of copyright to reproduce, issue copies to the public, perform it in public or include it in a cable programme (including online). These are what we call direct infringements of copyright.

Indirect infringements of copyright include importing, possessing in the course of trade, selling or exhibiting infringing copies in public and/or distributing them in the course of business.[4] These are obviously aimed at the distributor or retailer. They have to know or have reason to believe that they are dealing with an infringing copy.

MORAL RIGHTS

If the writer or composer of the lyrics and music is not identified, or the work has been subjected to derogatory treatment, then this may well be an infringement of moral rights if these haven't been waived (see Chapter 12).

4 Sections 22–26 CDPA.

TRADE MARKS

If the artist's or record company's trade mark name or logo is reproduced without permission of the trade mark owner then this is an infringement of the Trade Marks Act 1994.

TRADE DESCRIPTIONS

If the record has been misdescribed, or represents itself as something that it isn't, this may be a breach of the Trade Descriptions Act.

ENFORCEMENT

First decide on whom you are going to go for. Who have you got evidence against? You could try to take action against the pirate manufacturer but this may be difficult if it is based overseas. You could decide to try to stop distributors from starting or continuing to distribute pirate records. You'll have to move fast. If nothing has been distributed then you could try to get an injunction to stop distribution taking place. There is of course also the person retailing the product. When you've decided on whom you want to go for, what can you do?

CIVIL ACTION

You can apply for an injunction, although you have to move quickly. You can ask the court to make an order preventing infringement of your rights. The court can make orders preventing further sale, distribution and/or import of pirated products. You will probably also make a claim for financial damages.

CRIMINAL ACTION

You have to show that the defendant had reason to believe they were dealing with an infringing copy of a copyright work. The penalties are imprisonment and/or a fine. For this kind of action you need to involve the police, who may need to have explained to them how copyright exists in the product and how it is being breached. You also have to convince them that it is sufficiently serious for them to put resources into the case.

PRIVATE CRIMINAL PROSECUTIONS

The CDPA gives you the right to bring a private criminal prosecution.[5] This was first used successfully in a case run by my firm in 1994 to prosecute someone who was using computer bulletin boards to copy computer games illegally.

The CDPA also makes it possible for an officer of a company to be liable to prosecution for an offence committed by the company.[6] This is to avoid companies slipping through the net.

If someone is found guilty of infringement then the court can order that all the offending articles are handed over to you[7] and can order their destruction. I'm sure you will all have seen pictures of companies such as Rolex using a steamroller to crush fake copies of their watches that they have seized.

5 Section 107 CDPA.
6 Section 110 CDPA.
7 Section 108 CDPA.

TRADING STANDARDS OFFICERS

These are local government officials and they can be very helpful if you get them on side. A good friend of mine is an ex-Trading Standards officer and he tells me they like nothing better than a good raid on a pirate. They usually act to enforce breaches of trade mark using powers given to them under the Trade Descriptions Act among others. They can enter premises and seize goods. They can prosecute for offences such as fraudulently applying a trade mark[8] and the application of a false description to goods.[9]

TRADE BODIES

ANTI-PIRACY UNIT (APU)

The APU was set up by the BPI and also receives financial support from the Musicians Union and the British Association of Record Dealers (BARD).

The APU investigates complaints about piracy. They take information from record companies, musicians and members of the public. They also monitor new technology and how that might affect the record industry. The APU runs training courses and seminars for the police and Trading Standards officers.

The APU can assist in both civil and criminal actions and work with a number of other industry bodies.

THE INTERNATIONAL FEDERATION OF THE PHONOGRAPHIC INDUSTRY (IFPI)

This represents the international recording industry. If you are a member of the BPI you automatically become a member of the IFPI. It has about 100 members in over 70 countries. It is involved in the international fight against piracy. It lobbies governments for appropriate copyright protection and helps to ensure that the laws are enforced.

OTHER BODIES

Other bodies involved in the fight against piracy include the Federation Against Software Theft (FAST), which represents the software industry; the Federation Against Copyright Theft (FACT), which represents film and video producers; and the European Leisure Software Publishers' Association (ELSPA), which represents publishers of interactive software such as computer games.

FACT, FAST and the Music Publishers Association (MPA), which looks after the interests of music publishers, set up a hotline in the autumn of 1999 for people to report suspected cases of film, music or software piracy. You can also get legal advice on copyright and trade mark issues and they will tell you about their education and training initiatives.[10]

8 Section 300 CDPA.
9 Section 1 Trade Descriptions Act.
10 The hotline number is 0845 603 4567.

15: COLLECTION SOCIETIES

INTRODUCTION

As you know by now, copyright is the right of an individual and, in most cases, that right should be exercised as the individual decides and on his own behalf.

However, there comes a time when it makes more sense for these rights to be exercised collectively by an organisation set up to represent the interests of its members. To make doing business as easy as possible requires a one-stop service. For example, it wouldn't be commercially viable for the owners of a radio station to have to go to the copyright owners of the sound recording and of the rights in the songs on each of the records that the station bosses want to play on their programmes. It would be far too time-consuming and costly. Instead what the radio station bosses want to be able to do is to go to one body representing the copyright owners of the songs and to another body representing the broadcast rights in the sound recordings and get a one-off permission to use all the songs and all the records that these bodies control.

Over time, a number of these collective bodies have been set up. The first ones were set up to collectively license and administer public performance rights and others have come along as technological advances have brought newer means of using music. Given some of the current issues facing the collecting societies, it is going to be even more important in the future to have efficient and effective collecting societies offering one-stop global solutions.

WHAT ARE COLLECTION SOCIETIES?[1]

They are, in effect, organisations set up by the various categories of rights owners to administer their rights collectively as their sole, or one of their main, purposes.[2]

On the whole, collection societies are private as opposed to state-owned bodies but they are subject to some form of government or state supervision. In the UK that supervision is provided for partly by the 1988 Copyright Act, which establishes a form of compulsory arbitration in the shape of the Copyright Tribunal.[3]

The purpose of most collection societies is to provide a practical and economical service to enable its members to enforce and administer certain of their copyrights. These bodies make it easier for others to get licences to use copyright works. There is also certainty in that the payment for these uses will usually be at a fixed rate or one individually negotiated within certain guidelines. The idea is also that, by acting collectively, administration costs are reduced.

1 For a more detailed description of collecting societies and their history see Chapter 29 of *Copinger and Skone-James on Copyright.*

2 Section 116(2) CPDA defines a licensing body as 'a society or other organisation which has as its main object, or one of its main objects, the negotiation or granting, either as owner or prospective owner of copyright or as agent for him, of copyright licences, and whose objects include the granting of licences covering works of more than one author'.

3 Sections 116–123 CDPA.

There are, of course, possible dangers inherent in that these collection societies are, by their nature, monopolies. It is the job of the Monopolies and Mergers Commission to police whether that monopoly position is being abused.[4]

BLANKET LICENCES

One of the features of collection societies is that they grant so-called blanket licences for the right to use certain rights in all the works controlled by the society for a particular purpose, for a particular period of time and at a particular rate. Anyone wishing to take advantage of these blanket licences has to take a licence for the whole catalogue. For example, the Performing Right Society Limited (PRS) would negotiate a blanket licence with radio broadcasters for the right to broadcast to the public all the works controlled by PRS. The licence would be for a given period of time, say a year, and would then be subject to review. PRS would negotiate with individual radio stations, or more likely with their representative bodies, the rate that would be applied to these licences. It could be a flat fee per annum or it could be linked to revenue that the radio station earns, for example a percentage of the advertising revenue earned by commercial radio stations, or it could be a combination of both.

ADMINISTRATION

A main role for the collection societies is the administration of the rights, making sure that a member's interests have been properly registered, that people using the rights have the necessary licences and have paid the negotiated rate. They have to collect in the monies, allocate and distribute them. Most societies charge their members a fee of some kind for the administration of the rights, usually a percentage of the gross income they collect.

There is usually one society for each category of rights. A major exception is the US where three societies doing identical things compete for the right to administer publishing rights, namely ASCAP, BMI and SACEM.

Sometimes a society will administer more than one right. For example, in Europe a number of the collection societies administer not only the performing rights but also the right to copy or reproduce works. In fact, in the UK, the PRS and the Mechanical Copyright Protection Society Limited (MCPS) have now combined many of their managerial and administration functions while continuing to maintain separate identities.

RIGHTS GRANTED

The societies either take an assignment of certain rights from their members or they have a licence from their members or act as agents for them. The terms of membership of a collection society will usually dictate what form the rights granted will take. The idea is to

4 In the last ten years there have been two major reviews of individual collecting societies. The first, published in 1988 (HMSO Cm. 530), dealt specifically with Public Performance Limited. The second, in 1996 (HMSO Cm.3147), dealt with the Performing Right Society Limited. That report contained several criticisms of the Society, which has since altered its rules to try to deal with these concerns.

establish through these membership rules a clear mandate to grant licences to use certain rights. As we will see in the section on new issues below, there has been less certainty than is desirable in the mandate of some of the collection societies to deal with new technologies.

The collection societies usually have reciprocal arrangements with other societies so that they can protect their members worldwide. This system is still developing in the area of online licensing. These reciprocal arrangements mean that the UK societies can represent the interests of their UK members and of foreign artists, writers and composers within the UK. Both categories of writers must have the same treatment.

One of the main advantages of collective licensing is, of course, the greater bargaining power that you can get by being part of a collective effort. The rates and rewards for uses of your works that the collection societies can get for you should be better than what you could get on a one-to-one basis.

Collection societies have been around for over 150 years. The French Performing Right Society, SACEM, was the first to be set up back in 1852. MCPS and PRS were established in 1911 and 1914 respectively. Some are of more recent origin such as Public Performance Limited (PPL), which was established in 1934. A more detailed description of what each of these societies does is set out below.

OTHER COLLECTIVE BODIES

There are a number of other music business bodies that represent the interests of various parts of the business. These could be collective bargaining or interest groupings such as the Music Managers Forum (MMF). They also include unions such as the Musicians Union (MU) and Equity. More recent additions have been the two societies set up in the last couple of years to administer the income from exercise of the rights of performers, P@MRA and AURA.

What all these groupings have in common is that they act as a forum for debate and, to a greater of lesser extent, as a means of using collective bargaining power to get things for their members that as an individual it would be very hard to achieve (see Useful Addresses).

THE FUTURE AND CHALLENGES FACING THE COLLECTION SOCIETIES

The main challenges to the collection societies come from the development of new technologies, which is happening at a breath-taking pace. The societies are barely getting to grips with agreeing rates for the licensing of new formats such as Digital Versatile Disc (DVD) and CD-ROMs. Not all of the members of UK societies have given their members the mandate to negotiate and grant licences for these formats on their behalf. Getting the mandate requires, in many cases, a change of the membership rules and not all of the members have signed up to the new deal.

At least these formats are just new forms of providing physical copies of recordings of music. The collection societies are used to dealing with these sorts of things. Now they've got to get to grips with the challenges of online licensing and the commercial pressures that they are under to grant blanket licences for online uses. Many societies do not have the mandate from all their members to grant rights for online uses, although that is changing. Rates and possible pricing models for the new uses are being developed but have not yet found universal acceptance by any means.

An example of this is the rate for digital download of music off the Internet, which the MCPS announced on behalf of its members in 1999. It recommended 10 pence per download for up to 5 minutes of music and 2 pence per minute over that. The announcement was met with howls of protest from Internet Service Providers and content providers who felt that it was too high and would stifle business. But the MCPS was under considerable pressure to do something.

Another example is the situation that currently exists in the UK as to whether or not blanket licences are to be available for public performances of music online. Leaving aside for a moment the whole thorny question of whether many individuals each receiving music in the privacy of their homes is a public performance (see Chapter 7), there is the whole debate about whether or not the PRS can grant licences for any use of music online which involves any element of selection or choice on the consumer's behalf. In 1999 the PRS was issuing quarterly licences on a trial basis for the right to broadcast music online as a streamed 'live' broadcast. So, for example, when I was dealing with the rights issues surrounding the webcast of Robbie Williams's performance at Slane Castle last year I was able to get a blanket licence for the broadcast of the webcast on his own website from the PRS. What I couldn't have done then, and still can't do in early 2000, is get a blanket licence to 'broadcast' archived material online. So, for example, if you were running an Internet radio station in the UK you could get a licence from PRS to broadcast each of your radio programmes live. If, however, you wanted to give the listener the option to listen to the broadcast in his own time and to select which of the tracks he wanted to listen to then there is no blanket licence available. To do this legitimately you would have to go back to each individual owner and agree separate deals. This defeats the whole object of collective licensing and in my opinion is commercially unacceptable. I am told by the various UK collection societies that the situation is constantly under review, which I believe – but they do need to do something quickly.

The other big issue is the question of whether the societies can grant worldwide rights. We've already seen that there are reciprocal arrangements in place for a UK society to be able to grant worldwide rights for terrestrial uses of a song or a recording. With the Internet it is so easy to make your music available globally that it is going to be essential for the collection societies worldwide to put in place, as fast as possible, reciprocal arrangements for online uses so that these are afforded the same degree of protection. In January 2000 the major collection societies in the US, the UK and Europe announced that they were in accord over the need for a global solution and were working on a common solution but they did not expect to be able to finalise these arrangements until late 2000 at the earliest. In the meantime, online uses are going ahead globally and in many cases probably without the permission of the rights owners or the collection societies of which they are members. This is not such a problem when the use being made of the music or the recording is primarily promotional, but it will become a pressing problem when it takes off commercially because the rights owners will be losing out on valuable sources of income.

Even though global solutions are necessary to the problems of online licensing, there is still a need to deal with the fact that each country applies a different means of rewarding rights owners for different sorts of uses of the songs. For example, the mechanical royalty rate in Europe is on average slightly higher than in the UK but does vary between countries. If the rights owners are to be properly rewarded for these uses then there need to be systems in place that can identify where the use took place and calculate the rate of reward applicable in that country. These rights management systems are currently being developed but there is still a long way to go.

Another aspect of these rights management issues is the whole question of piracy. This is dealt with in more detail in Chapter 14. It is, however, a huge problem for all rights owners and for all the organisations set up to deal with these problems both on a domestic and international level.

All these issues will require flexibility from the various rights bodies so as not to stifle trade but at the same time to protect the rights of their members.

THE SOCIETIES

In the following section are brief descriptions of the structures and functions of some of the main bodies that exist in the UK as of March 2000. It tells you what they are, where they are and how you can contact them. It describes their basic aims and their basic criteria for membership. More detail can be obtained from the individual societies, most of whom publish brochures describing what they do for their members.

THE BRITISH PHONOGRAPHIC INSTITUTE (BPI)

Strictly speaking, this isn't a collection society as such but it is an organisation that represents the interests of UK record companies. It's a non-profit-making trade association that was set up in 1973.

The BPI is based in central London (see Useful Addresses) and its members are UK record companies. There are currently about 160 members. There is a fee to become a member and these fees mainly fund its activities. The subscriptions for full members are calculated on a percentage of the turnover of the member in the preceding calendar year. Turnover is defined as 'net sales of owned and licensed finished recorded music product to retailers and wholesalers in the UK'. There is a minimum fee. Any established record company able to afford the membership fee can join provided they agree to be bound by the membership rules and the Code Of Conduct that the BPI maintains. If you are a member of the BPI you automatically also become a member of the IFPI.

The Code Of Conduct deals with how the charts are drawn up and involves the BPI investigating alleged irregularities, for example if there is an attempt to buy up unusually large numbers of copies of a particular record in order to artificially gain a higher chart position. If the BPI finds that a member has been guilty of infringing the Code it can employ sanctions against that member, including expelling them as a member and/or imposing a fine.

Because it's a trade association rather than a rights body it doesn't take any rights from its members nor does it grant licences or otherwise administer or collect money from exploitation of rights.

The BPI provides a forum for discussion and acts for its members generally on matters in which they have a common interest. It also has a lobbying function in Westminster and Brussels. It also negotiates agreements with other groups such as music publishers, the Musicians Union or Equity.

Its Rights Committee monitors developments in the law and advises its members on implications for their businesses.

It is responsible for the collection of data on UK record sales and for matters relating to the profile of the record business through its Public Relations Committee.

A very important part of its job is to co-ordinate anti-piracy efforts through its very active Anti-Piracy Unit. Its role includes taking high-profile litigation cases against pirates and in giving publicity to successful seizures of pirate goods.

PHONOGRAPHIC PERFORMANCE LIMITED (PPL)

This is the record industry's licensing body. It licenses records for broadcasting and public performance.

It represents a large number of record companies, some of which, but not all, are members of the BPI. Approximately 80% of all UK record companies are members.

The PPL is also based in London. It was incorporated as a company limited by guarantee in 1934. (See Useful Addresses for contact details.)

The PPL negotiates collective agreements with broadcasters. It also protects the rights of its members and takes legal action to protect those rights. It doesn't, however, have its own anti-piracy unit or staff but relies on its members to bring infringements to its attention.

PPL has a number of different tariffs that apply to the various uses of the music in its repertoire. These are usually payable annually. There are minimum charges and how much is paid out to the members depends on the use. It does take assignments or exclusive agency rights of various rights from its members. These include broadcasting, public performance, dubbing of background music (a role it took over in 1985), multi-media uses and digital diffusion rights.[5]

The membership agreement allows the member to elect to assign all the rights or to keep some rights back. Most record companies assign broadcasting, public performance and dubbing rights to PPL. Many keep back the multi-media and digital diffusion rights. The fact that PPL doesn't have the mandate from all its members to grant digital rights is hampering its ability to negotiate licences for online uses of the repertoire. As at March 2000 the PPL does not have the right to grant blanket licences for online uses where any element of inter-activity or consumer choice is involved.

5 Dubbing is the right to 'copy, produce, reproduce or make records embodying a sound recording'. An example would be a television sports programme that has music in the background. The sound recording of that music is dubbed into the television programme.

PPL is also now charged with distributing a proportion of performing income to performers.[6]

VIDEO PERFORMANCE LIMITED (VPL)

This is a company associated with PPL. It is the record industry's licensing body for music videos.

Its members are the owners of public performance rights in music videos being publicly broadcast or included in a cable broadcast service.

It is a company limited by guarantee and has about 700 members. It is based at the same office as PPL.

Like PPL, VPL licences music videos for broadcasting, public performance and inclusion in a cable broadcast service. It applies a number of different tariffs to the different uses of the music videos.

Again like PPL, VPL takes an assignment of its members' public performance and dubbing rights in music videos and a non-exclusive licence of the broadcasting rights.

ASSOCIATION OF INDEPENDENT MUSIC LIMITED (AIM)

This is a very new association. It was first set up in 1999. Its members are drawn from the independent sector of the music business, mostly the record industry side but including publishers, production companies and manufacturers.

It's a trade association acting as a forum for debate and has a lobbying function. AIM is based in London and membership costs £117.50. Its function as a trade association means that it also has a collective bargaining role.

It provides a legal advisory service to its members with a number of checklists of points to look out for in negotiating various types of deals.

THE PERFORMING RIGHT SOCIETY LIMITED (PRS)

As we saw in Chapter 4, PRS is the UK collection society for composers, songwriters and music publishers and is charged with administering the public performance and broadcasting rights in music and lyrics. It also administers the film synchronisation right.

Both music publishers and songwriters are members. It was set up in 1914 as a company limited by guarantee. It also represents almost a million foreign music copyright owners through its affiliations with overseas collection societies.

PRS is based in central London. When you become a member of PRS you have to assign your performing right and the film synchronisation right to PRS. Although members assign rights, they can reserve some categories of rights or types of use of rights in all their works and the rules do allow members to request that PRS does not license the performing right in a particular work, for example if it is unlawfully sampled.

There are three categories of membership: provisional, associate and full. As of 1 January 2000 PRS has relaxed its rule on eligibility for membership of composers to just one

6 See Chapter 4 for performers' rights, and the description of P@MRA and Aura in the Appendix.

piece of work already or about to be exploited. The admission fee is approximately £50 for a composer or lyricist.

PRS grants both individual licences and enters into collective licence schemes with various categories of users.

In 1994 PRS was accused of being anti-competitive and in restraint of trade. The band U2 served a writ on PRS, requiring, among other things, that PRS change its membership rules and re-assign to the band their live performance rights. The band objected to the requirement of PRS that rights are exclusively assigned. They thought that members should have the freedom to choose whether to allow PRS alone to administer all or part of the performing right or to administer it themselves. PRS rules don't allow for members to 'opt out'. The equivalent societies in the US do allow their members to license individual music uses.

The group were dissatisfied with the administration by the PRS of live performances. The system that PRS operated meant that income from live performances could take over a year to come through and there were deductions for administration fees. U2 said they would rather administer the live performance right themselves. The trouble is that if big earners such as U2 pull out of the collective system then this would greatly weaken the collective bargaining power. It would also represent a huge drop in income for PRS. This could have a negative effect on the rights of less successful members who rely on their quarterly PRS cheques.

The case settled on the basis that PRS would allow U2 to administer the live performing right and U2 then apparently agreed that it would license the right to PRS in return for a reduced administration fee.

THE MECHANICAL COPYRIGHT PROTECTION SOCIETY LIMITED (MCPS)

This company was set up in 1911 in order to collectively license mechanical reproduction of music, i.e. the copying of music and the synchronisation of music with visual images (see Chapter 4).

MCPS has both publishers and songwriters as members. Its main area of activity is the negotiating and administering of collective licence schemes with record companies. It has reciprocal arrangements with similar societies worldwide.

MCPS is a subsidiary of the Music Publishers' Association Limited, a company limited by guarantee. MCPS has offices in Streatham, South London, although many of its day-to-day activities are now carried out at the same offices as PRS.

MCPS doesn't take assignments of rights but its membership agreement provides that the member appoints MCPS as their agent to manage and administer the mechanical copyright in the UK. It has the mandate to grant licences and collect royalties. It is also obliged to use its best efforts to prevent infringement of its members' rights. It can take legal action in their name and often does so.

There are three types of licence agreements with record companies. The AP1 agreement is given to those record companies who have a trading record and can satisfy the financial and accounting criteria set by MCPS. Under the AP1 agreement a record company can record any work in the MCPS repertoire provided MCPS is notified at least seven working days before its release. Royalties are calculated on the basis of actual sales and are payable quarterly in arrears. The AP2A agreement is the next best thing and is for record companies with a trading history but which can't satisfy the accounting and financial criteria. Record companies with this type of agreement have to notify the MCPS before manufacture. They are obliged to account for royalties on records manufactured even if they aren't ever actually sold. There is a 60-day credit period up to an agreed limit. The third type of agreement is the AP2 agreement. It's basically the same as the AP2A agreement but it is used for companies with a limited release schedule and there is no credit period.

MCPS has also negotiated blanket licence schemes with UK television and radio stations and many other types of specialist music providers.

MCPS charges its members a commission for administering the rights and collecting the royalties. This is between 4.75% and 12.5%. The average in 1997 was 6.01%.

As I explained above, both MCPS and PRS are moving towards new licensing solutions for new formats such as interactive CD-ROMs and the Internet. Since September 1998 MCPS has had a New Media Rate Card for such uses, which is under constant review.

Members are allowed to exclude certain uses from the rights that MCPS control. This must be notified on the registration form.

APPENDIX 1

GLOSSARY

A&R Man: the person in a record or music publishing company whose job it is to find and develop new talent. They may find it themselves or someone else may bring it to them. They develop the artists creatively, helping to find the right manager, record producer, musicians or co-writers. They are the artist's link with the company. The name stands for Artistes and Repertoire but no one uses the full title these days.

Album cycle: the period of time from when an artist starts writing songs to be recorded as part of an album, through to the last piece of promotion for that album, after it is released.

Artist: I use this term throughout the book as shorthand for performing artist. This could either be a solo artist or a group of artists.

Assignment: an outright transfer of ownership of rights by an owner to someone else. It is usually for the life of copyright although sometimes the rights are returned (reassigned) to the owner sooner than that. The assignment can be of some or all rights or have conditions attached.

Auditing: the process by which a specialist accountant called an auditor goes into a company and inspects their accounting books to see if the artists have been paid the correct amounts due under their contracts with that company.

Backstop: an end date by which something has to happen, or when rights come to an end.

Blanket license: a license, usually from a collecting society, which allows someone to use all the recordings or songs that that collecting society controls for a set payment.

Controlled Composition: a song composed by a writer that he or his publisher controls the rights to, as opposed to a song written by someone else.

Copyright: the rights that an author has to prevent anyone else doing certain things with his work without his permission. The basic rights of copyright are the right to copy the work; the right to issue copies of the work to the public; the right to rent or lend out copies of the work to the public; the right to perform, show or play the work in public; the right to broadcast the work or include it in a cable programme; the right to make an adaptation of the work; the right to do any of the above acts in relation to that adaptation. Before anyone can do any of these things with a copyright work they have to get the permission of the copyright owner.

Cover version: a song written and recorded by someone else, that an artist records a new version of.

Demo: a recording of an artist's performances or a songwriter's songs. It's the showcase (or demonstration) of their talents. It could be recorded in a professional recording studio or in your back bedroom on begged or borrowed equipment. The quality isn't expected to be good enough to release as a record, but it must be good enough to clearly hear the quality of the material (if you're a songwriter) or the performance (if you're a recording artist). The demo used to always be on a cassette tape but it's now just as likely to be on a recordable compact disc (CDR), mini-disc or digital audiotape (DAT).

Domain name: a unique name by which your website is identified on the Internet.

Dubbing: the right to 'copy, produce, reproduce or make records embodying a sound recording' for example, when music is played on the background of a television programme, trailer or advert.

Fiduciary duty: a duty to act in good faith and in the best interests of someone else. More often used in the music business in relation to the duty a manager owes to the artist to always put his interests first.

Intellectual property: the general term given to rights such as copyright, trademark, design and patent rights.

Key-man: a man or woman who is seen as essential to the success of a particular project. If the key-man were to leave or no longer be associated with the project, you may wish to have the right to end your association with that project. For example, if you expected to be managed by a particular person, that person would be your key-man and you would not want to be fobbed off on his deputy.

Licence: an agreement to allow someone to do certain things with the rights that an owner has to a particular product – a recording, a song and so on. A licence can be for as long as the life of copyright (see below) but is usually for a much shorter period. The owner continues to own the rights but gives someone else permission to use some or all of those rights.

Life of copyright: this is now the same throughout the EU. For literary and musical works (i.e. songs) it's 70 years from the end of the year in which the author dies. For sound recordings and performers' rights it's 50 years from the end of the year in which the recording was released or the performance was made.

Master Recording: the original fully finished, edited and mixed sound recording from which copies are made.

Mechanical reproduction: the making of a copy of a sound recording. Originally this was done by mechanical means e.g. the pressing of vinyl copies of a record, but now this term is also used to include the making of digital copies of recordings and digital transfer over the Internet in the form of downloads.

MP3: This stands for Mpeg3. It is the name given to a particular format for storing and transferring files of information – usually music – over the Internet.

Net receipts: the sum of money left after deduction of certain agreed amounts. For example, your record company may receive £30,000 from selling your records but after they have deducted the cost of making, distributing and selling those records there is £10,000 left. That is the net profit.

Override royalty: a royalty payable by one company or individual to another company in return for that other company giving up certain rights. For example your record deal with company A comes to an end. Company A has records of yours that it never released. You go to a new record company B and company B wants to release those records. In order to persuade company A to give up its exclusive rights over those records you or company B pays company A a royalty on the sales by company B of those records.

Pennies calculation: a means by which you compare one offer of a deal with another by asking each company to reduce their offer down to what you would receive in real terms of pounds or perhaps more usually pennies.

Performing rights: the rights performers have to prevent someone else from doing certain things with their performances or with recordings of their performances. The basic performing rights are the right to prevent someone making a recording of a live performance; the right to prevent the making of a broadcast or its inclusion live in a cable service programme; the right to prevent someone from making a recording of his performance directly from the broadcast or cable programme. Recordings of performances for personal use are allowed. The performer also has the right to refuse to let someone make a copy of a recording; to issue a copy of a recording to the public; to rent or lend copies of the recording to the public; to play a recorded performance in public or to include it in a broadcast or cable programme service. The performer's permission has to be obtained to do any of the above.

Pipeline income: income that is making its way through the system but hasn't yet reached either your account or the account of your record or publishing company. For example you have sold a lot of records in America but it can take up to 18 months for that income to come through to the accounts of your record company in the United Kingdom and even longer before it reaches your account. If you are asking your record company to advance you further sums of money it can have a look at what income is in the system (the pipeline) but hasn't yet come through before deciding what it can reasonably risk advancing to you.

Post-term commission: any fees payable to your manager or agent after the end of the term of your contract with him.

Remuneration certificate: a certificate that is issued after your lawyer's bill has been scrutinised, to state whether it is a fair amount to charge in the circumstances.

Restraint of trade: this is the name given to a legal doctrine that any contract that seeks to restrict a person's ability to earn a living is unenforceable as being contrary to public policy. Such contracts only become enforceable if they can be shown to be reasonable as between the parties to the contract. For example, if a record contract tries to tie you exclusively to work for that one company, but doesn't on balance give you a reasonable chance of earning a living from that contract, the contract would be unenforceable and you couldn't be held to it.

Retention period: this is sometimes also called a rights period. It is the period of time that a company or an individual owns rights in songs or recordings of your performances. For example a publishing company may retain the rights in any songs you write during the term of the publishing contract for a period of 10 years after the end of the term. That 10 years is the retention period.

Rolling advance: further advances that are paid once the first one has been recouped. For example if you received £10,000 and you were on a rolling advance form of payment you would receive a further £10,000 once the first £10,000 had been recouped from your earnings, your royalties.

Royalty: a payment made to a songwriter, author or performer by the person or company exploiting the songs, recordings or performances.
Scout: the person whose job it is to go around the country hunting out new talent. They are likely to be passionate music fans trying to get into the music business. They may work for nothing or for expenses only. If they are good at finding new talent they may be offered a job as an A&R man and get on to the first rung of the ladder.
Showcase: a performance – often a private one for one company or individual – at which a performer shows off his abilities as a songwriter or more usually a performer.
Synchronisation: this means to add sound to tie in in time with and in harmony with visual images. For example, putting a soundtrack or sound effects to the moving images in a film or video.
Trade mark: a mark – which can be registered or unregistered – which distinguishes your goods or services from someone's else's. For example Virgin has a trade mark in the name of Virgin to distinguish a Virgin plane, train or whatever they have applied the mark to from other planes, trains etc.
Webcast: the name given to a broadcast of a performance, either live or pre-recorded over the Internet.
White Label: a record which is released with a plain white label not bearing the record company's name or logo, which is made available in limited numbers or in a limited area as an 'underground' release or as review copies sent to DJs, journalists etc before full commercial release.

APPENDIX 2

USEFUL ADDRESSES

AIM – Association of Independent Musicmakers
Lamb House, Church Street, London W4 2PD
Tel: (020) 8994 5599
Email: info@musicindie.com

AMIA – Association of Music Industry Accountants
Becket House, 1 Lambeth Palace Road, London SE1 7EU
Tel: (020) 7931 3184
Fax: (020) 7401 2136

ANGLIA POLYTECHNIC UNIVERSITY
East Road, Cambridge CB1 1PT
Tel: 01223 363271
Email: degaalap@bridge.anglia.ac.uk
Website: http://www.anglia.ac.uk

ASCAP – American Society of Composers and Performers
8 Cork Street, London W1X 1PB
Tel: (020) 7439 0909
Fax: (020) 7434 0073

AURA – Association of United Recording Artists
1 Glenthorne Mews, 115A Glenthorne Road, London W6 0LJ
Tel: (020) 8741 2555
Fax: (020) 8741 4856
AURA was set up to administer and collect the performers' share of income from broadcasters and cable service programme providers. It is based at the same offices as the MMF and is closely allied with them.

BAND REGISTER
Oxford Music Central, 2nd floor, 65 George Street, Oxford OX1 2BE
Tel: 01865 798795
Fax: 01865 708796

BAR COUNCIL, THE
1 Deans Yard, London SW1
Tel: (020) 7222 2525

BMI – Broadcast Media Inc.
84 Harley House, Marylebone Road, London NW1 5HN
Tel: (020) 7486 2036
Fax: (020) 7224 1046
Email: london@bmi.com
Website: http://www.bmi.com

BOURNEMOUTH UNIVERSITY
Studland House, 12 Christchurch Road, Bournemouth, Dorset BH1 3NA
Tel: 01202 524111
Email: postmaster@bournemouth.ac.uk
Website: http://www.bournemouth.ac.uk

BPI - British Phonographic Institute
25 Savile Row, London W1X 1AA
Tel: (020) 7287 4422
Fax: (020) 7287 2252
Website: http://www.bpi.co.uk

BUCKINGHAMSHIRE CHILTERNS UNIVERSITY COLLEGE
Queen Alexandra Road, High Wycombe, Bucks HP11 2JZ
Tel: 01494 522141
Website: http://www.buckscol.ac.uk/bchome.html

CANTERBURY CHRIST CHURCH UNIVERSITY COLLEGE
North Holmes Road, Canterbury, Kent CT1 1QU
Tel: 01227 767700
Email: admissions@cant.ac.uk
Website: http://www.cant.ac.uk

CHAMBERS & PARTNERS PUBLISHING
23 Long Lane, London EC1A 9HL
Tel: (020) 7606 1300
Fax: (020) 7600 3191

CITY UNIVERSITY
Northampton Square, London EC1V 0HB
Tel: (020) 7477 8028
Email: r.s.broom@city.ac.uk
Website: http://www.city.ac.uk

CONCERT PROMOTERS' ASSOCIATION
54 Keyes House, Dolphin Square, London SW1V 3NA
Tel: (020) 7834 0515
Fax: (020) 7821 0261

DATA PROTECTION REGISTRAR
Wycliffe House, Water Lane, Wilmslow, Cheshire SK9 5AF
Tel: 01625 545745
Fax: 01625 524510
Email: data@wycliffe.demon.co.uk

DE MONTFORT UNIVERSITY
The Gateway, Leicester LE1 9BH
Tel: 0116 255 1551
Website: http://www.dmu.ac.uk

EQUITY (British Actors' Equity Association)
Guild House, Upper St Martin's Lane, London WC2H 9EG
Tel: (020) 7379 6000
Fax: (020) 7379 7001
Email: info@equity.org.uk
Equity is an independent trade union representing not only actors but also other performers including singers and dancers. Equity negotiates industry agreements with TV and radio broadcasters, theatres and record companies (through the BPI).

FACULTY OF MEDIA, MUSIC AND PERFORMANCE
Adelphi Campus, Peru Street, Salford, Manchester M3 6EQ
Tel: 0161 295 6112
Fax: 0161 295 6113

GAVIN
140 Second Street, San Francisco, CA 94105
Tel: +(415) 495 1990
Fax: +(415) 495 2580
Email: gstaff@gavin.com

GLOBAL ENTERTAINMENT GROUP, THE
Music Training Division, HMS President (1918) Victoria Embankment, London EC4Y 0HJ
Tel: (020) 7583 0236
Fax: (020) 7583 7221

IAEL – International Association of Entertainment Lawyers
c/o Julian Turton of The Simkins Partnership
45–51 Whitfield Street, London W1P 6AA
Tel: (020) 7631 1050
Fax: (020) 7436 2744

IFPI – International Federation of the Phonographic Industry
54 Regent Street, London W1R 5PJ
Tel: (020) 7434 3521
Fax: (020) 7439 9166

ILEX – Institute of Legal Executives
Kempston Manor, Kempston, Bedford MK42 7AB
Tel: 01234 841000
Fax: 01234 840373
Email: jburns@ilex.org.uk
Website: http://www.ilex.org.uk

KEELE UNIVERSITY
Keele, Staffs ST5 5BG
Tel: 01782 621111
Email: aaa20@admin.keele.ac.uk
Website: http://www.keele.ac.uk/depts/aa/homepage.html

KINGSTON UNIVERSITY
River House, 53–57 High Street, Kingston-Upon-Thames, Surrey KT1 1LQ
Tel: (020) 8547 2000
Email: d.milner-walker@kingston.ac.uk
Website: http://www.kingston.ac.uk

LAW SOCIETY, THE
113 Chancery Lane, London WC2A 1PL
Tel: (020) 7242 1222
Fax: (020) 7831 0344
Website: http://www.lawsociety.org.uk

LONDON SOCIETY OF CHARTERED ACCOUNTANTS, THE
53 Tabernacle Street, London EC4 4NB
Tel: (020) 7490 4390

MCPS – Mechanical Copyright Protection Society Limited
Elgar House, 41 Streatham High Road, London SW16 1ER
Tel: (020) 8604 4400
Fax: (020) 8769 8792

MELODY MAKER
IPC Music Magazines, Kings Reach Tower, Stamford Street, London SE1 9LS
Tel: (020) 7261 6229
Fax: (020) 7261 6706

MIRACLE PUBLISHING LIMITED
1 York Street, London W1H 1PZ
Tel: (020) 7486 7007
Fax: (020) 7486 2002
Email: info@audience.uk.com

MMF – Music Managers Forum
1 Glenthorne Mews, 115A Glenthorne Road, London W6 0LJ
Tel: (020) 8741 2555
Fax: (020) 8741 4856
Helpline: (020) 7351 7763
Email: office@imf-uk.org
Website: http://www.imf-uk.org
Training Officer: Stuart Worthington
Tel: 0161 228 3993
This is the UK trade association for artist managers. It was set up approximately five years ago as the International Managers Forum to act as a representative body for managers, to act as a forum for debate on matters of interest to its members and as a lobbying body.

MUSIC WEEK
40 Beresford Street, London SE18 6BQ
Tel: (020) 8855 7777
Fax: (020) 8317 3938
Website: http://www.dotmusic.co.uk

MUSICIAN'S ATLAS, THE
33 Porter Place, Montclair, NJ 07042-2036
Tel: +(973) 509 9898
Fax: +(973) 655 1238
Email: MRGroup3@aol.com

MUSICIANS UNION
60–62 Clapham Road, London SW9 OJJ
Tel: (020) 7582 5566
Fax: (020) 7582 9805
The MU is the only UK trade union solely representing musicians. It was formed in 1893. It has about 40,000 members and about 100 local branches. It acts as a collective body by seeking to improve the status of musicians and the money they earn. The MU makes national agreements with various organisations including the BPI (for recording sessions and promotional videos) and television companies (for broadcasts).

NET SEARCHERS
Nick Wood
Tel: (020) 7565 4090
Fax: (020) 7565 4099

NEW MUSICAL EXPRESS
IPC Music Magazines, Kings Reach Tower, Stamford Street, London SE1 9LS
Tel: (020) 7261 5813
Fax: (020) 7261 5185
Email: nme.com

OXFORD BROOKES UNIVERSITY
Gipsy Lane Campus, Headington, Oxford, Oxon OX3 0BP
Tel: 01865 483040
Website: http://www.brookes.ac.uk

P@MRA
29–33 Berners Street, London W1P 1AA
Tel: (020) 7580 5544
Fax: (020) 7306 4340
P@MRA is a non-profit-making company limited by guarantee and is appointed as an agent to collect and administer the performing right income and also to enter into reciprocal arrangements with producers' and performers' organisations overseas.

PINNACLE
Electron House, St Mary Cray, Orpington, Kent BR5 3RJ
Tel: 01689 870622
Fax: 01689 873144
Website: http://www.pinnacle-records.co.uk

PPL – Public Performance Limited
1 Upper James Street, London W1R 3HG
Tel: (020) 7534 1000
Fax: (020) 7534 1111

PRS – Performing Rights Society Limited
Copyright House, 29–33 Berners Street, London W1P 4AA
Tel: (020) 7580 5544
Fax: (020) 7306 4455
Email: info@prs.co.uk
Website: http://www.prs.co.uk

REGIONAL PROMOTERS' ASSOCIATION
Riverside Promotions, 7–15 Pink Lane, Newcastle upon Tyne NE1 5DW
Tel: 0191 232 9729
Fax: 0191 261 4129
Email: andyhockey@yahoo.com

ROEHAMPTON INSTITUTE LONDON
Roehampton Lane, London SW15 5PU
Tel: (020) 8392 3000
Email: admissions@roehampton.ac.uk
Website: http://www.roehampton.ac.uk

SOUTH BANK UNIVERSITY
103 Borough Road, London SE1 0AA
Tel: (0)20 7815 8158
Email: enrol@sbu.ac.uk
Website: http://www.sbu.ac.uk

SQUARE CENTRE, THE
Alfred Street North, Nottingham NG3 1AA
Tel: 0115 947 0044
Fax: 0115 941 8866

THAMES VALLEY UNIVERSITY
911 University House, Ealing Green, London W5 5EA
Tel: (020) 8579 5000
Email: christine.marchant@tvu.ac.uk
Website: http://www.tvu.ac.uk

UCAS – University Clearing Advisory Service
Rosehill, New Barn Lane, Cheltenham, Gloucestershire GL52 3LZ
Tel: 01242 222444
Email: app.req@ucas.ac.uk
Website: http://www.ucas.org.uk

UNIVERSITY COLLEGE NORTHAMPTON
Park Campus, Boughton Green Road, Northampton NN2 7AL
Tel: 01604 735500
Email: admissions@nene.ac.uk
Website: http://www.nene.ac.uk

UNIVERSITY OF GREENWICH
Wellington Street, Woolwich, London SE18 6PF
Tel: (020) 8331 8044
Email: p.fisher@greenwich.ac.uk
Website: http://www.gre.ac.uk

UNIVERSITY OF SUNDERLAND
Edinburgh Building, Chester Road, Sunderland SR1 3SD
Tel: 0191 515 3000
Email: student-helpline@sunderland.ac.uk
Website: http://www.sunderland.ac.uk

UNIVERSITY OF SURREY
The Registry, Guildford, Surrey GU2 5XH
Tel: 01483 300800
Website: http://www.surrey.ac.uk

UNIVERSITY OF WESTMINSTER
Metford House, 115 New Cavendish Street, London W1M 8JS
Tel: (020) 7911 5000
Website: http://www.wmin.ac.uk

VITAL DISTRIBUTION
Unit 6, Barton Hill Trading Estate, Herapath Street, Bristol, Avon BS5 9RD
Tel: 0117 988 3300
Fax: 0117 988 0600

APPENDIX 3

FURTHER READING

Burgess, Richard James, *The Art of Record Production*, Omnibus Press.

Chambers Guide to the Legal Profession, Chambers & Partners Publishing.

Chitty on Contracts, Sweet & Maxwell.

Copinger and Skone-James (1998), *Copinger and Skone-James on Copyright*, Sweet & Maxwell.

Cornish, William R, *Intellectual Property*, Sweet & Maxwell.

Dann, Allan and Underwood, John, *How to Succeed in the Music Business*, Omnibus Press.

Drummond, Bill *et al*, *The Manual: how to have a Number One the easy way*, Ellipsis London Ltd.

Flint, Michael and Thorne, C D (1997), *Flint: User's Guide to Copyright*, Butterworth's.

Frascogna, Xavier M Jr and Hetherington, H Lee, *The Business of Artist Management*, Billboard Books.

Gertler, Nat and Underhill, Rod, *Complete Idiot's Guide to Music on the Internet with MP3*, Que.

Gibson, David and Peterson, George (eds), *The Art of Mixing: a visual guide to recording, engineering, and production* (Mix Pro Audio Series), Hal Leonard Publishing Corporation.

Golvan, Colin (1992), *Introduction to Intellectual Property Law*, Blackstone Press Limited.

Harrison, Tom (1998), *Music Deals: a guide to making contracts in the UK popular music industry*, Harrison Law Publishing.

Kanaar, Nicholas (ed.) (1998), *Bagehot on Music Business Agreements* (2nd edition), Sweet & Maxwell.

Krasilovski, William M and Shemel, Sidney, *This Business of Music*, Billboard Publications.

Laddie *et al*, *Laddie, Prescott and Vitoria: the Modern Law of Copyright and Designs* (2nd edition).

Lathrop, Tad and Pettigrew, Jim, *This Business of Music Marketing and Promotion*, Watson-Guptill Publications.

Legal 500 UK Edition, Legalese (published annually).

Leikin, Molly-Ann, *How to Write a Hit Song: the complete guide to writing and marketing chart topping lyrics & music*, Hal Leonard Publishing Corporation.

Passman, Donald S (1998), *All You Need to Know about the Music Business*, Penguin Books Limited. This is a US attorney's perspective on the music business.

Pattenden, Sian (1998), *How to Make It in the Music Business*, Virgin Books, London.

Purce, Teresa, *Copyright, Designs & Patents Act 1988*, The Stationery Office.

Schwartz, Daylle Deanna, *Start & Run Your Own Record Label*, Billboard Books.

Schwartz, Daylle Deanna, *The Real Deal: how to get signed to a record label from A to Z*, Billboard Publications.

Stone, Reuben (1993), 'Plagiarism and Originality in Music: a precarious balance', in *Media Law & Practice*, vol. 14, no. 2.

Strong, William S, *The Copyright Book: a practical guide* (5th edition), MIT Press.

Wall, Raymond A (1998), *Copyright Made Easier*, ASLIB.

Webb, Jimmy, *Tunesmith: inside the art of songwriting*, Hyperion Books.

APPENDIX 4

WORKING IN THE MUSIC BUSINESS

Here is a brief overview of some of the information available on the music business. It is not meant to be a complete list; it is information I've come across when researching this book. All the contact details are in Appendix 2.

If you're interested in more formal training in the music business then there are a number of courses now available. If you have access to the Internet then this is an excellent resource for finding out about courses. The University and College Clearing Site at www.ucas.co.uk is a good start point. Or do a general search, using any good search engine, for education/music. For short or evening courses, check Floodlight and Local Authority publications for courses outside London.

My own researches have turned up the following universities and colleges that run courses either in media or the music business. Qualifications vary from NVQs, through HNDs, to degrees. Some don't offer a nationally recognised qualification but more of an overview with a certificate when you complete the course. Check the course details to make sure they meet your requirements. The list isn't a complete one by any means, and neither is it a recommendation of any particular course.

HIGHER EDUCATION

Legal and business courses

Kingston University and Gateway offer short evening courses giving an overview of the music industry. They also offer two-year higher diploma courses in music business studies.

The University of Westminster offers a BA (Hons) degree in Commercial Music and Music Business Practice.

Buckinghamshire Chilterns University offers HND and BA (Hons) full-time courses in Music Industry Management.

City University, London, runs a number of introductory courses such as Making Music Work: An Introduction to the Music Industry. It also offers distance-learning courses in Music and the Law and An Introduction to the Music Industry.

Greenwich Community College, South London, offers short courses in Making it in the Music Industry.

Anglia Polytechnic University offers a BA in Law and Music.

Canterbury Christchurch University College offers a module, within other courses, in Business Studies with Music.

Darlington College of Arts runs a BA degree course in Music with Arts Management. Although this isn't a law course it may suit those looking to being a manager.

De Montfort University, Leicester, offers a BA in Law and Music Technology.

Keele University has a module within its main degree course in Law and Music. University College, Northampton, offers a similar subject but as a full degree.

Oxford Brookes University offers a number of combined modules involving music including Law/Music and Business Administration and Management/Music, which may suit those more interested in a general as opposed to a specific legal course.

Roehampton Institute, London Southlands College, has a module in Business Studies and Music within its Business Studies Combined Honours courses. These are either full- or part-time courses leading to either a BA (Hons) or BMus (Hons).

The South Bank University, London, offers BA/BSc courses in Law and Music as three-year full-time degree courses.

The University of Sunderland offers a number of combined BAs including Business and Music and Business Law and Music. Intriguingly, it also offers a course entitled Gender Studies and Music.

Technical courses

For those looking for a more technical emphasis there is a highly regarded Tonmeister course at my old university, the University of Surrey. This is a BMus degree course in Music and Sound Recording. It's a four-year sandwich course with time spent out in work placements.

Thames Valley offers various two- and three-year full-time courses covering Music Recording and aspects of the music business, for example Advertising with Sound and Music Recording.

Salford offers a BA (Hons) course in Popular Music and Recording. Its professional patron is former Beatles producer George Martin and the Honorary Master of Arts is ex-Genesis vocalist Peter Gabriel. The emphasis is on popular music and music technology but it also aims to prepare you for a career in the music business or in the recording industry. They say you'll be directed towards modules as a Studio Performer or Producer depending on your aptitude and interests shown in entrance tests, interviews and by your profile. Mature students are welcomed and they say they accept those who don't have formal academic qualifications if they have 'the right attitude'.

The Nottingham Foundation for Music and Media is offering further and higher education courses, as well as commercial training courses, for the music and multi-media industries. Their courses are validated by New College, Nottingham. They offer BTEC First Certificate, National Diploma and Higher National Certificates in Music Technology. These are one-year intensive courses that have modules on the music business as well as technical recording skills. They also run a number of short courses during evenings and weekends. These are of a technical nature, for example Digital Recording and Editing and Midi Sequencing. You can check out their website on www.the-foundation.org

Masters degrees

Westminster and Bournemouth Universities are both offering Masters degrees in the Music Business. In the case of Westminster it's in Music Management. The University of Bournemouth is offering an LLM/MA in Media Law from this year.

COMMERCIAL COURSES

There are also courses run by commercial organisations that aim to give practical overviews of aspects of the music business. One of the more established organisations is the Global Entertainment Group. They are offering evening courses over eight weeks as a Music Industry Overview. This can be taken together with their Skills Link programme, which provides more specialised subjects such as Music Marketing, PR and Promotion or Successful Artist Management.

The Music Managers Forum (MMF) offers short courses to its members on aspects of music management and the industry. These are either short evening courses or week-long intensive ones.

The British Phonographic Institute (BPI) occasionally offers one-day training workshops.

BECOMING A SOLICITOR

If you want to become a solicitor, the Law Society can give you information. If you already have a first degree in law, you need to complete a one-year Legal Practice course and a two-year training contract. A fast track to qualifying may be available for those who already have relevant business experience.

The Law Society now includes Media Studies as optional courses as part of the Legal Practice course. The Law Society also requires practising lawyers to keep up-to-date on the law by undertaking further training during their working life.

If your first degree is not in law, you'll need to do an additional one-year conversion course called the Common Professional Examination.

In-house or private practice?

Once you've qualified as a solicitor you can choose whether to work in a private law firm or in-house as a lawyer in a record or music publishing company. Managers don't usually employ an in-house lawyer, nor do small labels or publishing companies. They usually use lawyers in private law firms.

The competition between specialist music business lawyers is intense. It takes considerable effort, both in and out of normal working hours, to build up a 'practice' – a body of clients who use you regularly for legal advice. Without a practice you are unlikely to be promoted to Associate, salaried or full partner sharing in the profits (or losses) of the business. The financial rewards and job satisfaction can be considerable.

Those of you who think you'd find it difficult to build up a practice or who aren't interested in becoming a full profit-sharing partner or owning their own business may decide to work in-house instead. That isn't to say that this is an easy option. The work in-house can be very intense. There's no job security and you have to follow company policy, the corporate line. The up-side is that the working atmosphere can be more relaxed, you don't have the stresses of building a practice or running your own business and it can be a very good way to move into management positions.

It is possible to move between the two. A partner in Harbottle & Lewis left to go in-house at one of the big music publishing companies and now runs the whole of their European operation.

BECOMING A BARRISTER

Instead of being a solicitor you could choose to do a law degree, a follow-up course at a recognised Bar School and a minimum of one year's training to become a barrister. Barristers can't be partners in law firms without re-qualifying as a solicitor but they can, and often do, work as in-house lawyers. For further information on becoming a barrister contact the Bar Council.

BECOMING A LEGAL EXECUTIVE

You can also get a qualification as a legal executive. For information on legal executive qualifications, contact the Institute of Legal Executives. It doesn't entitle you to become a partner in a law firm but it does give you a legal qualification. It can be done in evening and day-release classes while you're working and it can be a stepping-stone to becoming a fully qualified solicitor, although this would take many years. You find legal executives in support roles in media law firms. In the smaller firms their role isn't that different from that of fully qualified solicitors. Legal executives also work in-house and to all intents and purposes they do the same work as qualified solicitors. However, there is often the view in music companies that unless you're a fully qualified lawyer, or have an additional business qualification such as an MBA (a masters degree in business administration), you are unlikely to get promoted to a management role. You may not have any desire to go into management and may be happy with a non-management role.

NON-LEGAL JOBS

For a general overview of types of careers available in the music business, a good place to start would be Sian Pattenden's book on the music business (see Further Reading).

You could also refer to your Careers Advisory Service and government-backed enterprise and job advisory centres. The Jobseekers scheme now extends to specialist advisers dealing with the music business and the particular needs of musicians. There is now even a scheme called 'Fair Deal for Musicians' – for details ask at your local job centre.

It's less easy to learn about jobs in other areas of the music business by going on formal courses. Those wishing to become A&R contacts will generally start as hopeful 'scouts', running around the country, often for little more than out-of-pocket expenses, chasing down likely new bands. Another way in is if you've already had some kind of success as an artist and then you cross over into the business side. A common quality is a passionate love of music.

INDEX